Recollections of Squatting in Victoria, then called the Port Philip District, from 1841 to 1851.

Edward Micklethwaite Curr

Recollections of Squatting in Victoria, then called the Port Philip District, from 1841 to 1851.
Curr, Edward Micklethwaite
British Library, Historical Print Editions
British Library
1883
xii. 452 p. ; 8°.
10491.ee.22.

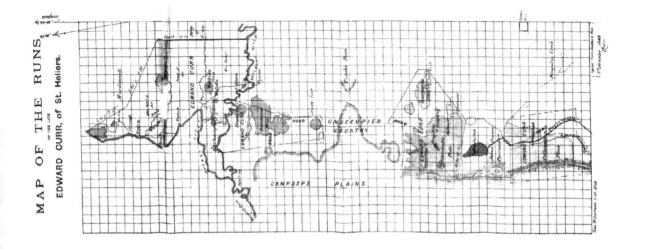

MAP OF THE RUNS OF THE LATE EDWARD CURR, of St. Heliers.

RECOLLECTIONS

OF

SQUATTING IN VICTORIA.

RECOLLECTIONS

OF

SQUATTING IN VICTORIA

THEN CALLED THE PORT PHILLIP DISTRICT

(From 1841 to 1851)

BY

EDWARD M. CURR

GEORGE ROBERTSON

MELBOURNE, SYDNEY, AND ADELAIDE

MDCCCLXXXIII

PREFACE.

In laying the following pages before the public the writer has little to say by way of preface. An excuse for the publication of mere personal matters will, it is hoped, be found in the contrast their relation exhibits between the past and the present state of things in Victoria. The champagne-loving little town of Melbourne in 1839, for instance; the ways of its jolly denizens; the Blacks; the expiree-convict shepherd; the Commissioner of Crown Lands, who ruled it so bravely in bush matters; the life of the squatter in the forties, are (even when seen through the medium of individual experiences, possibly of not a very representative sort) features so markedly different from those of the present time, that a sketch of them may, it is hoped, find some interested readers.

Having devoted his leisure hours for the last ten years to the collection of information from gentlemen resident in the bush on the subject of the aboriginal tribes spread over our continent, the writer takes this opportunity of informing such of his contributors as may chance to see this work, that he has succeeded in obtaining vocabularies of over two hundred of our languages, and detailed accounts of about one hundred of our tribes; there being at present in print, scattered through many works, only sixty vocabularies and accounts of about twenty tribes. This accumulation of material the writer expects will be ready for publication in a few months, when it will be at the disposal of our Government, or of any scientific body which might desire to print it. Collating the information on this subject which the writer has in his hands with the languages and accounts of the other dark-skinned people, no possible doubt seems to remain that the aboriginal race of Australia is of African descent. Other important facts connected with the past history of the Australian race also become evident.

CONTENTS.

CHAPTER XII.
A VISIT FROM THE COMMISSIONER OF CROWN LANDS.

CHAPTER XIII.
CORROBOREES, AND GIVING IN MARRIAGE.

CHAPTER XIV.
THE DESERTED CAMP.

CHAPTER XV.
STEELE'S CREEK.

CHAPTER XVI.
THE MOIRA.

CHAPTER XVII.
CHANGES IN CONNECTION WITH FLORA AND FAUNA.

CHAPTER XVIII.

A VISIT TO THE MOIRA IN COMPANY WITH THE POLICE.

CHAPTER XIX.

A SUMMONS.

CHAPTER XX.

CORAGORAG.

CHAPTER XXI.

THE BANGERANG TRIBE.

CHAPTER XXII.

THE WARS OF THE BANGERANG.

CHAPTER XXIII.
COLBINABBIN TAKEN UP.

CHAPTER XXIV.
A MAIL ON THE LOWER GOULBURN—NEWS-PAPERS AT TONGALA — OUTCRY AGAINST THE SQUATTERS.

CHAPTER XXV.
PROGRESS IN SHEEP-FARMING AND DAILY LIFE ON THE STATION.

CHAPTER XXVI.
HUNTING WITH FOX-HOUNDS.

CHAPTER XXVII.
LAW IN THE BUSH—AN INTRUDER ON THE RUN.

CHAPTER XXVIII.
OLD DAVIE.

CHAPTER XXIX.
RAMBLES IN UNOCCUPIED COUNTRY.

CHAPTER XXX.
MY SERVANTS.

CHAPTER XXXI.
CONCLUSION.

RECOLLECTIONS OF SQUATTING IN VICTORIA.

CHAPTER I.

ARRIVAL IN MELBOURNE.

My first visit to Melbourne was in August or September, 1839. I had come in company with my father from Circular Head, in the schooner *Eagle*, which was freighted with cattle, horses, and sawn timber. We had a pleasant run of twenty hours across the Straits, and after a delightful sail up the Bay we anchored off Williamstown, at eight o'clock in the morning. After breakfast we got into a whaleboat, which had come alongside, and proceeded up the Yarra Yarra (as the river was always called at that time) to Melbourne. The day, I remember, was crisp and exhilarating, and well fitted to give favourable first-impressions ; the stream bright and clear, and clad with the verdure of the ti-tree and other shrubs to its edge, vistas of grassy land presenting themselves here

2

and there. What struck me most—though birds
were not wanting—was the stillness of the bush.
As for signs of civilization, they were as completely absent from the lower portion of the river
as when Batman first steered his boat to the Falls.
They were, however, close at hand; and we
were not long in reaching the bustling little town
of Melbourne, where one of the crew, in the
absence of a wharf, fastened our boat to a friendly
stump, and we jumped on shore, carpet-bag in
hand, and proceeded to take up our quarters at
the British Hotel, which, if I recollect rightly,
was one of only three inns then in Melbourne,
and stood at the south end of William-street,
at about a hundred yards from the landing-place.
Arrivals in Melbourne not being quite so numerous then as they are now, ours soon became
known to some of my father's friends, who came
to our hotel to welcome him to the new colony.
Invitations to dinner; to take up our quarters,
during our proposed stay in Melbourne, at the
houses of friends; and to the gaieties of the hour,
were numerous and cordial. Our little sitting-
room was soon filled, and conversation became
animated, there being notably prevalent a general
tone of high spirits, based, as it appeared, on the
unexpected prosperity and unbounded hopes of
the young community, which was as delightful as
it was infectious. The next day my father removed
to the Melbourne Club, of which he had been

elected an honorary member; whilst I went to take up my quarters at the cottage of a friend (a few months before a fellow-passenger from England), who resided *en garçon* on the Yarra, close to its junction with the Merri Merri Creek, his family not having yet arrived to join him.

Of course I felt a good deal of curiosity to see Melbourne, which I had heard much talked of in Tasmania, whence it had already seduced a good deal of the enterprise and capital. It was also the first colonial town I had been in since boyhood, and was already spoken of as destined to become the leading city of the Australias.

CHAPTER II.

MELBOURNE IN 1839.

MELBOURNE has had its alternations of activity and depression, like other cities, of course ; but, on the whole, I think we may say that it has been a bustling, stirring sort of place from the very pip. Going back to the days of its founders, we find that they had hardly got their tents pitched, and local quarrels properly established, when they raised a hue and cry and insisted on the Government of New South Wales unlocking the lands, having the site of the future city surveyed, allotments put up, a police magistrate sent down, and who knows what besides; so that, evidently, the youngster was in a hurry. Of course, all this impatience was quite irregular, and probably to the official mind (if current ideas concerning it are correct) must have seemed very much on a par with a three-days-old baby declining its pap and clamouring lustily for beefsteak and bottled ale. No doubt officialdom in the good city of Sydney must have groaned from every pigeon-hole *(ab immo pectore)*; and if the eccentricities of the new-comers did not bring on their devoted heads a visitation of gubernatorial displeasure, and the pioneers had their wishes complied with (after a year or two), it may no doubt be attributed to the fact that the prospect of a speedy contribution to the Treasury, from land sales, was at the bottom of the business. However that may be, we know that the first sale of town allotments took place in Melbourne in June, 1837, or about two years subsequent to the first settlement, and rather more than two years prior to the period of which I write, and that the half-acre allotments realized on the occasion an average of some £33 all round. As characteristic of how things had gone on during these two years I may mention that, on the occasion of this visit, I was present at what was known as Ebden's sale, when three of these allotments sold at auction for something over £10,000, from which an idea may be formed, not only of the rise in prices, but of the insane spirit of speculation at that time rampant in the colony.

The town allotments sold in 1837 had, as a rule, generally been built on when I saw them, displaying structures of every variety of plan which might suit the tastes or the pockets of their owners, those which could not boast of a tenement being generally enclosed with a two-rail fence. Any approach to continuous rows of uniform or similar buildings such as one expects to find in streets there was none, as everyone built as he liked, in the most independent way, and to suit the requirements of the moment. Here and there houses were of brick, some of one, and a few of two stories; others were of weatherboards, wattle-and-dab, or slabs. In some cases there were two cottages on the same allotment, in others one; some of the buildings hugged the footpath which was to be, and others stood back from the street, amidst trees and stumps, in semi-rural retirement; whilst here and there considerable intervals occurred entirely destitute of buildings. The size, too, of the structures, in many cases, could hardly be considered commensurate with the uses to which they were put; the operations of the Bank of Australasia, and of the Post-office, for instance, were each carried on in a small four-roomed brick cottage, in which some at least

of the officials connected with them also dwelt.
In another instance, the front of a wooden hut of
the dimensions of eight feet by twelve, which
stood near about where the *Argus* office now
is, displayed on a signboard in large letters the
waggish announcement " Universal Emporium,"
and in its window a few pipes and sticks of
tobacco arranged crosswise. As regards the
streets, no attempts had yet been made to
pave or macadamize them, and very little to
separate the footpath from the roadway; whilst,
in the absence of drains, chasms, in many places—
notably in Elizabeth-street—some eight feet deep
and fifteen or twenty feet wide, had been excavated
by the rains. At the intersections of streets the
perpendicular banks of these gullies were broken
down by drays, and tolerably practicable crossing-
places established, which answered well enough
except during heavy rains, when they got flooded
six or eight feet deep, and had to be crossed somewhere north of Lonsdale-street. In most of the
streets stumps were plentiful, and in all but one
or two, trees were occasionally to be met with;
whilst by no stretch of imagination could the
limits of the town be said to extend beyond the
area enclosed by William-street, Lonsdale-street,
Swanston-street, and Flinders-street. Straggling
houses, of course, there were outside that area,
and Collingwood—at that time called Newtown—
was a rising suburb of a dozen or two houses.

But if the appearances of the streets and buildings were unlike those of the old country towns, the ways of the inhabitants, as far as they met the eye, were not less decidedly dissimilar. Perhaps the first thing one noticed was the almost total absence of women from the streets, as well as the paucity of old men. In those days anyone over thirty was spoken of as old So-and-so. Of the gentlemen one saw, a good sprinkling were *squatters*, who had brought their flocks and herds from New South Wales or Tasmania. As a variety of the *genus homo* they were distinguishable by their hirsute appearance; whiskers, beards, and moustaches being decidedly in the ascendant among them. Many of them, I noticed, indulged also in blue serge shirts in lieu of coats, cabbage-tree hats, belts supporting leather tobacco-pouches, and in some few cases a pistol, which, with breeches, boots, and spurs, completed the costume. The horse, too, seemed an animal all but inseparable from the young gentlemen I am attempting to describe, who, if not engaged chatting in twos and threes at the corners of streets, or in the act of coming out of or going into one of the inns, might generally be observed hurrying on horseback from one end of the little town to the other, occasionally, to avoid detours, taking their nags over one of the gutter chasms which intersected the streets. One young squatter, I remember, was particularly noticeable, as it was his custom to

have a black boy in livery mounted on his horse's
croup. Nor did such little eccentricities seem to
surprise the residents or attract much notice, the
accepted idea seeming to be, that bushmen were
not by any means amenable to the slow ways of
the dwellers in towns, and that many things
were proper enough in them which might have
been esteemed strange, or even objectionable, in
others.

The squatters of that period—generally new
arrivals from home, and young men who had
brought with them more cash than experience—
were a good deal discussed by the townsfolk,
and more especially by the ladies, who, it struck
me, had vague and curious notions concerning
them. As far as I could gather, the prevailing
notion seemed to be that the squatters' *habitat*
in all cases was some fearfully remote and lonely
locality which it would be quite impossible for
ordinary persons to reach ; that without his horse
the squatter could not exist ; that he wore habitually Hessian boots and spurs, of which it was
uncertain whether he ever divested himself ; that
he was much given to emu and kangaroo hunting ; had constant encounters with hordes of
blacks ; rode as a rule fifty miles a day, chiefly at
a gallop—a performance which seemed as necessary to his horse as to himself—and at night slept
anywhere, with his saddle for a pillow. It was
also surmised that some sense, peculiar to the

young squatter, enabled him to find his way in the most unerring manner through trackless forests and waterless wastes; that (when out of town) he lived solely on tea, mutton, and damper, and enjoyed, when in the saddle, a perfect immunity from fatigue. All this of course was mere surmise; what townspeople really did know about the squatter was, that in town he was lavish in his expenditure, affected tandem driving, had a decided *penchant* for beer and brandy, smoked continually, and was not as a rule over-punctual in his payments, or versed in the ways of merchants or bankers. His peculiarities, however, real or imaginary, did not survive the very early days of the colony; he was too lively a bird for our forests, so that, eventually, lawyers and courts of justice put out many a shining light of those times. In the early days the young men took to the bush and the neighing steed, as naturally as they now become bank clerks, lawyers, and cricketers.

But if the squatter was what perhaps first attracted the attention of a stranger in the streets in 1839, he was not by any means the only subject of remark. These were numerous. Amongst other noteworthy matters which one met with in Melbourne at that time was the champagne lunch. To account for this institution (which, by-the-bye, was thought worthy of mention by Sir George Gipps in one of his despatches to the home Government), it must be borne in mind that the moneyed portion of the population consisted in the main of individuals of a more or less adventurous turn of mind, who had left Great Britain in search of new homes; or of unquiet spirits wearied with the jog-trot ways of the elder colonies, already effete after their prolonged existence of fifty years, who had come to Port Phillip to take possession of a magnificent territory ready for immediate use; and that from the congregation of such a population, the elements of pastoral wealth ready to hand, the too facile accommodation afforded by the banks, and the artificial stimulus which resulted from Sir George Gipps's system of land sales, a spirit of speculation, as hair-brained as ever the world saw, had taken root in the colony, at that time known as the Port Phillip district.

The consequences of this state of things pervaded all the relations of life, and a general mental inebriety seized on the people. I suppose we may say they were drunk with speculations and visions of wealth. That a man had bought a horse for £100, or a town allotment for £1,000 one day, seemed almost to be accepted as a guarantee for their purchaser realizing at auction £150 or £1,500 on the next; and champagne lunches seemed the natural adjuvant and appropriate stimulant to business conducted on such sparkling principles. People said it " kept the steam up," and so lunches were to be met with daily, at one auction room or another, cold fowls, hams, beer, brandy, and champagne being provided for intending buyers, and in fact for anyone who chose to partake of them. Without such accessories it would have been thought imprudent to put property on the market—the *mise en scène* would have been critically wrong; and so they became an " institution," as the Yankees say. To these spreads (there were usually one or two daily), in addition to those who proposed to buy, anyone who was disengaged seemed to saunter in ; no questions were asked, but as a rule each one seemed to take a bottle of his favourite beverage for himself (no matter how many stood open to his hand), knocked the head off with a knife, drank, chatted with his acquaintance for a few minutes, stayed to see a lot or two disposed of, had another drink, pronounced the champagne refreshing, or the brandy "nippin" (as the term was), lit his pipe or cigar, and left. Why people always knocked the heads off the bottles in those days I cannot say, but I remember I used to incline to the belief that there were no corkscrews in the colony at the time. Whether the colonists, in their hurry to reach Australia Felix, had neglected to supply themselves with that time-honoured utensil, or whether they had worn out on the passage those with which they had left home, or whether they were contraband of the Customs, I never learnt. Whatever the cause, however, a corkscrew was certainly seldom seen in public.

Another thing which struck the stranger in connection with business matters was, that the community seemed urgently bent on ascertaining, by the test of auction, the value of every horse, house, and acre in the colony. I was the more confirmed in this view by observing how few persons seemed to have any idea of retaining permanently any property purchased, as it was no sooner acquired than the new owner seemed to set himself to calculate what it would fetch when put more advantageously on the market, and resold at the expiration of a week or two. This seemed to be specially the case as regarded town allotments, and people were always arguing that the value of that commodity increased in proportion to its subdivision, and hence buying large lots, subdividing, and reselling was constantly going on. In connection with this business I remember there was a grey-haired old man who was quite a character about the town. Mounted on an old white horse, this individual might be seen daily perambulating the streets between the hours of nine and twelve a.m., ringing a bell, and carrying a red flag elevated on a staff, a few feet above his head, on which appeared in large letters the word *Auction*; whilst two boards, on which were posted bills of the sale to which the old man drew attention, dangled at his back and chest. As he rode down Collins-street, I often noticed that the board which hung in front rested on the pommel of the saddle, and, coming under the rider's chin, elevated his line of vision far above the horizon. As he could see little of what was passing around him, and hear nothing for the noise made by his bell, his look naturally became abstracted, if not solemn. Somehow this old man, always gazing upwards, apparently at some distant hills, with banner upreared and locks floating in the wind, has become mixed up in my mind with Longfellow's Alpine hero—whimsically and improperly enough, I admit—and when I think of him, the poet's verses seem to vary into something of this sort :—

> Onward the old man spurred his horse;
> Adown the street he took his course,
> Bearing a banner with strange device,
> *Re* town allotments at a price,
>
> Excelsior !

This old man, with horse, flag, bell, and board, served, it might be, more than one useful purpose; and I certainly, as the result of a limited experience, came to consider that, at the auction announced by him, the beer and champagne would be found cooler and more choice than elsewhere; indeed, I was often led to debate in my mind whether he did not carry out a hospitable device of the jovial dwellers of the town for letting strangers know where the principal commercial spread of the day would be, at which, *sans façon*, their company was expected.

The Melbourne Club, which at that time occupied the corner of Collins-street and Market-street, was another object of note. The number of its members seemed considerable, and it was at the club door—which stood what I may call three-quarters face to the street—that the orderlies and horses of the Commissioners of Crown Lands (the former in spruce uniform, and the latter be-holstered and be-cavessoned) were to be seen in attendance several hours daily; their masters being probably engaged with brandy and cigars within. Those were the palmy days of Commissioners, when licenses for runs, the settling of disputed boundaries, &c., depended on their *fiat*. They were also in command of the mounted police, and in some instances, at least, displayed in their costume and manner decidedly military proclivities. Another peculiarity of the town at that period was, that the time-honoured black hat and dark clothes of the old country had given way to straw hats and white suits; and I well remember, later, a few men donning dark clothes and black hats, and bringing back the old country costume. On the first day of my arrival in Melbourne (of which the population was estimated at about 5,000 souls) I remember being somewhat struck by the leading article in the newspaper, which was a diatribe on the doings of the wife of the principal merchant. From the article in question it appeared that the lady had given a ball the night previously, to which all the *élite* of the place had been invited, and congenially, perhaps, with the advanced lights prevalent at the moment in the future capital of Australia Felix, she had thought fit to receive the company seated on a chair, which stood on a dais beneath a canopy. The name of the editor, however, from some cause or other had been omitted from the list of invitations, and, to mark his disapproval of such treatment, he had indited a leader, making savage sport of the lady and her doings. The scene, no doubt, was provocative enough of mirth, and the editor's explosion was the more interesting to me as I was that evening to be a guest of the fair hostess of the dais and canopy, who, I may remark, dispensed very pleasantly the hospitalities of her house, in which the *tout ensemble* of furniture, wines, cookery, attendance, &c , would have passed muster in a more settled country, and was little to be expected on the spot where, not four years previously, Batman had stepped from his whale-boat into the primeval bush.

But at this epoch the Melbourne craze, *par excellence*, was town allotments. On this subject ran conversation principally, and probably dreams entirely—a circumstance not to be wondered at

when we remember that in two years favourite
lots had increased ten or twenty fold in value, and
were still steadily rising. With this mania men
and women were all bitten alike, and it was per-
petually cropping up in the most ridiculous and
unexpected ways. My father used to relate,
as an instance, a conversation he heard one
evening at the club. The parties conversing were
a doctor and a lawyer. The doctor, whose im-
ported blood-horse was daily paraded about the
streets in the usual bravery of ribbons and rugs,
was talking over his grog to his friend the solicitor
on the subject of a profit of £8 per head on a lot
of mares on which he reckoned.

"Look here!" said the doctor, holding the palm
of his left hand before his friend's eyes, "look here!
here are eighty mares at £8 a head," and he
accompanied the words with an invisible writing
of the figures on the outstretched palm. His
friend bent his energies on the aerial figuristic
statement, under which the doctor proceeded to
draw a line in the time-honoured way. "That's
clear," said the doctor. "Quite," replied the
lawyer, with that air of thorough assent which
people not infrequently put on when what they
should understand appears at the moment a hopeless muddle. "Well then, eight times nought are
nothing—put down nought and carry one," and
the doctor drew a nought with the index finger of
his right hand on the palm of his left, which the

lawyer carefully noted, winking his eyes to clear his sight, as the calculation was growing intricate.

"Eight times eight are sixty-four, ar'nt they, C—?" "Quite so," said the lawyer approvingly.

"Just so; eight times eight are sixty-four, and one are sixty-five. Six hundred and fifty pounds in three months," continued the son of Esculapius, and he turned the *quasi* slate full to the light, so that his friend might more clearly discern the interesting calculation. The lawyer, my father used to assert laughingly, gazed for a moment on the hand, as if thoroughly enjoying the beautiful demonstration, and then turned his face, radiant with groggy good-humour, on his friend, exclaiming "Nippin!" and a slight hiccough disturbed his utterance, "nippin, doctor; so come on *and let us have another glass of town allotments!*" The horsey allurements had seduced the steadfast mind of the man of briefs but for a moment from their accustomed shrine.

But though my father amused himself with the oddities of the town allotment mania, some purchases which he made during his visit seemed to show that he himself had not quite escaped the malady. Fortunately, however, he only took it in a mild form.

It was also on the occasion of this visit that I was present at, I believe. the first land sales at Pascoeville and Sandridge, or the Beach, as the

3

latter was then called. To arrive at Sandridge
the Yarra had to be crossed on a punt. Of
those who went there, some rode and others
drove, the pace of the horses being decidedly
fast, and so far in keeping with the ways of
their owners. A carriage or two, and dog-carts
galore, whirled along, and there was a considerable sprinkling of ladies out to see what was
to be seen. One eminent lawyer I noticed driving
several of the fair sex in an ammunition waggon,
with a pair of horses with which he had got into
difficulties; in fact, the steeds, which did not
appear to understand the man of briefs, had
demurred to his pleadings to proceed. Altogether
he was not happy with horses, for I remember
hearing some time afterwards that one of them
had broken his leg with a kick—his " polka leg,"
as he said. Arrived with a friend at the future
Sandridge, we met, as usual, hams and turkeys,
beer and champagne. I do not recollect seeing
any land sold. It might have been that the
company had only come to view the allotments,
which were shortly to be offered for sale in
Melbourne. What I do remember is that the
gathering was a very pleasant one; everyone
seemed in the best of spirits, and several tents
had been set in a prominent position, in which
the company lunched as they arrived. That important preliminary over, we broke up into twos
and threes, some strolling on the beach with the

ladies, some examining the surveyor's lines in the future township, whilst others sat down to enjoy their cigars in the shade. Altogether, anything more like a picnic, and more unlike the usual routine of business, I never saw. In these ways two or three hours were passed, when by degrees the ladies and their escorts left to return home, after which town allotment talk flowed for a time triumphant; except in the case of a few young squatters, who got up races on the sands, or tried their horses over a jump of boughs which they had improvised.

When people could tear themselves from town allotments, the leading topics of conversation in Melbourne at that time were the expected arrival from England of the Superintendent, Mr. Latrobe, and the position he would take up with respect to the local revenue, which heretofore had been expended in Sydney. Then there was the anticipated news from Adelaide of Messrs. Hawden and Mundy, who had left town in a tandem to explore a route between the two capitals. The uncertainty of whether these explorers would succeed in passing through several hundred miles of unexplored country beset with blacks, or whether they would get their brains knocked out on the way, was, of course, the principal feature of interest in the affair, and that which commended it to the sympathies of a society, the daily transactions of which might fairly be placed midway between the chance of the dice, pure and simple, and the cold prudence which regulates the business of more staid communities.

Another feature of Melbourne was the blacks, who constantly wandered about in large numbers, half-naked, and armed with spears in the usual way. To hear them cooeying and shouting to one another, in shrill voices and strange tongues, in the streets had a strange effect. These once free-born lords of the soil seemed to make themselves useful under the new *régime* by chopping firewood, bringing in brooms for barter, and occasional buckets of water from the Yarra; and might be seen a little before sundown retiring to their camps on the outskirts of the town, well supplied with bread and meat, and followed by packs of half-starved mangy dogs, which had spent the day in performing scavengers' duty in the streets, in which employment they were clearly not without their advantages. But whilst speaking of the town, I must not forget the cottage of the kind friend who had asked me to make it my home during my visit. It was a rustic-looking little wattle-and-dab building of three rooms, well shaded by trees, and situated within ten yards of the bank of the Yarra, at about three hundred yards from its junction with the Merri Merri Creek. The floors were the ground, ceiling there was none, and around the outside was a verandah, up the posts of which were trained creepers. In front there were three French windows, which looked on the river flowing by amidst lovely wattle trees. As a servant my friend had a rough man, not used to the ways of towns; in fact, a bush hutkeeper, who baked our damper, fried our chops, and went to town once a fortnight to purchase groceries and get drunk. The kitchen and servant's room were detached, and a little further off was a stable. The approach was across a thickly grassed alluvial flat studded with handsome and shady trees—some of them blackwoods —and the Merri Merri Creek was crossed by a stony ford. Nothing, in its way, could be prettier than this spot; more Australian, or more secluded. One of its features was the great quantity of birds congregated thereabout. The voice of the bell-bird—"which never was mute"—I heard there for the first time, ever ringing amidst umbrageous river trees. Magpies and other songsters dwelt there also in considerable numbers; and as I sat alone in the verandah one evening watching the sun go down, I heard, for the first time, the laughing-jackass's nightly adieu to that luminary.

CHAPTER III.

JOURNEY TO WOLFSCRAG.

My father had formed a very high opinion of the colony in 1839, and being again in Melbourne in January, 1841, he purchased a sheep station which was situated on the Major's line,* about seventy miles from Melbourne, and five miles south-west from where the town of Heathcote now stands. This station, which was called Wolfscrag, had been taken up for an absentee Tasmanian proprietor by his overseer, and had been represented at the sale to have improvements on it to the value of some £300 or £400. The number of sheep depasturing at Wolfscrag was said to be 2,300, more or less; and my father, who had not seen the property, purchased it at the price of 15s. a head on the sheep delivered to him—a figure then unprecedentedly low.

As regards the value of runs or stations at that time, it must be borne in mind that anyone was at liberty, on payment to Government of a yearly fee of £10. to "squat" on country not already occupied; so that, as there was plenty of country

---

* The "Major's line" is a term signifying the track, or line of road, formed by the drays of Major (afterwards Sir Thomas) Mitchell in his explorations. In some localities the track or road which his drays left behind is called "the Major" to this day.

vacant, the selling value of a run was very little more than the cost of the improvements—that is, huts, fences, woolsheds, &c.—which had been erected on it.

On his return to Tasmania, my father sent me over to take delivery of the sheep, and manage his new purchase, directing me to engage a competent overseer, from whom I should be able to learn sheep-farming, of which I knew nothing, and for which, at that time, I had little inclination. Accordingly, I left Tasmania without delay, and reached Melbourne on the 9th of February, 1841. On arriving there I met the person who was to give delivery of the sheep and run ; and, though I was not at all prepossessed with him, I was glad to engage him as my overseer for three months at a salary of £100 per annum, as servants of any sort were most difficult to obtain ; which being arranged, I directed him to return to Wolfscrag, where I purposed following him in the course of a few days.

Being, as I have said, perfectly ignorant of everything connected with sheep and their management—never having, in fact, seen a station or counted a flock of sheep, I was very desirous of getting some friend experienced in such matters to accompany me to see delivery taken, as well as to obtain an opinion of the property ; the more so as I had got an idea into my head, during my interview with my overseer, that I should find things on the station very different from what they had been represented at the sale. In this, fortunately, I succeeded, as I met a friend of my father, who was on the point of starting with a companion to his own station, and who kindly consented to make a *détour* and see me through my first difficulties at Wolfscrag.

I had brought an excellent saddle mare with me from Tasmania, and set out accordingly with my two companions about three o'clock one evening, a few days after my arrival, our destination that night being the Bush Inn, distant some thirty-five miles from Melbourne. As the weather was excessively hot, and our horses fat, we rode slowly, and did not reach the inn until a couple of hours or more after sundown, when my experience of Australian bush life began. The inn, we noticed as we approached, was somewhat noisy, and on going up to it, a hostler, summoned by the barking of a bloodhound, came out of the front door, and, taking possession of our horses in a very free-and-easy manner, directed us to enter the house at the door by which he had left it. Having got rid of our horses, a step took us into the sitting-room, which opened on to the verandah. The building was of slabs, roofed with shingles in the usual way ; its dimensions were about thirty-five feet by twelve, with a skillion in addition in the rear, which ran the whole length of the structure. The exterior and division walls were seven feet high. The ceiling was of white-washed canvas, and a covering of the same material lined the walls in lieu of plaster. The sitting-room, into which we have found our way, was about fifteen feet long. In the middle of it was a deal table, one end of which was laid with washing utensils for the morning. In the centre of the table was a large brass bell, such as is used by criers, and a single tallow candle in a disreputable candlestick, which guttered complacently on to the oilcloth covering. On the mantelpiece were a few gaudy ornaments, Phillises in china with lambs to match, and the figure of a Spanish bull-fighter or two, if my memory serves me.

There were also in the room four sofas, of the poorest sort, on two of which beds had been made, the one having an occupant who was already asleep. He was probably a squatter, travelling between his station and town. His boots, hat, and clothes had been thrown on the floor beside him; a tobacco-pouch hung suspended by a leather belt from the head rail of the sofa or bed-stead (the one by day, and the other by night), and from under his pillow protruded the end of a valise and the butt of a horse pistol. Besides visible discomfort, a conglomerate aroma of tobacco, beer, and mutton-birds, new to me at that time, pervaded the atmosphere; whilst now and then the canvas ceiling, shaken by a pass-ing air, which fortunately found ingress under

the eaves, gave a sort of plunge which reminded one of the sails of a ship in the light
weather of the tropics. Two of the sofas, as I
have said, were doing duty as beds, in one of which
the occupant was asleep. On the second was a
man who had apparently been laid down shortly
before, but was now sitting on the edge of his bed
in strong *déshabille*. He was evidently of the
working class; his shirt was unbuttoned at the
throat; he had on slippers and trousers; his hair
was dishevelled, and his suspenders hung down
behind him. To our entrance this character paid
no attention, if, indeed, he saw us at all, but
continued smoking his pipe with an abstracted
look, his eye being wild, haggard, and restless.
Now and then he strode up to the fireplace,
wrung his hands with the air of a maniac giving
vent *sotto voce* to a string of bitter imprecations
on some, to us, unknown individual, and then
reseated himself in his former position. The
feeble cry of a child from the adjoining skillion we
soon noticed to be in some manner connected with
his excitement, and, indeed, to judge from appearances, it only required the presence of a sharp
razor to ensure a case of suicide before morning!
From the tap, in the meantime, which was within
a yard of us—the only separation being the walls
and ceiling already particularized—proceeded the
wrangling, laughter, and oaths of half-a-dozen
drunken men.

Such was the *coup-d'œil* which presented itself to us on our entering the sitting-room of the Bush Inn, which might, at the period, have been considered, in the main, a fair specimen of bush inns in the colony generally at nine o'clock in the evening. Supper being desirable after our ride, the startling sound of the big brass bell, which stood on the table, brought the barmaid into the room, who having promised us some bacon and eggs and tea without milk, and tried with a spoon, which she happened to have in her hand, to stop the candle from guttering, removed the washing utensils to a corner on the floor, and proceeded to lay the table. Having supped, we adjourned to the open air for a smoke; after which two of our number took possession of the vacant sofas in the sitting-room, on which beds had been made in the interim, whilst the third was accommodated for the night in some other part of the house. Our rest in such a place, it may easily be imagined, was of a very equivocal description; in fact, the songs and shouts of those drinking in the bar, which continued till nearly daylight; the remonstrances of the landlord, the cries of the child, the mutterings of the dishevelled one, and the unsavoury odour of our mutton-bird feather pillows, together with certain animalculine inconveniences, made sleep all but impossible.

When morning came, having performed our ablutions in the creek (doubly welcome after a

feverish night) and our toilet on its banks, we
called for our bill, whilst discharging which, an
account of the dishevelled occupant of the sofa
was elicited from the landlord. From him we
learned that this mysteriously excited individual
was an overseer on a station about ten miles from
Wolfscrag, on which his brother, a lately married
man, had also resided in the capacity of stockman.
This stockman, it appeared, had died not long
since from a wound received in an encounter with
the Blacks, leaving a young widow and a child
behind him; the former of whom, after bemoaning
her loss with great constancy for six weeks, had at
length dried her tears and consented to become the
wife of her brother-in-law. In consequence of this
arrangement, the young widow had started for
town with the proprietor of the station, who had
obligingly offered her a seat in his dog-cart, the
bridegroom-elect being to meet her at church two
or three days later. In the meantime, it appears
that the capricious fair one was wooed by her master
on the road down, and wedded forthwith on their
arrival in town, and was on her return to the
station in all the glories of a new bonnet and
husband, when the pair met the discarded lover
face to face at the inn door ; who, in ignorance of
what had occurred, had just been experiencing
that delicate badinage to which "happy men"
have been victims from time immemorial. A
stormy *éclaircissement*, under circumstances so

embarrassing to all parties, had, it seems, taken place and as what had occurred was past remedy, the disappointed overseer had flown for consolation to brandy-and-water, of which the landlord informed us "he had taken a heavy lap" before going to bed.

Mounting our horses after hearing this little relation, we rode over to the quarters of the Crown Lands Commissioner, which, with the barracks of the mounted police under his command, were only a mile or so from the inn, and, in exchange for his breakfast, gave him an account of our miserable night, of which that official, I remember, took a more serious view than we had done ; debating whether he would renew the license of a publican who allowed his customers to drink and conduct themselves uproariously after 10 o'clock p.m., as that seemed to him the hour at which travellers who were not drunk should be allowed to go to sleep.

After leaving the Bush Inn, it took us two days of leisurely riding, and following wrong roads, to reach Wolfscrag. The hour of our arrival was a little before sundown, and certainly the aspect of my new home and its surroundings was anything but inviting. The run, a good deal of which we had passed through on our way to the huts, might be described as a mass of barren quartz ranges, between which were a few long narrow flats, watered by small creeks, and very poorly grassed. The establishment consisted of two slab huts, each about fifteen feet by ten; one occupied by the men, and the other by the overseer and his servant. They stood on a hillside not far from the creek, and a little removed from them, in the flat below, were three flocks of sheep in hurdle-yards; a movable watch-box, in which the hutkeeper slept, standing in the space between them. On the side of the range, some three hundred yards off, the shadows of the trees fell on a tumble-down edifice, constructed of bark and poles lashed together with thongs of bullock hide, which I learned was the shed in which the shearing and wool-pressing were carried on. From the huts no grass or herbage could be seen; the dust from the lately yarded flocks slowly drifted in a cloud down the desolate valley, and the whole scene, from a sheep-farmer's point of view, was as disheartening as could well be imagined. The sterility of the spot indeed was more noticeable, of course, when contrasted with the rich country through which we had travelled from Melbourne, and it will be easily imagined that my companions offered no congratulations on my prospects.

Having unsaddled and tethered our horses in one of the gullies on some coarse grass, we entered the overseer's hut, the interior of which was scarcely an improvement on its outward appearance. It consisted of three rooms, one of which was a store, in which were kept the flour, tea,

sugar, meat-cask, &c., of the establishment;
another was the bedroom of the overseer's female
servant; whilst the principal apartment did duty
as kitchen, diningroom, and overseer's bedroom,
and was arranged in this way :—On one side, and
close to the fireplace, stood a rough bedstead, an
opossum-rug spread over, which concealed the
bed-clothes beneath. In the centre of the room
there was a large sea-chest, which served as a
table; and at the fireplace, which occupied the
whole of one end of the building, and was almost
as large as one of the smaller rooms, the supper
was being cooked—to the no small increase
of a heat already excessive. Against the walls,
around which were hung a pair or two of horse-
hobbles, a gun, stock-whip, some tin dishes,
pannikins, a rickety looking-glass, and other odds
and ends appertaining to the gentle craft of
squatting, were set three rough stools; and on
the mantelpiece were disposed, evidently with
some regard to effect, a couple of Hall's powder
canisters, of a flaming red colour; a horse's hoof;
some blue paper boxes containing seidlitz powders
(the overseer's substitute for sodawater); a
meerschaum pipe, with a large glass-stoppered
druggist's bottle as a centrepiece, containing
some three pints of a sherry-coloured liquid, and
labelled *butyr of antimony*. In one of the walls
of the hut there was an aperture of about a foot
square, cut through the slabs as a window, before

which was drawn, on strings, a little curtain of white calico. The outer door, which always stood open by day, was secured at night by a bar; and a couple of woolpacks, nailed to the tie-beams and reaching the ground, supplied the place of doors to the two smaller apartments.

On arriving, we had been met by the overseer, who ushered us into the hut, and formally put me in possession of the premises, with the air of one who was relinquishing what he evidently looked on as a very complete little establishment. Of the correctness of his views on this subject it hardly needed the smile, which I thought I detected on the faces of my friends, to remind me that some diversity of opinion might exist. There was a momentary lull as we sat down, and the eyes of each wandered involuntarily over the hut, and took stock of its contents. It was clean in its way, but very comfortless as I thought then; later on I got used to things still rougher. After a moment, the friend who accompanied me broke the silence, remarking, as he turned towards me—"The hut is well enough, though rather small; I assure you we don't think this bad in the bush."

"As tight as a nut, sir," said the overseer, interposing and looking up at the ridge-pole, evidently pleased; "I had it new barked in the spring. You'll find everything very comfortable and dry," continued he, addressing me. "A grand thing, sir, a dry hut; a grand thing! My old one at Western Port used to leak like a sieve, and we were always wet. But, I dare say, gentlemen, you are hungry after your ride." And, turning to the servant, he ordered supper.

In due time the sea-chest table was covered with a clean towel; three willow-pattern plates, in more or less dilapidated plight, were placed on it; an old pint pannikin, partially filled with clay and topped up with mutton fat from the frying-pan, with a bit of old shirt wrapped round a stick stuck in the centre for a wick, did duty as a lamp; some odd knives and forks made their appearance from the store-room, whilst a round wooden box (marvellously like a lather box) supplied the place of a salt-cellar. Beside each plate the servant laid a pint tin pannikin and a slice of damper; and a large tin dish was placed in the centre of the table. Everything was clean at least, and the tinware bright as silver. After these preliminary steps had been taken, some rather coarse brown sugar was put in the pannikins, which were then filled with tea from an iron kettle which was simmering by the fire, and finally a leg of mutton was transferred on the end of a large iron skewer, amidst clouds of vapour, from the iron pot in which it was boiling, to the tin dish on the table, the overseer at this stage of the proceedings inviting us cordially to "sit in" and have supper whilst it was hot. It certainly was hot, and so

were we,—and no danger of us, at least, getting
cool. The atmosphere of the room, the fire, the
vapour, the odour of the "fat lamp," the scalding
hot tea and reeking mutton, were neither pleasant
nor inviting; but as there was no preferable
alternative, we did "sit in" to the edge of the
sea-chest on our three-legged stools, and, setting
to work manfully, acquitted ourselves as well as
could have been expected of novices under the
circumstances. "*Messieurs, vous êtes servis!*" said
one of my friends, laughing, as we began our meal;
probably some hotel on the *Boulevards* suggesting
itself to his mind as a contrast!

CHAPTER IV.

PROSPECTS OF SHEEP-FARMING AT WOLFSCRAG.

VERY anti-Capuan were the couches of Wolfscrag,
and conducive to early rising; and before the sun
was two hours high the sheep had been counted
by my friend, delivery of the station had been
taken, and I had shaken hands with my late companions, and watched them as they rode slowly
down the grassless valley, which extended some
distance before the hut which I was now to call
my home. A momentary spasm of regret, I must
say, passed over me as I stood at the door watching their departure, and thought of the altogether

uncongenial surroundings amidst which I was to
remain behind. But indulgence in such feelings
could serve no purpose, so, as my mare was tired,
and there seemed heretofore to have been no
recognized pastime or occupation at Wolfscrag—if
I except smoking negro-head tobacco and drinking
green tea—I thought it desirable to innovate a
little, and vary my amusement and that of my
overseer by turning our attention for a short time
to the financial matters connected with the establishment. Before, however, laying the result of
my investigations before the reader, I may premise
that the sheep on the station (which were badly
scabbed and suffering from foot-rot) were depas-
tured in three flocks, each of which was under
the charge of a shepherd, who, as was the custom,
took it out to feed from sunrise to sunset, when
he brought it home and put it into a fold of hurdles
for the night. The care of the three flocks during
the night, and their protection from wild dogs, de-
volved on the watchman, or hutkeeper, who slept
in a movable watch-box close to them; whose further duties also were to remove the folds daily on
to fresh ground, and to cook for the shepherds.

The number and description of my three flocks
were about as follows :—

> 650 very old ewes.
> 650 two, four, and six-toothed ewes.
> 800 { 300 wethers.
>   { 500 weaners of both sexes.
> ————
> 2,100

I may add that there were belonging to the station neither horses, dray, nor bullocks, and that the small supply of rations in store was, by the terms of sale, to be paid for at invoice prices, cartage added.

As regards the wages current on the station, they were as follows :—

Overseer, per annum	£100	0	0
Three shepherds, at £1 per week each	156	0	0
One hutkeeper do. do. ...	52	0	0
Bullock driver do. do. ...	52	0	0
Overseer's servant, per annum ...	40	0	0

In addition, I also found that the following outlay would be necessary :—

A team of bullocks, with dray, &c. ...	£100	0	0
One mare (already purchased) ...	75	0	0
One horse	55	0	0
Twenty rams (those which had been on the run having been destroyed for scab)	80	0	0
Rations for eight persons, flour being £60 per ton ; and tea, and sugar, and tobacco at corresponding rates	200	0	0
Yearly license of run	10	0	0
Assessment on 2,100 sheep	8	15	0
Sheepwashing, shears, woolpacks, &c.	12	0	0
Shearing 2,100 sheep	21	0	0
Dressing materials for scab and foot-rot	10	0	0
Expenses, travelling and unforeseen ..	100	0	0
Total estimated expenditure for the year ... ...£	1,071	15	0

Against this outlay, the only asset to be looked

forward to was the wool on the sheep, which might be estimated at the price of 1s. per lb., each sheep yielding about 2½ lbs., which brings out £262 1s., which would leave a deficit, if everything went on well, of £809 14s.—certainly a very charming prospect for a beginner !

As regards fattening my 300 wethers for market, I found, next day, that the scarcity of feed on the run made this quite out of the question. Indeed, the bare keeping the flocks alive seemed to me very problematical, as they appeared to be existing in a state of chronic semi-starvation; as a proof of which, if any were needed, it appeared that from the 1,300 breeding ewes only 500 lambs had been weaned after the last dropping.

On talking to the overseer of this ruinous position of affairs, he informed me that I should find on inquiry that the number of sheep in each flock, as well as the rate of wages paid to the men, were the same as on all the runs in the neighbourhood, which, in fact, I afterwards found to be the case.

Such a state of things could not, of course, last for ever, and in the next and subsequent years, as I shall have occasion to show, produced the only possible results—viz., embarrassment to the sheep-owners generally, and ruin to a large proportion of them. Why flocks depasturing on ground so flat, open, and richly grassed that

5,000, or even 7,000 sheep, could be easily kept in
sight by a single shepherd, as was really the case
in many parts of the colony, should be limited to
500 or 700 (though it did not interest me
pecuniarily at the moment amidst the scrubs of
Wolfscrag) was a matter which often suggested
itself to my mind, and it was not until long
after that any probable solution of the question occurred to me.   I then learned that the
localities in which sheep were first kept in
New South Wales being generally scrubby
and difficult to shepherd in, it had been decided by the country police magistrates that
shepherds (who were chiefly convicts) should
not be held responsible for sheep lost from
flocks which exceeded 520; and that the
flocks had, consequently, in order that the
shepherd might be made responsible for their
safety, in almost all cases been limited to that
number.

This custom having obtained in the elder
colony, had, it seems, been brought by the
overlanders to Port Phillip in spite of the
difference of the circumstances, of its rich open
plains and free shepherds; indeed, it was long
argued by old Sydney colonists that depasturing
any number in a flock over the time-honoured
520 could only lead to loss; one of the reasons
advanced being, that larger numbers defiled and
wasted the grass over which they daily travelled,

whilst the strong sheep in the flock got all the best of the feed.

My stay at Wolfscrag on this occasion did not, I think, extend much over a week, three or four days of which I passed shepherding with my overseer, who, waiting the arrival of some passer-by looking for work, was obliged to take charge of the flock of one of the shepherds who had demanded his wages and taken his departure the second morning after my arrival on the station. Whilst so employed, I naturally picked up some information on the subject of sheep-farming generally, and I became thoroughly convinced that my father's seemingly cheap purchase was in reality a very bad one: in fact, that the sheep were of bad quality, diseased, and one-third of them worn out; that the run itself was as bad as could be; that very vigorous measures would need to be taken to put matters on a proper footing; and that in any case a considerable loss would have to be submitted to. What steps could be taken I was at that time unable to decide. One thing was very clear, that nothing could go on properly until the sheep were removed to more suitable country than Wolfscrag. This I was informed was impossible for the present, as scabby sheep, which mine undoubtedly were, were prohibited from travelling, under a heavy penalty, except during the month of February, which was now drawing to a close.

Under these circumstances, I determined, waiting further experience, to put off any radical measure until I could hear from my father, and in the meantime to apply myself to the work in hand. Having so decided, I proceeded to town after a few days, where I purchased a dray, a team of bullocks, a horse, a supply of rations, sheep-dressing, tobacco, &c., at the prices already particularized, and engaged for six months a lot of fresh men at the rate of £45 per annum, thus making some slight reduction, at least, in the current expenses of the establishment.

CHAPTER V.

TROUBLES OF A BEGINNER.

I have just said that shortly after I took charge of Wolfscrag, I engaged a fresh lot of servants. I may add that hiring men in Melbourne in 1841 was not by any means an agreeable job, as wages were high, and labourers (almost all old gaol-birds and expiree convicts) exceedingly independent and rowdy, so that my first experiences in this line were anything but pleasant. They occurred in this way. Having learnt from my acquaintances in town that the only places at which men were to be found for

hire were the public-houses at which they were
accustomed to spend the proceeds of their labour,
I went, about ten o'clock one morning, to one of
these establishments, and walked into a front room
I saw open. In it a scene presented itself which
surprised me not a little; the more so as this was
the first time I had ever been in a place of the
sort. The room into which I had found my way
was a lengthy apartment, in the centre of which
was a long narrow deal table, on which stood, here
and there, a number of bottles of ale, brandy,
champagne, &c., together with tumblers, glasses,
and pewter-pots. On each side of the tables,
against the walls, were benches running the
length of the room, on which were seated some
thirty men in every stage of intoxication, from
maudlin imbecility to that of the maddened
bacchanal, vigorous and rampant, in the first
stage of his debauch. Some of the men were
drinking out of pots and glasses, and others out
of the bottles; some were singing, others quarrelling; one, with vacant lack-lustre eyes, sat
silently staring on the ground, another into an
empty pannikin; whilst three or four were
trying to dance to an air which was being played
on a fiddle by a man seated in a corner of the
room—a sort of resident musician to the establishment, I believe, whose bestial face was a study in
itself. Many also were smoking, and others trying
to smoke. As far as I observed, the conversation

of these heroes seemed to be carried on in a yell. One man cut a ludicrous caper when he saw me enter the room; but it was a last effort, for he staggered and rolled under the table, where he probably fell asleep. Another burly ruffian, who stood in the centre of a small group near the door and was flattening a pewter-pot with his fingers probably for a wager, turned on me, and accosted me in a savage and impertinent tone with " What the —— devil do you want, bloke, eh ?" " A bullock-driver," I replied, looking him in the face, and grasping firmly the hunting-whip which I held in my hand. My answer elicited from the company a roar of laughter, with oaths, yells, and imprecations. " Bonnet him, Tom ; bonnet him !" screamed one. " Break his —— back !" yelled another. " Come on, young 'un, have a drink," shouted a third. Whilst one poor fellow, with sodden wasted features and stony eyes, kept drawling out in a hoarse undertone, frothing at the mouth as though he were going to have a fit, " Put him out and break his neck, I say. Put him out and break his neck ;" which words he never ceased spluttering forth for the short time I remained in that pandemonium of debauchery.

Having neither seen nor heard of such sights previously, I was naturally astonished and disgusted at what was before me. Fortunately, no one laid hands on me, though several threatened to do so, when the publican came to the rescue, and, withdrawing me from the room into which I had stumbled, bundled out for my inspection, into a dingy back parlour, some six or eight men, whose money being spent, were no longer of any use to him, and only remained on the premises on sufferance. From amongst these worthies I hired the number I required—making each of them an advance of a pound. The same day I purchased a team of bullocks, and also a dray, which, with infinite trouble, I got loaded with supplies the day after, and then accompanied on the road a few miles out of town, having my patience cruelly exercised for some hours by my drunken servants, who tried hard to induce me to buy them a bottle or two of brandy. Having got them so far, and seen that they were getting sober, and knowing that there was no public-house within several miles of them, I returned to Melbourne for a day or two, reaching Wolfscrag just in time to see my dray arrive without accident, install my new servants and discharge the old ones. But though I had now got a dray and bullocks (indispensable requisites on a station), fresh men, and a supply of rations, I only came home to encounter new troubles. In the first place, my men were anything but satisfied with their master's run—for servants in those days were fastidious and outspoken—and mine complained that the station was scrubby, without feed, and almost impossible to shepherd on;

telling me that they had never seen so miserable
a station, such a lot of " crawling" sheep, and so
forth. The bullock-driver, too, was not less dissatisfied than the shepherds, complaining that
there was no grass, and that he would walk his
legs off trying to keep his team from straying.
As far as the shepherds were concerned, getting
them to their work was a matter requiring some
tact, and it was only effected, after much trouble,
by the overseer and myself going out with them
for a day or two so as to accustom them a little
to the run, and to some extent talking them out
of their objections to the place. As for *compelling*
them to perform their agreements, under which
they had all received money advances, it would
have been simply impossible under the circumstances. The bullock-driver was more easily
managed than the shepherds, as I rendered his
duty easy by directing him, as there was no
stockyard, to chain the bullocks to a tree at night
until something better could be done with them,
and take them out to feed during the day on what
little grass there was on the scrubby ranges.

Having arranged matters in this way as well
as I could, I proposed, partly on the advice of a
friend of my father, whom I had consulted in
town, but principally because I did not see how
things were to be put on a better footing, to
endure a while longer the troubles of sheep-
farming at Wolfscrag. For some time after I

got home I was glad to find that my business
went on more comfortably than before, though of
course, as I have already pointed out, the whole
concern was a losing one, and I did not see how
it could be made otherwise. To me a squatter's
life was a great change from my previous experiences; my not very delightful occupations at
this period being helping to dress the sheep for
scab and foot-rot, a little bullock-driving, learning
to find my way about the bush (an art which had
been sadly neglected in my education), getting
used to the ways of my men, and in the even
ing reading Youatt's book on "The Sheep."

Things were in this position, and scab and foot-
rot were being pretty well got under, when an
incident occurred, provoking enough at the time,
the results of which were to lead eventually to a
very decided and advantageous change in my
prospects as a sheep-farmer. I allude to the loss
of four of my six working bullocks. These
wretched animals— in those days always a source
of trouble—had seized an opportunity for ab-
sconding, taken to the bush, and gone no one knew
whither. To the uninitiated this may appear a
very small matter; but it was not so in reality,
as horses and bullocks are, in fact, the principal
means by which station work is carried on.
Without them little can be done, so their recovery
was a matter of necessity. In this emergency,
the overseer, the bullock-driver, and myself rode

out daily to try and find the truants, each going
in a different direction into the bush ; and a most
tiresome business it was, this weary looking for
tracks, examining creeks, and following gullies.
For my part, whilst attempting to find the missing
animals, it was only with great difficulty that I
managed not to lose myself. The country being
rangy, somewhat scrubby, and destitute of prominent features, was exceedingly perplexing to a
" new chum," so that, if I rode ahead for four
hours looking for the bullocks, I generally found
that it took me six, with good luck and all my
ingenuity, to retrace my steps. But to anyone
who knows anything about the bush I need not
dilate on the subject of bullock-hunting. Day
after day for a fortnight we persevered in our
search from daylight till dark, when, being
unsuccessful, I gave it up as hopeless, concluding,
new-chum like, that the wretched animals had
made good their escape into those boundless
forests, as yet unexplored by civilized man, on the
verge of which Wolfscrag was situated, and out of
which their recovery was hopeless. How differently I should have thought and acted a twelve-
month later !

This was my first real dilemma, and sadly I
pondered on it ; not that I had any work for
bullocks on the station at the time, but that there
loss rendered my leaving Wolfscrag impossible,
which, notwithstanding the Scab Act, I hoped to

do in one direction or another at no distant date. Of course, the animals might be replaced, but to do so would cost £40 ; and though the funds at my disposal had not got so low as that, they were getting sensibly less, and I was unwilling to ask my father for more money. After worrying myself in vain, and turning the matter over in every way, I made up my mind to wait as patiently as I could for a few weeks, before buying a new team, and see what chance would do for me in the interim, consoling myself with the reflection that, at all events, I was getting day by day more conversant with my business, of which, indeed, on my first arrival I knew absolutely nothing.

Affairs were in this position, and my sheep, which were to lamb in three months, were becoming daily more reduced in condition, when chancing to inquire one evening of my overseer whether it was not possible that a little more feed might be found in some distant corner of the run, he said to me, with an expression of face which I could not understand, but noticed at the time—— "Oh! you should take the sheep over the ranges ; there is lots of feed there now." And on my expressing some surprise that as often as I had spoken to him on this subject he had never suggested that step before, he replied, " that on the part of the run he spoke of the grass had been burned by a bush fire just before my arrival, and

that before this it had not had time to grow
again."

In consequence of this information he and I
set out next day and followed up the creek to the
range referred to, climbed its rather rugged side,
and, on descending its southern slope, found ourselves in the midst of an abundance of grass and
water. Gently sloping hills, which as far as the
eye could see had been run over by a bush fire
a few months ago, were now clothed with the
greenest and freshest of kangaroo grass, inter-
spersed with yams, murnong, and other herbs in
which sheep delight; whilst two small creeks, well
supplied with water, met in the valley in which
we stood. To my inexperienced eye no track of
foot or hoof was visible, whilst the grass-covered
hills, lovely as a view, were doubly so in the eyes
of an owner of three famishing flocks. To make
up my mind to bring my sheep to the spot
required, of course, no lengthened consideration :
so, after gazing on the beauties around me, we remounted our horses to return, and on our road
home I saw from the top of the range, far away
to the north, a large tract of open country, concerning which my overseer could give me no
information. Later on I found this to be the
Colbinabbin and Coragorag plains, little dreaming,
when first I saw them, that the rocks and scrubs
of Wolfscrag were one day to be exchanged for
that then unexplored country. Having thus dis-

covered an abundant supply of feed and water for
present use, a day sufficed to bring my sheep
to the spot, and the scanty requirements of an
out-station of the sort were quickly supplied.
Merrily with saw and axe we felled the trees
around, and with them constructed the required
yards, a tarpaulin and a few forked sticks and
poles being all that was necessary in the way of a
hut for the shepherds. Then, having stripped for
the men a sheet of bark each, on which to lay
their beds, I left them almost as pleased with the
change as the sheep themselves, and returned
with my overseer to the head station.

CHAPTER VI.

ALONE AT MY HUT.

For a time after I had got my sheep on to the burnt
feed just spoken of I had very little to do but
revel in the reflections that my miserable flocks,
with dressed backs and pared hoofs, had at length
their wants fully supplied; that I should have
some prospects of a tolerable lambing; and that
my shepherds were no longer discontentedly
scrambling up and down the sides of grassless

5

ranges after their hungry wandering charges, but were now watching their sheep feed around, and in the enjoyment of that thorough idleness which, everyone knows, of course, is so congenial to the pastoral mind. As for me, I could not help wondering that such feed existed on the station, and that I had never heard of it; and this set me thinking about the boundaries of the run, a subject upon which, up to that time, I had never been able to obtain any information, the overseer having always told me that he was the last comer in the neighbourhood, and that the question of boundaries had never turned up, remarking that when my flocks met those of my neighbours some day in the bush it would be time enough to move in the matter.

It was a few days after my sheep had been located in the midst of plenty, that the term for which I had engaged my overseer expired; and as I had found that instead of making himself useful, or giving me an insight into the business, he had systematically tried to deceive me on every occasion, I determined to pay off both him and his servant, and let them go. This I did. We had no words on the occasion, however, and I gave him the use of my remaining pair of bullocks, dray, and driver to remove his luggage to town. As he had four bullocks of his own running on a neighbouring station, the team was made up with them, and it was agreed that

I should have the use of the lot to bring back a small load of supplies for the station.

The departure of my overseer forms one of the little epochs in my reminiscences which are particularly stamped on my memory, as it was on that occasion that I took on myself the responsibility of management. It was on that occasion, also, that I first found myself quite alone in the bush; all my servants, with the exception of the bullock-driver, who was now leaving with the dray, being stationed, as the reader is aware, with the sheep some six miles away, so that there remained no one but myself to look after the stores and plant at the head station.

First impressions of things generally remain, and I well remember seating myself on a log near the hut, the morning the overseer left, and watching the dray as it toiled slowly and noisily up the gully which led to the road. For some time I could see the many-coloured bullocks; the driver, in his cabbage-tree hat, walking near them with his whip over his shoulder, and the overseer and his servant following a little in the rear. I thought they were a long time getting out of sight. At last they disappeared into the scrub; and when no longer visible, I still sat and listened to the creaking of the wheels, the voice of the driver, and the crack of his whip, till the sounds, growing fainter and fainter, at length ceased altogether. What appeared to me an unusual stillness and

loneliness then seemed to settle around me.
Afterwards I got used to be alone, and very indifferent on the subject, but it was not so then;
and I don't know whether it will strike the reader
that the position in which I was placed was a
nervous one, bearing in mind that with very little
experience of the bush I was suddenly left by
myself, probably for three weeks, in an unfre-
quented spot, and in a neighbourhood in which a
considerable number of exasperated and hostile
Blacks were known to be. At all events I was
not without anxiety, knowing, as I did, that not
many months since the owner of a station not
ten miles away had been wounded, and some of
his men killed, by the Blacks, and that four or
six soldiers had been sent from Melbourne for his
protection, whilst I, a lad just out of my teens,
was here without a comrade, indifferently armed,
and quite inexperienced. It should also be remembered that at this time I had never seen the
Blacks, except in Melbourne, and was totally
ignorant of their ways. These circumstances,
which I had hardly thought of the day before,
now came distinctly to my mind. My reflections
on them were not, however, of very long duration,
for the sounds of the retiring dray had not long
ceased, when I set to work to put myself into a
position to meet whatever danger might occur.
To effect this my preparations were simply—
loading carefully my two guns, chaining up my

pair of kangaroo dogs in such positions as to render surprise impossible, and seeing that the door of my hut could be effectually and easily secured.

The first day of my solitude passed over slowly enough, the stillness around weighing a good deal on my spirits, whilst such occasional sounds as did occur made me start involuntarily. The wind, the noise of a falling bough, the cawing of a crow, or the whistle of a hawk—which yesterday failed to arrest attention—made me now look carefully round. Unused to solitude and to the feeling of my life being in danger, I was much on the alert, and in a very prepared state of mind for fighting, magnifying a good deal the risk I was running. At that time I realized (though from boyhood I have always been satisfied to be a good deal alone) how necessary to me were a certain amount of conversation and fellowship. As regards my occupations when left to myself, some of my time of course was taken up with cooking (a novel industry to me at the time), with chopping wood for my fire, and other little household jobs; as well as looking after my two horses, which were hobbled about half-a-mile from my hut. These I used to bring to water twice a day. In the morning, as generally happens to those who live alone, I rose with the sun, when the monotonous routine of the previous day recommenced. A good deal of my time was naturally passed in read-

ing; and, when tired of my occupations, my only
resource was to walk up and down before my hut,
sometimes watching the few almost voiceless little
birds that disported themselves on the trees
around. If a flight of cockatoos passed screaming
over the valley, I used to wonder whether they
had been disturbed by anyone; and if so, by
whom—by a White man or Black? and look carefully around to see if I could descry anyone
coming.

After the first day or two, however, my feelings
of loneliness and apprehension in a great measure
left me. I got used to the position, and though I
continued to live, as it were, gun in hand, my
mind occupied itself with other thoughts, and
dwelt but little on the subject of danger. The
forced confinement to one spot troubled me, indeed,
more than anything else, and I used often to
regret that I could not now and then spend a
morning in hunting or shooting. About ten days
had passed in this manner, and I was sitting at
my door with a gun in my hand, smoking my pipe
and watching the sun go down, when I caught
sight of a horseman riding at a walk up the
valley. The prospect of having some one to talk
to for the evening pleased me not a little, and I
anxiously kept my eye on the stranger to see that
he did not pass by without coming to the hut.
My visitor, when he arrived, turned out to be a
mounted policeman doing patrol duty, who came

to ask a night's lodging. This, of course, I very willingly granted, putting him in possession of the men's hut, and giving him whatever provisions he required. Before going to bed, I also went to the hut and had a long yarn with him, when I learnt amongst other things, that four bullocks with yokes on, such as I had lost, and which from his description I made no doubt were mine, had been seen on the Goulburn, and were then running on a station about eighty miles from Wolfscrag, where they could easily be had. This of course was great news for me. The trooper also informed me that the Blacks had been committing depradations in my neighbourhood down the M'Ivor creek; that he had been sent to look after them, and recommended me to be on my guard, as he said that if they came upon me unarmed they would certainly kill me in revenge for some of their people who had lately been shot at a place about fifteen miles off, on the banks of the Campaspe.

In the morning the trooper got on his horse and started for his station, near the old crossing-place of the Goulburn, which he told me was about thirty miles distant, and I was again left to my own devices.

I think some three or four days must have passed after this visit, when I noticed, as I was dressing about sunrise, some wild ducks alight in a water-hole not far from the hut. A drizzling

rain was falling at the time—the first I had seen
at Wolfscrag—and, without waiting to finish my
toilet, I hastily put on a cloak, and, taking one of
my guns, sallied out to try if I could get a shot at
them; but though I took some pains to stalk
them, they proved too wary for me, and flew off
without my being able to get near them. After
returning to the hut I had scarcely washed and
dressed when the same, or a similar flight, of ducks
again settled in the water-hole. Being in doubt
whether the gun which I had had in the rain
would go off, I hastily took up the other and
again sallied out, and had a second time to return
unsuccessful. Replacing my gun, I proceeded to
cook my breakfast, and was thoroughly intent on
that interesting occupation, when the kangaroo
dog, which I had tied up at the back of my hut,
suddenly sprang to the end of his chain and
commenced barking furiously. Feeling sure that
something unusual was afoot, I laid down my
frying-pan, and, taking up one of the guns, stole
cautiously around the hut, keeping close to the
slabs, to ascertain what was the matter. Arrived
at a position from which I could see behind the
building, I discovered the cause of the commotion
was a small dog close at hand, which, in my
ignorance, I supposed to be a wild one. This
seemed to me a lucky chance for a shot; so, quite
inapprehensive of danger, I levelled my carbine
and was about to fire, when something which

moved amongst a clump of bushes a few yards off attracted my attention. Quick as thought I turned the muzzle of my gun from the dog to the bushes, at which, though I could distinguish nothing for the instant, I nevertheless held it pointed, keeping myself still partly covered by the hut. This proceeding, I have no doubt, saved my life, for the next moment I caught sight of a pair of spears quivering amongst the boughs, from which, after a moment's delay, lowering their weapons, there stepped two Blacks, stark naked, and in all the beauties of war-paint. If any confirmation of their murderous designs were wanted, the expression of their faces supplied it. Laughing in a confused way, and in a hollow, unnatural tone trying to make some joking sort of apology for being found in such an equivocal position, the two worthies sauntered easily towards me, I, dropping my carbine into the hollow of my arm, keeping my finger always on the trigger. Though we began to talk on both sides in a friendly way, and as if things were just as they should be, I never saw anyone more put out than these two savages, who had probably been watching my movements since daylight, and counted on my falling unarmed into their hands. They seemed more put out than I was, and I was a good deal "*skeared*," as the Yankees say, and more, perhaps, by the murderous looks which even now my two friends were unable to get rid

of, than by the thought of the danger which I
had escaped. The hatred which their looks could
not hide disconcerted me, whilst the effect of
their painted faces and chests, white circles round
the eyes, and ribs like those of a skeleton, first
seen under such circumstances, was most striking
and forbidding. Whatever the reason of their
attempted attack, and whatever might be the
result of their visit, I made an effort to conceal
my feelings, and, well on my guard, walked
side by side with the two Blacks to my door,
which (saying " *Stop a minute, my boys*," and
without turning my back to them) I entered
at once ; a savage dog which was chained to
the door-post preventing them from following
me.

The reader will readily believe that I drew a
long breath of relief when I reached my stronghold. The Blacks, spears in hand, wearing the expression of men who had been sorely baulked, stood
quietly beyond the reach of the dog, which made
furious efforts to get at them, and I took up my
position a little within the doorway. My visitors, I
fancy, still entertained hopes that, being young and
evidently unused to their ways, I should sooner
or later expose myself, when they would kill
me. If so, however, they reckoned without their
host, for I had made up my mind to trust myself
with them no more, but to fight it out, when the
time came, at the doorway, where I should have

the assistance of the dog, and where two could not get at me at once. Had I known the ways of our aboriginal race I might have been quite certain that no attack of the sort would be made, as open warfare is not their system. My sable friends seeing, I presume, at last that I intended to stick to my cover, began protesting their friendly intentions, and asking me for food. Stepping back, as if to reach the damper on the table, I seized a tomahawk and placed it beside me, ready for the hand-to-hand fight which I anticipated would follow, being in great doubt whether either of my guns, which the reader is aware had been in the rain, would go off. In reply to their demands for food and assurances of friendship, which were made in quite intelligible English, I told them to be off; that I would give them nothing; that I knew they had come to kill me, and that if they came an inch nearer my door I would shoot them. In return they threatened to spear me, but did not raise the points of their spears from the ground; so, with my gun at my hip, covering myself partly with the door I invited them to come on. In this manner we stood confronting each other for a bit, both sides hesitating to begin—I, because I was afraid the gun would not go off, and they, because they were sure that it would. Had it not been for my doubts on this score, I should have shot one of them at once in self-defence, as it seemed to me that blows were inevitable. Ever afterwards I was glad that I had not done so. Had the Blacks had an older man to deal with, I have no doubt they would have retreated at once; but probably they did not like being baffled by a very young man, combatants of that age not being much respected amongst themselves.

Finally, however, the prudence of the two worthies got the better of their valour, and seeing that nothing was to be got without running the risk of being shot, not even a smoke of tobacco, for which they begged hard, they retired to some bushes behind which they had left their opossum-rugs and other effects, and after a few minutes I had the pleasure of seeing them disappear in the scrub. When all was over, I wondered that when I reached my hut I had not shut the door and brought the matter to an end; but it never occurred to me. It was a great relief to me when I got rid of them. That they did not succeed in killing me I have always looked on as a special interposition of Divine Providence, for which, I trust, I have been grateful.

After the Blacks had fairly gone I tried my guns, *which both missed fire.* Of course I was not long in drawing the charges, rubbing out, and reloading them. I had had a narrow escape, and took it as a warning which never required repeating, being from that time scrupulously attentive to the state of my fire-arms. When next in Melbourne I also purchased an excellent pair of pistols, which I learnt to use well, and had constantly at hand for several years—in fact, as long as danger existed.

CHAPTER VII.

BULLOCKS RECOVERED, AND A NEW RUN DISCOVERED.

WITHIN a week after the visit of the two Blacks my dray arrived from town, bringing a married couple with two children, whom my agent in Melbourne had engaged for me—the woman as domestic servant, or hutkeeper, and her husband as shepherd. After my lonely time, these few persons and the little business of unloading the dray made Wolfscrag seem by contrast a centre of population; and of course it was quite a blessing to be relieved from my solitude, though I had still no one to converse with.

The servant woman, an active body, seized at once on my not very extensive *batterie de cuisine*, and transported it in a trice to the kitchen, whilst a course of sweeping, dusting, and arranging my hut was instituted forthwith. Fearing that I myself might be whisked off by my inexorable domestic, I was fain to give up possession temporarily to the new arrivals; so, mounting my horse, it being yet early, I proceeded to visit my shepherds, of whom I had only once heard during the absence of the dray. In the flocks I found that the succulent feed of the burnt hills, and the quiet which they had enjoyed for the last month (being able to get their food without much walking), had brought about a very perceptible change, so as to lead to the probability of a tolerable dropping of lambs. I also found, as I rode along on the flats near the head station, from which my sheep had originally been removed, that the grass was springing nicely after the late rains. The shepherds, who had seen nobody in the interim, were glad to have me break upon their solitude, hear a little news, and get a newspaper from which they might learn something of what was doing in the world; so, after chatting an hour with them, I cantered home in the twilight, not altogether indifferent to the prospect of a little change of food and cookery.

After allowing matters at Wolfscrag to settle down a little, taking rations to the shepherds, and initiating my new arrivals into the routine of their work, I determined to start with the bullock-driver and make an effort to recover my lost cattle, of whose whereabouts, the reader will remember, I had heard from the passing trooper. On my last visit to Melbourne, finding the showy grey mare which I had brought from the clover

fields of Tasmania but ill adapted to the rough starvation ways of Wolfscrag, I sold her, and bought
instead, for £55, a powerful old horse, well bred
and used to the country, and a hardy little Timor
pony, for which, with the saddle and bridle, I paid
£35. Giving the pony, therefore, to the bullock-
driver, who was a light-weight, and taking the
horse myself, we set out on our travels.

Our first day's stage of about thirty miles
brought us to the old crossing-place of the Goulburn, some seven miles lower down that river
than where the town of Seymour now stands.
Our road so far was the Major's Line.

The stillness, so common a feature in Australian
woods, I constantly noticed during my ride.
Equally characteristic was the sinuous creek,
and not a bit like what I had seen in Tasmania.
I saw nothing to remind me of the Blacks, and
yet they must have wandered along the creek,
built their huts on it, killed opossums on its
banks and ducks on its waters, for who shall say
how many ages? whilst the single party of white
men who had passed that way had left a road
behind them which one might follow unaided.

At one of the ponds (so round that they might
have been the work of man) which occurred
every here and there in the bed of the creek my
companion and I, availing ourselves of a shady
wattle-tree, sat down at midday to eat our lunch,
and allow the horses an hour to feed, as is the

custom with travellers in the bush. Mounting
again and beguiling the way with a little conversation and a good deal of smoking, we arrived
shortly before sundown at our destination for the
night. This was an eating-house on the banks of
the Goulburn, which, with a log punt, were kept
by the owner and his two servants for the convenience of overlanders travelling with sheep or
cattle to Port Phillip or South Australia. With
him we put up for the night. Hearing from my
host that an overlander and his party were
camped close by, I strolled out after sunset to
have my first look at a bushman's camp, a sort of
thing of which in after years I was destined to
have a good deal of experience.

The sound of the bullock-bells soon guided me
to the spot, where, on some four acres of ground,
surrounded by a number of large fires, I saw
encamped a flock of five thousand sheep Passing
by a host of dogs which sallied out to meet me,
two teams of bullocks, and six or eight saddle-
horses grazing in hobbles. I got to the fire,
where the men of the party—about a dozen in
number—were eating their supper. They were all
seated on the ground except the head of the
party, for whom the water-keg did duty as a
stool. Having quieted the barking of the dogs,
the master invited me warmly to " have a feed;"
but, as I had already supped, I was obliged to
decline his invitation to join in the attack which

was being made on some fried mutton, and a damper of about the circumference of the front wheel of a phaeton. Altogether the scene was picturesque enough, and the overlanders seemed to be enjoying themselves. The camp-fire, made against the butt of a fallen tree, was on the brink of the river, which ran noiselessly through the towering gum-trees which over-shadowed its course. Around the fire were the shepherds and bullock-drivers of the party, seated, as I have said, at their suppers, each expectant sheep-dog waiting for his share from his master. Before us, contentedly chewing the cud, were the sheep, gazing at us by the light of the fire, and in the background were two tents; whilst scattered around, or hanging from neighbouring branches, one noticed bridles, bullock-gear, saddles, and other articles of that sort. A couple of guns leaned against a stump close at hand, and the large fire threw its mellow light alike on the leafy arches overhead and on the travellers and their belongings beneath.

In the course of conversation I learned from the head of the party that he had started with his stock from the neighbourhood of Bathurst; that he had already been over ten weeks on the road; and that it would still take him several months to reach his destination in South Australia.

By eight o'clock the smoking and yarning of

6

the overlanders had nearly come to an end; the horses and bullocks had been looked to, and their whereabouts reported to the leader; the first watch was set; and as some of the shepherds had retired to one of the tents, and I saw others making their beds under the drays, I thought it time to retreat to my own quarters. The party were of course accustomed to their airy lodgings, and I noticed that they were in good spirits, and in the enjoyment of superlative appetites.

In the morning I mounted my horse, and, followed by my little bullock-driver, Dan, on his Timor pony, took the road which led from station to station down the river. We rode slowly, and about midday, I remember, were passing a station, when Dan trotted up and asked me if I would not call and get dinner; which, in my ignorance of bush customs, I declined to do, being unwilling to trespass needlessly on the hospitality of strangers. Accordingly we rode on, my follower seeming somewhat downcast, until a little before sundown we reached the Protectorate Station, at which any aborigines who chose to locate themselves were supplied with food and blankets at the public cost. This establishment, which consisted of several slab huts in the occupation of the Protector and the half-dozen white men in his service, and, in some cases, of their wives and families, was prettily situated on the banks of the river. The buildings were neatly constructed, and surrounded by trim gardens, with cultivation and horse paddocks, the whole giving promise of comfortable accommodation, as well as of dinner, a matter at that moment not without interest in my eyes.

In this way we went jogging on from day to day, and from station to station, with little variety. But though I have so far—in order to give some idea of the life of an early squatter in Port Phillip—entered into details about all sorts of trifles, it is clear that I must have some regard for the reader's patience, and carry on my narrative with longer strides. In view of this, then, I will cease to drag him with Dan and myself along our monotonous road through endless gum forests and over far stretching plains, contenting myself with noticing what is important in relation to the results of my journey.

After the delays usual in such cases—any amount of cattle-hunting and going from one station to another—I succeeded in recovering my bullocks, and having accidentally met a fit person out of employment, I engaged him as overseer, put him with Dan in charge of the truants, and directed him to take them back to Wolfscrag by the road which I had just travelled. In the meantime I had learnt from the stockman at Wyuna, the station at which I had found my bullocks, which was also the outside station in that direction, that there was abundance of excellent unoccupied country close at hand, which, with the consent of his master, he volunteered to show me. This was quite a godsend to me, and of course I accepted his offer, and, the day after my new overseer left with the bullocks, rode over Tongala Plain in his company; and, as it appeared to me well adapted for stock. I made up my mind to abandon Wolfscrag, and take it up as a run with the least delay possible. To do this there were, in those days, no hindrances of any sort, the custom being to drive one's stock on to any unoccupied country, and then apply to the Commissioner of Crown Lands for a license to depasture, the application being granted as a matter of course. The extent of land licensed by the Commissioner was proportioned, in a rough way, to the quantity of stock owned by the applicant; this permission to occupy country being renewable yearly, until the ground should be required by Government for other purposes, on the annual payment of £10 into the Treasury. Besides this fee for a license, which, except in the vicinity of Melbourne, everyone thought would last for a generation or two, there was also a small capitation tax payable yearly on the sheep. The extent of country which I applied for, when I got back to Wolfscrag, was fifty square miles, half of it on each bank of the River Goulburn.

Having determined to remove my flocks from Wolfscrag to Tongala, as I called my new run, I started with the stockman (to whom I gave £5 for his trouble) direct for the former run through the bush, by the places now known as Bundari, Coragorag, Colbinabbin, and Redcastle. By this time, as is usual with a little practice, I had become a tolerable bushman for a new chum, and the distance saved by the route I took going home, across entirely unexplored country, was about fifty miles, the distance through the bush from Tongala to Wolfscrag being about eighty miles.

Hence the reader will see that the most fortunate thing which befell me at that time was the loss of my bullocks, as it was the means of making me a bushman, and of my getting an excellent run; so right glad was I to leave the barren scrubs of Wolfscrag and its wretched creek for the well-grassed plains of Tongala and the ever-flowing Goulburn. The occasion was one of unmixed satisfaction; and the country between the two places being unoccupied, I took it for granted that the "Scab Act" offered no obstacle to the removal of my flocks in the proposed direction.

CHAPTER VIII.

REMOVAL TO TONGALA.

The ride from Wyuna to Wolfscrag, which should have occupied two days, took in fact three. owing to the Timor pony which I now rode (as I had mounted my overseer on my old horse) having knocked up, or nearly so. Punch, as he was called, was rather a character in his way. Bay, with black points, he was but little bigger than a full-grown sheltie, with a beautiful head, a thick tail which reached the ground, and a perfect cloud of mane, from which pricked out just the tips of his restless little ears. Nothing in the shape of horseflesh could be more beautiful in its way, nor more thoroughly put together. Head, neck, legs, shoulders, quarters—in fact, the whole animal— might have served as a model. Though I rode over twelve stone. sixty miles in a day on an occasion hardly overtaxed the little fellow, nor a hundred miles in two days : but, on the other hand, he was so incurably wild, self-willed. difficult to catch even when hobbled. and so addicted to rearing over when mounted, that few could even saddle, let alone ride him. when in condition ; so that, on a journey in the bush, it became impossible to let him take full advantage of the feed which offered, and hence his failing me on this occasion.

The first night after leaving Wyuna, we camped without water at the end of thirty miles, near Paboinboolok, or Lake Cowper as it is now called, the day having been pretty hot, and the next day Punch gave in, on the head of the Colbinabbin Creek. Indeed, matters just then were not going altogether smoothly with me. A drizzling rain, which seemed likely to continue, had begun to fall; the ground was soft, the sun obscured; my compass, which was too small, had proved useless, and declined to traverse; my pony, as I have said, had jibbed; the small supply of food with which we had started was nearly consumed, and the face of my companion, the stockman, was becoming a sort of standing reproach to me, too clearly conveying the impression that he thought me a very unsafe guide in the bush, and likely to get him into all sorts of difficulties. However, as I knew we could not be more than thirty miles from home, to which, in the absence of sun and compass, I knew I could find my way by the watershed, it did not seem to me that anything very serious could occur. Things being so, I proposed to the stockman that we should camp for the rest of the day and rest the pony, who would then take me home well enough on the next. To this I found him rather averse; and I have often noticed that men of his class commonly never think of camping in the bush until their horses have come to a complete standstill.

However, I turned a deaf ear to his suggestions; so, hobbling out our nags on excellent grass, with abundance of water at hand, the stockman undertook to make a mia-mia to keep our camp dry, whilst I sallied forth on foot with my dog and a brace of pistols to look for something to eat, in which I was so far successful, as to secure an old-man kangaroo, whose tail and a few steaks fully supplied our wants. On my return to camp I found that my companion had made the mia-mia with forked sticks, some pieces of bark stripped from a fallen tree, and our saddle-cloths, in which we should be very well sheltered from the cold, drizzling rain which was falling; so that, with a roaring fire, a bed of boughs, and a saddle and a blanket each, plenty of tobacco and a kangaroo, a morsel of bread and a pot of tea, we stretched ourselves out in luxury for the night. Our nags, too, were enjoying great times amidst the plentiful feed; my dog had a haunch of roasted kangaroo for his supper, so that I think on the whole we might be regarded at the moment as a decidedly happy family. The conversation of my companion also was not without interest to a new chum, being made up of accounts of fights with the Blacks on the Upper Murray, and relations of his doings amongst wild cattle. In this way, smoking and yarning, we passed the hours till bed time; and, after a good night's sleep, were awakened by a fine sunny morning, of which we took advantage, reaching Wolfscrag that evening without further let or hindrance. Home, after absence, even to the dweller in a slab hut, and in despite of there being only the "watch-dog's honest bark," and no bright eyes "to mark his coming and look brighter when he comes," still brings feelings of pleasure, as I found on this occasion, though I was about to leave the old home and make a new one.

Matters had, I found, been going on all right in my absence; my sheep had now got into good condition, and I anticipated a favourable lambing. It is true I found awaiting me a short but trenchant note from a neighbour, requesting me to remove my sheep from what he termed "the very centre of my Emu Flat station," which annoyed me a little at first; but when I came to reflect that he had failed to discover my involuntary intrusion with three flocks of sheep for several weeks, I contrived to make myself easy with the conclusion that if my sheep had benefited exceedingly by the trespass, his cattle could not possibly have been much the worse for it. At the same time, the cause of my late overseer's sinister manner, when he suggested the removal of my sheep across the ranges, became now obvious enough. In fact, he was proposing to me, in his usual style, what he knew was a trespass, which possibly might be the cause of a quarrel with my neighbour.

I had, I think, been only three or four days at Wolfscrag, during which period I had despatched a letter to my agent in Melbourne, directing him to take at once the necessary steps for securing me a license for Tongala, when my lately-engaged overseer gladdened my heart by arriving with my four lost bullocks. As I had determined to effect my migration at once, for which I had also explored a route, I lost no time in bringing my flocks from the " Emu Flat " to the head station, and loading the dray with my stores and effects. This took only a day to do, and on the next, a little after sunrise, in the most hopeful of moods, I started with my possessions for the banks of the Goulburn, leaving behind for the time at Wolfscrag, where the grass was now tolerable, one of my ewe flocks, which had already begun to lamb. The order of march was as follows :—Knowing how the country lay, I led the way for Dan and the bullock-dray. On our tracks followed the two flocks of sheep at short intervals, each driven by two men, looked after by the overseer. I had almost forgotten to notice that my servants, from fear of the Blacks,* were exceedingly averse to the journey which I was beginning.

* It happened that several of my men were fresh arrivals from Tasmania, where the Blacks were a very hostile race, and much dreaded.

The shepherds, indeed, who as a rule are the persons who get speared in new country, had tried to persuade me to pay them off and let them go, a proposal which I could not entertain, as procuring fresh hands would necessarily entail expense and loss of time ; besides, I counted on the wages I owed these men as to a certain extent a guarantee for their good conduct, which I should not have in the case of servants newly hired.

My party on setting out consisted of eight persons, each of whom I armed with a carbine and half-a-dozen buckshot cartridges, as much perhaps to give them confidence as from any likelihood of a collision with the Blacks. At starting our route lay along the Major's line for about five miles, when we crossed the *Pinch*, after which I struck north-east, in the direction of the head of the Colbinabbin watershed, camping for the night after having accomplished about eight miles, which is a fair journey for sheep. The spot selected for the camp was on the bank of one of the tributaries of the Major's Creek ; and after having something to eat, and the never-failing cup of tea, I proceeded to have things arranged on the plan of the overlanders' camp which I had seen. Of course, now, after many years of diversified bush experiences, I look back with amusement to my youthful ignorance of such matters, and can only attribute my not coming to grief in one way or another to

the fact that there was more luck than good
management in my affairs just then. The spot
at which we had camped—a very suitable one, with
abundance of feed—appeared not to find favour
with my shepherds, who were not in a frame of
mind to be satisfied with anything. They not
only objurgated it as "*wild*," but I overheard one
of them appealing to his neighbour as to whether
the water in the creek, which they were drinking
at the time, was not "the wildest water as ever
was." At that time I was unable to guess what
it was which was affecting my men disagreeably
about the camp, and in what the uncongenial
"wildness" consisted—and, indeed, why wildness
should be thought objectionable. Since then,
however, I have often remarked that unoccupied
country produces very opposite effects on different
persons, either raising or depressing the spirits as
the case may be. This fact may be noticed in
the printed accounts of our explorers. Some,
when the country they were travelling through
was remote from the settled districts, or its
features on a large scale, such as extensive forests
or horizon-bounded plains, got quite dispirited,
and have described such districts (we all know
now how incorrectly) as destined to be for ever
useless to man. The Darling, Lachlan, and
Murray countries are instances of this, and notably
the Cooper's Creek and Barrier Range districts.
Sturt always speaks of such country as a *region*,

and Mr. Giles uses the same word in a like sense.
Others, again, the further from civilization, the
more satisfied they seem to become, and the more
roseate their descriptions of the land. On my
men, all of them old hands, unoccupied country
had a very depressing effect, their idea being that
we should be all killed by the Blacks.

In this way we kept on without anything
worthy of notice occurring for two or three days,
accomplishing about eight miles a day; some of
the party, as I regretted to notice, getting apparently more nervous and dejected as we proceeded.
It was after supper, I think on the fourth day, as
I was about to turn into my blanket, that the
men in charge of the sheep formally complained
to me that they knew we should be killed by the
Blacks; that they objected to proceed any further,
and that they were determined that I should pay
them off and let them go. Being probably somewhat excited, they displayed a good deal of temper
in what they had to say, telling me that I was too
young to lead them, and that they would not be
trifled with. Though it was unpleasant to hear
expostulations from my *ci-devant* convicts, backed
up as they were with an implied threat of employing force if necessary for obtaining compliance with
their demands, I thought it prudent to reason a
little with them on their groundless timidity, and to
endeavour to shame them into a more courageous
frame of mind. My efforts, however, though

prolonged for some time, proved quite ineffectual;
in fact, the men had made up their minds to bully
me into paying them off and letting them return
to the settled districts.   At the moment I could
think of nothing better to say to them than that
I would take the night to think over what they
had said; that in the meantime two of them must
keep the first watch as usual, and call the overseer
and myself at midnight.   Without further remark
I then turned in under the dray, where I lay for
some time reflecting on the course I should take.
The position of affairs was not pleasant, as I could
not hope to get any men where I was going to;
besides, huts had to be built, shearing was drawing
nigh, and it was most desirable to meet the
Murray and Goulburn Blacks, who bore the
reputation of being numerous and troublesome,
with a fairly strong party.   On the other hand,
to pause was to upset all my plans; water would
be getting scarce on the plains which I had to
cross, and my ewes would be beginning to lamb.
Things, it is true, might have been worse than
they were, as the overseer, the bullock-driver, the
cook, and myself could have continued the journey
well enough by boxing the flocks, though we
should not have been able to put up the necessary
buildings and do the shearing.   Having pondered
the matter for some time, I made up my mind as
to the course which I would take, and then, with
the happy facility of youth, forgot my troubles and

fell asleep. The determination to which I had come was to proceed on my journey; to coerce the men, if possible, to accompany me, as they were bound to do by their agreements, and, failing this, to go without them.

At midnight the shepherds, who had been watching the sheep, called the overseer and myself as they had been directed; and I heard them declaring, as they betook themselves to their beds, "that they had kept their last watch this heat." During the night I had a long talk with my overseer (who, with the bullock-driver and cook, remained thoroughly staunch), and told him what I intended to do; and, though he thought there might be some risk with the Blacks, he agreed to support me. To enforce my views on the shepherds, and to compel them to fulfil the terms of service for which they had hired, I had determined to seize the guns with which I had armed them, and lock them up in a large chest which I had in the dray, so as to leave my refractories no choice but to proceed with me on the journey, or to leave my camp without arms, food, or wages. Accordingly, when all was still, I took the guns, drew their charges, and locked them up, taking special care to see that those of the overseer and myself were fit for immediate use, as it was possible that my gaol-birds might resort to violence. By sunrise the bullocks and horses were brought up as usual,

when we all sat down to presumedly our last
fryingpan of chops together, a dogged silence
prevailing on both sides. When breakfast was
over, the sheep being still on the camp, I thought
it time to bring matters to an issue, so I spoke to
my four rowdies, all Tasmanian expirees, saying,
I understood it was their intention to abscond;
if they were so determined, of course they must
have their way for the present, but at their own
risk; that I should not prevent them removing
their "swags" from the dray, but food or wages
they should have none; and that they would have
to take their chance of being speared by the
Blacks, who, even now, for anything I knew,
might be watching us from the scrub, as I would
not allow them to take any of my fire-arms; and,
finally, that on the first convenient opportunity
I would proceed to take out warrants for them.

This announcement of my intentions coming
unexpectedly on my recalcitrant worthies took
them somewhat by surprise. I ordered the
bullock-driver, without more ado, to yoke up his
bullocks; the cook took charge of the sheep,
and the overseer and I lit our pipes and sat
smoking with our arms in our hands. Of course,
threatening speeches were made, and there was
loud grumbling, but no violence; and just as the
dray was about to move on my four shepherds
gave in and returned to their duties.

After this little *fracas* things went on quietly

enough, more especially as at night I held out the
olive branch, by declaring that I would allow
any of my men to leave me, who might wish to
do so, as soon as I could get fresh hands to
take their places. I think, also, that emerging
from the scrubby country on to the beautiful
plains of Colbinabbin and Coragorag tended to
raise the spirits of the party and allay their dis-
content, which arose entirely from fear; in fact, I
heard some of them declare the plains to be less
" wild" than the scrub, and more homely—an idea
which, of course, I did not call in question.
Though between the spot on which Mr. Winter's
house at Colbinabbin now stands and Tongala—a
distance of thirty-five miles—no water was to
be found at that time, except in one or two
crabholes, still the country was most pleasant
to travel over, differing somewhat in its aspect
from that which it now presents. Altogether,
fences and tree-ringing have not improved the
scene. At the epoch of which I write the
grass, though at a distance it presented the
appearance of a sward, consisted of sparsely-
scattered tussocks of the primest descriptions:
the wire-grass, however, largely predominating
over the kangaroo grass. As it was then
winter, the interstices were filled with luxuriant
herbage: the yam generally, and in some cases
the myrnong, or native carrot, prevailing. The
bed of Paboinboolok, which seemed to have

been long dry, was almost one field of myrnong,
whilst the inferior grasses and weeds—now unfortunately abundant—were almost, if not entirely,
absent. Colbinabbin was a handsome piece of
country, with its timber-dotted ranges, richly-
grassed plains, and pleasant little creek embowered
in gum-trees, and so superior in the matter of
grass to Tongala that I should have ended my
travels there had it not been for the scarcity
of water. As it was, I was very loath to
leave it.

Allowing my party to follow down the creek, I
galloped over to the ranges, to obtain from their
summit a view of the country through which my
route lay. From them I first saw Lake Paboinboolok—waterless, as I have said, at the time, and
covered with myrnong. The features of the landscape were sunshine and stillness; my little party,
now and then discernible amongst the lines of
trees on the banks of the creek, was creeping
slowly on in a northerly direction; here and
there a flock of emus, or a few bustards, were
feeding on the green herbage; and on the eastern
side of the plain, fifteen or twenty miles away, I
could just make out a faint line of smoke, rising,
no doubt, from a native encampment on the edge
of the forest.

With no further inconvenience than a scarcity
of water, which was obviated to some extent by
carrying a small supply for the use of the party

in a harness cask on the dray, we arrived in due
time at Tongala, the journey having occupied
altogether about ten days.

CHAPTER IX.

A STATION FORMED AT TONGALA.

It was in the month of July, 1841, that I arrived
at Tongala, as I called my new station.* Whether
Punch on the occasion " bounded beneath me as
a steed that knows his rider" or not, I cannot
say—probably not, however, for as a rule neither
horses nor ponies indulge themselves in that way
at the end of a journey, whatever they may do
at the beginning, especially when their riders are
on the sunny side of twenty. Punch's master,
however, I remember, rejoiced in the best of
spirits on that particularly bright and sunny
morning, when he pitched his tarpaulin on the
little plain of Thathumnera (as that particular
portion of Tongala was called, and for the first
time watered his sheep, now pretty thirsty, at the
Goulburn River.

Of course, on arrival there was much to be done,

* The name was not by any means an apt one, as it is the
Bangerang name for the River Murray.

so, after a hasty dinner I set all hands to work to make a bough yard for one of the flocks, as it was important as early as possible to get rid of the nuisance of watching the sheep at night. To effect this the men went to work, some with their axes felling the small trees on the edge of the plain, the bullock-driver with his team drawing them to the spot selected for enclosure, the rest of the party building the fence as the materials came to hand, so that by sundown we had one substantial yard completed.

Whilst engaged at this work, my attention was attracted by a cooey, and, looking in the direction whence it proceeded, we saw three Blacks on the opposite side of the stream. Their appearance on the scene caused some little trepidation in my old Tasmanians, whose idea, as I heard one of them express it, was " to kid (entice) them over and shoot the lot." Walking to the river, close to the perpendicular bank of which our yard was being constructed, one of my men, a Sydney hand, who was accustomed to the Blacks, called out and asked them what they wanted; to which they replied, in very broken English, that they had come to see us, and would cross over the river if we liked. On learning that I should be glad to see them, they laid down their bags, drove the blunt end of their spears into the ground, and, after examining the trees at hand, set to work to cut a canoe, in which to

float themselves and their effects over the water.
This operation was speedily effected, and in
about half-an-hour I saw them in Indian file
briskly approaching the camp-fire, at which I
had seated myself. They were all muscular,
active men, two out of the three being about
five feet nine inches in height. Their dress
consisted of an opossum-skin cloak, which was
fastened at the chest, passing over the left
and under the right shoulder, so as to leave
the right arm at liberty. The fur was worn
next the person, and the skin, which was outside, was painted in various carpet-like patterns
with a sort of red clay which the Blacks burn
and make use of for this and other purposes
of ornamentation. The garment fell in not un-
graceful folds as low as the knee, and around their
necks they had necklaces of small reeds, cut into
lengths of about an inch and a half, and strung on
twine made from wild flax. In a sort of rude
kangaroo-skin bag carried on the left shoulder,
which opened out so as to be available for sitting
or sleeping on, were conveyed their tomahawks,
shields, waddies, and other utensils; their spears
and throwing sticks being carried in the hand.
Their hair, which was straight and black, was
confined round the forehead by a narrow net,
through which were thrust the barbed switches
with which they extracted the edible grubs from
the trees; and around their arms, near the

shoulder, were twisted strips of opossum-skin with the fur on. Erect as reeds, my new acquaintances stalked in grave silence up to the camp-fire, and on my invitation, after warming their feet for a moment in the blaze, took their seats before me.

The crash of the trees falling on the edge of the little plain which had so long been their property, and of which we were unceremoniously taking possession, and the general devastation which accompanies the white man, naturally attracted their attention. Their eyes seemed to take in what was being done, and every strange object around them, but neither word nor gesture of curiosity or surprise escaped them. All three of them, no doubt, had had some little communication with whites, and picked up—chiefly at second-hand, from their neighbours, the Ngooraialum Blacks—a smattering of English, so that we were able to understand each other to a certain extent. After they had come to comprehend that I was going to remain permanently at Tongala, and heard what I had to say about the heinousness of sheep-stealing and shepherd-spearing, the power of fire-arms, and the beauty of my kangaroo dogs—which they very much admired— I thought it well to address myself to the better feelings of my guests by directing the cook to give each of them as much meat, tea, and damper as would serve two ordinary whites for a meal.

On his handing it to them, they seemed much pleased, and began to eat, but without hurry or the interruption of our conversation. In fact, their manners generally were easy and pleasing, and there was a sort of propriety about their ways, and an absence of awkwardness which I little expected to meet in savages; besides a certain politeness, which made them, for instance, prepare a firestick when they saw me cutting up tobacco, and offer other little attentions.

What with their erect carriage, dignified bearing, graceful postures, novel appearance, and the frank and courageous way in which they had entrusted themselves amongst armed strangers, I found myself considerably interested in these children of the woods; though I still bore vividly in recollection my late unpleasant interview with two of their colour. Having got through what seemed the proper preliminaries of an acquaintance (they having, as it were, come to leave their cards on the new arrivals), I thought it well to utilize my new friends a little, lest they should come into the erroneous idea that my camp was an elisium of food, leisure, and tobacco-smoke. In fact, as I had determined to transport one of my flocks across the river, for which purpose a canoe would be necessary, I thought the present a favourable occasion for supplying myself with that indispensable article, and proposed the matter to the Blacks, who at once acceded to my request, and stripped to the work. As they stood before us in ebony, tomahawk in hand, their well-proportioned busts, strong shoulders, and light but sinewy arms at once attracted the attention of the party. I also noticed their well-curved spines, a formation on which, I fancy, grace of carriage and elasticity of motion chiefly depend, and which seems more common to the savage than the civilized man. It occurred to me, also, how much less unpleasantly the nude strikes one in the Blackfellow than in his white brother, leading one to contrast the perfect *aplomb*, solid tread, and disregard of the wind or sun of the first, with the hooped back, colourless skin, and ill-assured step with which the latter painfully shambles over the pebbles from his clothes on the brink to the stream hard by in which he is about to bathe. Possibly it was in such a predicament that the rhymer gave vent to the

> " Oh, ye gods and little fishes,
>   What's a man without his breeches?"

which we all remember.

As the reader may be interested to know how the Black makes his boat, I will take this opportunity of describing the process, as so doing may serve to illustrate not only the ready way in which he obtains from nature all that he requires, but also the skill with which he avails himself of the few implements of which he is possessed.

And it is in such little matters that one is particularly led to contrast the ways of the savage and the civilized man. The first, arriving at a stream, with the aid of a stone tomahawk provides himself in half-an-hour with a boat—frail and perishable, no doubt, but sufficient for the occasion, and passes over; whilst the white man, checked for the time, sits down deliberately, and after a long delay produces an article of wood or iron which may serve him for years.

In the first place, then, as the canoe required was to be large and durable—that is, fit to last several months—an old tree was selected, as well for its size as for the thickness of its bark, and also a little curved, in such a way that the canoe, *which was to be peeled off it*, might have its bow elevated a little above the water; the entrance of water at the stern being usually prevented by a little wall of well-kneaded clay in that part. The tree chosen (an old river-gum of about twenty feet in circumference), a few notches were cut with the tomahawk, one above the other, in its bark just outside of what was to be its edge, or gunwale of the canoe. The operator having then roughly marked out on the tree the lines of his vessel, commenced cutting the bark along them with his tomahawk down to the wood, so as to detach from the tree an unbroken sheet of bark, which would be the canoe. To effect this the tree was ascended gradually, by placing the big toe in the notches before mentioned, which were used as steps, the Blackfellow holding on with one hand and one heel, whilst he plied the tomahawk with the other hand. He also, I remember, assisted himself by rearing against the tree a stout branch which happened to be at hand, and using it as a ladder to stand on whilst he chopped. The bark thus cut all round, it only remained to detach it from the tree, to which it still adhered. This was effected, as the sap was not well up, and the bark clung to the wood, by hammering the future canoe gently with the butt of the tomahawk, and by forcing the end of a pole here and there under the edges of the bark and prizing steadily. Gradually, in this manner, it was neatly detached from the tree. The canoe being a heavy one, my sable friends then produced a cord which they passed round the centre of the canoe and round the tree, and then tied somewhat loosely, in order to prevent the canoe from coming down with too much violence. The last bit of bark by which it was suspended was then severed, and the little skiff gently lowered to the ground. Once landed, it was placed in the position of a boat turned upside down; some dried leaves and boughs were put under it and set fire to, the object being to dry up the sap, and so toughen the bark as to allow of its being moulded into the required shape. In a minute or two the fire had burned out, the canoe was righted and placed on a level spot; two or three pieces of stick were inserted after the manner of *thwarts* to keep the sides distended; the bow was permanently elevated, being forced into the required position by means of a log placed under it, and in this way the canoe is usually left for a day or two to set and harden. The canoe I speak of (which could have been used as soon as it came off the tree) was about 18 feet long by 2 feet 6 inches wide, floated eight inches clear of the water, and would carry five persons.

Having thus got a canoe, I set to work in the morning to erect yards at a convenient place on the bank of the river, and the next day, with the assistance of my men and the three Blacks, I got one of my flocks transported across the Goulburn. The operation was performed by placing the sheep, six at a time, in the canoe with their legs tied, when a Black punted them over. This wet and troublesome job accomplished, my men set vigorously to work to provide the first necessaries of a station, which consisted in a hut for themselves as well as yards for the bullocks and the other flock, the completion of which occupied about a fortnight. The hut was made in the usual way, the walls being of slabs, and the roof of bark stripped by the Blacks and carted in on the dray. The erection of a hut for myself, a store for my supplies, a woolshed, and a paddock for my horses and bullocks, works which it would

take some time to complete, I left, together with
the care of the flock, which had just begun to
lamb, to my overseer to look after, and, accompanied by Dan, I started with my dray and
bullocks once more to Wolfscrag to bring up the
flock which I had left there, as well as the woolpacks and other stores necessary for shearing,
and, I may add, some fresh hands to supply the
places of those who wished to leave. Of the
Blacks, of whom my Tasmanian servants were so
"skeary," considerable numbers gradually made
their appearance and camped at the station, which
I encouraged them to do, both because I found
their services useful, and thought them far less
likely under such circumstances to attack the
shepherds, or steal my sheep, than if I drove them
away and placed myself in a hostile attitude
towards them. In order, however, that no temptation to violence might be given, from the very
beginning I kept my party armed, and insisted
on the shepherds carrying guns and keeping them
in a serviceable state—which, after their first fears
were lulled, they would have neglected to do, had
I not insisted. In this course I persisted for
several years—in fact, until danger was at an
end.

From the first I had a good deal of curiosity
about the aborigines, constantly observed their
ways, talked a good deal with them, and rapidly
picked up a smattering of their language. What

struck me, on first acquaintance, was their freedom
from all the business cares and responsibilities of
the white man. They constantly reminded me of
children, whose anxieties were about matters to
which the average white man is not called on to
pay much attention. Besides, they had but little
care of the future, their existence being literally
from hand to mouth.

But notwithstanding many differences between
the Black and the White man, their sympathies,
likes, and dislikes were very much what ours
would have been if similarly situated ; so that
a very limited experience enabled both parties
to understand and appreciate the position of the
other. This fact only gradually dawned on me,
as I had somehow started with the idea that I
should find the Blacks as different from the
White men in mind as they are in colour.

Whilst on the subject of my sable neighbours,
I may mention a characteristic brutality which
occurred in the neighbourhood a day or two
before I left for Wolfscrag. As I was dressing
one morning rather late, I saw a Blackfellow
sitting alone at some distance from my camp. On
going up to him I found him rather a stupid-
looking fellow, who knew nothing of English, and
was turning away, when I noticed a spot of blood
on his opossum rug. On examining I found that
he had a wound through the thick part of his
arm, and, calling one of the other Blacks, I

learned that Nosie—as he was named—had been
that morning to the cattle station at Wyuna,
about three miles off; that he had laid down his arms
before going up to the hut, and that the hut-keeper,
who was alone, had apparently ordered him off.
Nosie, understanding neither his words nor gestures, remained where he was, inapprehensive of
danger, when suddenly a gun was protruded from
the hut; then followed a great noise, as he
described it : he saw smoke, and a part of his
beard was torn with considerable force from his
chin.   Greatly frightened, the unfortunate, it
seems, took to his heels and ran off as quickly as
he could ; but he had not gone far when he heard
a repetition of the loud noise, and something
which he did not see tore through his arm.

Having got the poor fellow's wound bound up,
I rode over to Wyuna in the course of the day,
where the hut-keeper, who had been both a convict
and a soldier, under the impression that neither
shot had taken effect, related what had occurred,
apparently with much satisfaction.   As I told him
roundly what I thought of his cowardly and
barbarous act, he replied, looking at me with the
most self-satisfied air, his hands in his breeches
pockets, " As many of them as comes here when I
am alone I'll shoot."

" And if it comes to my ears," said I, " that you
do anything of the sort, I shall certainly report
the fact to the Government."

At this speech "Jack the soldier," as he was called, seemed quite taken aback! At first he appeared to doubt his ears, and I believe weighed within himself the propriety of making all safe by shooting me on the spot. Ever after, I dare say, he looked on me as a sort of dangerous lunatic for troubling myself about the lives of a few Blacks, which he evidently thought he had a perfect right to dispose of as he chose, so long as he did not get into trouble. What expiree convicts meant by "*getting into trouble*," the reader may be told, was simply their being brought in contact with the "cat," the gaol, or the hangman's rope ; presumably because nothing short of such stern realities ever did trouble them.

CHAPTER X.

SHEARING, AND THE RESULTS OF MY FIRST YEAR'S SHEEP-FARMING.

ONE journey with sheep across a country is so like another that it will be unnecessary to enter into particulars respecting the removal of my last flock from Wolfscrag to Tongala ; and, indeed, except that I had very nearly lost a large number of lambs at the source of the Colbinabbin Creek from poisonous herbs, which produced a swelling of the head and ears, which I cured by copious bleeding, very little occurred on the trip which, even amongst a squatter's not very exciting reminiscences, might pass muster for relation.

On reaching Tongala I found my sheepwash and woolshed, such as they were, nearly ready for use. Of course, in these days of sheds replete with conveniences, and usually much surpassing the village church in dimensions and cost of construction, one can hardly look back without a smile on the humble ways of the early times. My first shed, for instance, was nothing but a common bark building of about twenty-five feet by twelve, with a wool-press of split-stuff outside, to match. Nor was I behind the times in this particular, for if some were better provided, there were others who were worse. Of course the artificial reservoir, which one now meets everywhere, had not then been thought of; nor those luxurious shower-baths, hot water soaks, douches, &c., supplemented with soap and soda, with which the sheep's summer toilet is now made in Victoria. Indeed, twenty years ago, however it may be now, I fancy few towns in England had half the accommodation for human bathing that is provided for sheep at one of our first-class Victorian washingpens of the present day. Neither did one see in the old days those retinues of washers, shearers, wool-pressers, &c., which crowd the modern shed; so that in fact I thought myself very fortunate, under the circumstances, in being able to muster just three extra men for shearing and washing, and to avail myself of their services with the humility which became a master of those times.

These three worthies of course fixed the rate at which they were to be paid, which was, in addition to their rations, one pound sterling per hundred sheep, with four glasses of rum a day. The last requirement I thought very hard and arbitrary, as rum, or spirits of any sort, formed no part of my stores; and I tried hard to get it commuted to double its money value. But for the moment the men were masters of the situation, and their ultimatum in this particular, immutable, on the approved pattern of the celebrated laws of the Medes and Persians. Of course, I felt myself to be a much abused master, and should, no doubt, have struck employing men entirely, had it been possible to conduct the business of sheep-farming without them.

Inwardly groaning under the tyranny to which I was subjected, I found myself obliged, very much *contre-cœur*, to mount one of my men on poor Punch, now in very low condition, and start him off furnished—not with money, for none was ever kept at stations, but with an order for six gallons of rum, addressed to the nearest publican, who lived rather more than a hundred

s

miles away, and with whom I was totally unacquainted. For this duty I selected a man who had some £20 of wages coming to him, and who, fortunately, was not so immoderate a drunkard as the generality of my party. His instructions were to ride to the public-house and get the rum in a pair of three-gallon kegs, one of which would hang on each side of the saddle, with which load he was to lead the pony home.

As Punch was weak, I allowed my messenger ten days to do the two hundred miles; and as regards time he was punctual enough, but instead of getting the spirits put into two small kegs, he was only able to obtain one large one, which he balanced on the other side of the saddle with a bag of stones. I also learned afterwards that this worthy had himself ridden on the top of this load, and made all the shepherds on the road drunk, replacing with water in the morning the spirits abstracted for the evening's jollification. This sort of thing, however, I had calculated on; nor was it of much consequence, as the spirit was strong and fiery—fit, as they say, to give D.T. at fifty paces, so that a little water did no harm.

The wishes of my servants having been thus complied with, I had to put up with one or two rather boisterous scenes, as I found that the covenanted dose of rum made my men drunk, when fights and disturbances ensued. However, I got the first flock washed, and in due time commenced shearing with one man, as the other two could not attend until the next day. I will leave the reader to imagine what a bother it was to look after one man shearing, and yet I thought it prudent to do so and make a beginning. Whether or not it was the effect of the four glasses of rum on this occasion I cannot say, but instead of the sixty or one hundred ewes which are usually shorn by each man, poor old Tom with difficulty got through twenty-five, after completing which he complained of having a headache, and certainly was very red in the face ; in view of which abnormal symptoms I thought it desirable still further to dilute Messrs. Young and Nicol's rum, which I did liberally, and with the best results.

As the sheep-owner's financial year closes with his shearing, it will not, perhaps, be out of place here to state succinctly the result of my first year's sheep-farming. In a former chapter the ruinous conditions under which squatting was at that time generally carried on have already been particularized, so that the reader will be prepared to hear that, irrespective of interest on the purchase-money, the outgoing in wages, the purchase of horses, bullocks, rams, and supplies exceeded my receipts on wool by about £1,000 ; against which there was to be placed a thousand lambs—worth, say, a shilling a head—and the difference in value, whatever it might have been, between the excellent country which I had taken up and the scrubby desert which I had abandoned. In addition, I may also mention that I found, when I arrived in Melbourne with my clip of wool, that the depreciation which had occurred in station property since the date of my father's purchase was not less than *fifty per cent*. In fact, a stagnation of business was preceding the commercial storm which was just about to burst, and the sins of reckless speculation, easy-going banking, champagne revels, and fast living were about to be atoned for by something very like the general insolvency of the community. Town allotments were rarely mentioned now; for the time people had had enough, or, perhaps, too much of them. Even the old bellman, " Excelsior," had, like his prototype, struck his flag. Everything was very dull. The merchant and squatting agent seemed to have nothing to do but trot from one bank to another, " financing," as it was termed. Champagne, that once too familiar libation, was now a thing of the past; in fact, the drawing of a cork of any kind was now as startling from its rarity as the report of a pistol. The squatter who formerly strode so gaily up Collins-street in his Hessian boots, with the " action" of one who, even when on foot, could not altogether get rid of the feeling of having a horse between his legs, was now seldom seen. Probably he had returned to his hut in the bush to philosophize on life in general and his own outstanding acceptances in particular. As regards the merchants in the old country who had made consignments of goods to Melbourne—well, I presume they might as well have consigned them to the "vasty deep" at once, and that "writing off" must have been very common in their counting-houses just about that time.

CHAPTER XI.

A RIDE TO THE MUDDY CREEK.

In after years I had plenty of experience of a business I very much disliked—I mean looking after the wool-shed—but on the occasion to which I have referred in the last chapter, a better fortune befriended me. I was sitting, I remember, in front of my hut, a little after sundown on the second or third day of shearing, taking my evening smoke, when a traveller on the look-out for work (the first who had found his way to Tongala) put a letter into my hand, and called my attention to an endorsement on the back of it, which ran—"*Please give the bearer half a pound of tobacco.—R. C.*" The letter I found was from one of my brothers, who, it appeared, had come from Tasmania some weeks before to join me, and, waiting for an opportunity of writing, had accepted an invitation to the station of a squatter

friend on the Muddy Creek, about one hundred
and twenty miles from Tongala.   Delighted at
the prospect of having a companion, I made
up my mind to go in search of him at once.
As regarded leaving the shearing, I felt no
misgivings on that score, as my overseer was a
thoroughly competent person, and would be
assisted in picking up fleeces, wool-packing, &c.,
by some of the Blacks, who had already begun to
make themselves useful about the place.   Neither
was any further difficulty anticipated with the
shearers, as they had now got fairly to work, and
the talisman of a properly-watered rum keg in
the overseer's possession (not to speak of wages
due) was an ample guarantee for their good
behaviour.   Accordingly, next morning I mounted
my old grey horse, Sweepstakes, and leading
Punch for my brother, set out on my travels—
glad, I own, of an excuse for getting away.   Men-
tioning the old grey reminds me that in those
days, when horses were scarce, and many persons
had only one, on whose back they were also
pretty constantly, that with the estimate of the
rider the capacity and peculiarities of his horse
were often whimsically mixed up.   Everyone
in the neighbourhood knew all about his neighbour's nag, and the animal's powers and speciali-
ties, even to the minutiæ of his saddle and
bridle; so that, as much of our work was done
on horseback, an active man, ill mounted, with

difficulty escaped the character of a " Crawler."
In this way I remember a neighbouring
squatter, of rather cantankerous temper, whose
horse, Dangerous, was constantly throwing him,
acquiring the *sobriquet* of "The Buckjumper,"
a name which was laughably thought suitable
to the rider as well as the horse.

In those days bush business altogether was
carried on very differently from what it is at
present, for squatting has now, for many years,
become in all parts of the continent, however
remote, what the Yankees term " an institution,"
and is conducted in a well-understood routine
way by persons brought up to the occupation;
so that now one only sees about stations what is
suitable to the circumstances. But in the early
days of inexperience, not only was stock ill
managed, and comforts as a rule little thought
of, but the establishments of new arrivals from
home frequently exhibited the most amusing
incongruities. Few of our immigrant squatters,
indeed, had at all correctly forecast what their
new homes would be like, or what they would
require for use or comfort in the bush; whilst
just as few (I refer particularly to the neighbourhood in which I lived) thought of availing themselves, at the outset, of such natural advantages
as further experience proved to be abundantly at
hand. Hence discomfort and a ludicrous inter-
mixture of the useful and inappropriate were

constantly met with. For instance, on the bark table of a hut in which the rafters were begrimed with soot, the earthen floor in holes. and the slab walls anything but weatherproof, might be noticed occasionally, cheek by jowl with the poorest table knives, some handsome silver forks ornamented with the family crest. Occasionally, also, hanging on the rude walls with more suitable articles, might be seen a cavalry sabre or a hunting horn, or perhaps some handsome volumes arranged on a box turned sideways, which, suspended from the tie-beams by thongs of bullock-hide, did duty as a bookshelf; whilst a complex coffee-pot, an expensive canteen, or a stretcher for buckskin breeches were consigned ignominiously to some out-of-sight corner. Looking on such tell-tale articles, the accuracy with which De Foe realized in his " Robinson Crusoe" the exigencies of bush life has often struck me as remarkable.

On this journey I passed the first night after leaving home at the hut of a squatter newly arrived in the colony, who had, unfortunately, fallen into very bad ways. I believe he had been a small land-owner at home, and brought out £1,000 with him. The hut. which he occupied in common with his men, consisted of a single apartment, with the addition of a skilling, which served for store and master's bedroom. Around the common room were several bunks, or bed-places in board-of-ship style; the table in the

centre being a sheet of bark nailed on to the
top of four posts driven into the earthen floor.
On each side of the large fireplace was a rough
wooden bench, which was moved to the table
at meal times ; two or three joints of meat were
simmering in an iron pot on the fire, and a
quart-pot for tea was set to boil for each person,
after the old Sydney fashion.   Kettle, cups, or
teapot there were none.   It was nearly sundown
when I arrived, and in the hut were several of
the station hands, some smoking, some dozing on
their nasty beds ; one had pulled a boot off, and
was mending it, whilst the master—a rough
diamond, in no wise distinguishable from his
servants in the matter of dress—was busy cal-
culating something on a slate, most likely the
yield of his coming clip of wool.   In keeping with
the rest of the establishment were three or four
semi-domesticated black picaninnies seated on
the ash-heap before the door, who were engaged
in sucking the canes of a discarded sugar-bag—a
delicacy, the enjoyment of which a swarm of flies
disputed with them.   They were naked, or, if you
like, dust-clad, big-bellied, rheumy-eyed, disgusting little urchins, who, nevertheless, eventually
grew to be strong men.   An oldish lubra (woman)
also sat a little apart from the sugar-cane group
with her boy of about three years of age, whose
only article of clothing was an old sock which he
had picked up somewhere, and who seemed to

divide his time pretty equally between the pipe, which he was smoking, and the maternal breast. However, if my host was living in an altogether exceptionally rough way—indeed, in almost more discomfort than I recollect ever to have met anywhere else—there was no want of hospitality about him, and whatever was to be had, either for myself or horse, was frankly placed at my disposal.

Shortly after my arrival the cook lit the fat lamp and announced supper, when all hands came forward to help themselves from the smoking mass of meat which had just been extricated from the iron pot. The master sat at one end of the table, on a sheepskin-covered stump, which had been conveniently planted in the floor for his accommo-. dation, and I took up my position on the bench by his side. Quart-pots of tea, here and there at random, one for each person, were on the table, which stood four inches or so higher than is usual, probably as a security against the dogs. Of plates and knives and forks the supply was limited. and the patterns various. Indeed, the arrangements altogether were charmingly simple. Some of the men ate off plates at the table, others put their meat on a slice of damper and took their seats on their beds, or stood in the fireplace, whilst quite a little pack of dogs assisted at the ceremony, to secure the scraps which were thrown on the ground. Supper did not detain us very

long, and we passed the evening smoking and
drinking tea, conversation running on the prospects
of sheep-farmers, and afterwards on some passages
in the history of Scotland (of which country my
host was a native), concerning which he and I did
not quite agree. In this way we got on till bed-
time, when my host, with his clothes off and his
pipe lit, ready to turn in with, summed up the
"Young Chevalier," whose doings we had been
discussing, by vociferating in rather an excited
way, "You may talk of Prince Chairlie and Prince
Chairlie, but I say hang Prince Chairlie! If it
had na been for Prince Chairlie I'd a bin Lord
Oliphant the day!" with which exclamation for a
climax he betook himself, pipe and all, to the
blankets, and was no doubt soon asleep. Poor
C—— ! he ever kept a keen look-out after the
lawbees, and soon got to have a considerable
share of the world's gear; but it must be now fully
thirty years since the "barley bree," which he
loved so well, sent him to join the departed
Oliphants and Prince Chairlie.

The next morning I was approaching the Protectorate station when I overtook a gentleman
riding a magnificent Peter Fin horse, whose
grand legs, superb carriage, and aristocratic head
were a pleasure to look at. Of course we
entered into conversation, as people always do
who meet in solitary places. My new acquaintance turned out to be the doctor to the Protec-

torate station, and he very kindly insisted on my
spending the night at his quarters, which I did.
Naturally he had a good deal to say about the
Blacks ; and he mentioned, amongst other circumstances, that a large number of them had been
employed a few days before, under the supervision of a white man, in planting potatoes for
the future consumption of themselves and
families, receiving for their labour a ration of
flour and meat as usual. It appeared, however,
that these primitive worthies, not being well
versed in agriculture, thought the burying of
food in the ground (a proceeding unheard of in
their annals) a gross folly, so they turned out
during the night and surreptitiously dug up, as
far as practicable, the potatoes planted during the
day, and made a late supper off them. The
doctor also told me that they were very much
subject to panics, and that on the occurrence of
a death, some time back, the tribes had deserted
the station for several months : that they took
but indifferently to civilization ; and that the
best of them were incorrigible wanderers.
Leaving the Protectorate late in the morning
for Baylestown, the next station (as I was only
making short stages), I had jogged on quietly for
some miles, when a kangaroo dog I had with me
bounded past in full pursuit of a kangaroo. As
Punch led like a shadow, I joined the chase,
and, cutting off the turns, was close up to the

kangaroo when he took to water. Into the
lagoon he went with a glorious bound, the dog
close behind him; when a Blackfellow, who had
seen us coming, stepped from behind a tree and
plunged in after the pair. Hand over hand the
savage seemed to slide along the surface of the
water, so that he soon overtook the kangaroo.
He then seized him by the tail and steered him
quietly towards the other bank, on which was his
camp, and knocked his brains out with his nulla-
nulla, which he had brought with him, just as he
was on the point of getting bottom. After
obtaining my consent, he and his lubra dragged
the animal on shore, and no doubt a great feast
ensued. On reaching Baylestown Station I was
hospitably received by the owners, two brothers
from one of the midland counties of England,
who had been some time in the colony. Their
hut, which they had built themselves, was a com-
modious, substantial structure, and was looked
after by a female servant; the establishment
being in marked contrast to my lodgings of
two nights before, and well supplied with
vegetables, dairy produce, and horse-fodder.

After dinner, or supper, as some called it, we
smoked, of course, and brandy and water took the
place of tea, which was not of course. Then
ensued conversation about sheep and horses, and
what the *neighbours* (any stock-owners within
forty miles) were doing. One of my hosts, who

was quizzically inclined, related with a good deal
of humour a colloquy which he had overheard at
an inn on his way from town.   The inn was a hut
of many rooms without ceilings.   The inter-
locutors on the occasion (two canny Scots, whom
we'll call Fraser and Forbes) were, it seemed, the
joint owners of the inn, and it was the custom, as
the narrator said, for Mr. Forbes, the junior
partner, to rise a little before daylight to attend
to the wants of such early birds as desired " to
pick the worm" at the bar, whilst Mr. Fraser
made his appearance a little after the grand
luminary had risen.   On this particular occasion
it seems that the senior partner, before emerging
from his bedroom, recognized, proceeding from
the tap, the voice of a customer, the last of whose
money had been invested in grog some forty-
eight hours before, and concerning whom he
proceeded to call the junior partner to account.

" Mr. Forbes! Mr. Nichol Forbes!" shouted
the senior partner, in an authoritative manner.

" Aye, Mr. Fraser," replied Mr. Forbes, in a
tone of voice which our host described as
obstinately assertive of an equal importance on
the side of the junior partner, " What is it?"

" How is this, Mr. Forbes?   That fly-blown
party (person whose money was all spent) not
gone yet?   I will not have it, Mr. Forbes!
Give him a nobbler of brandy, if you please, and
start him at once."

"Nobbler!" said Mr. Nichol Forbes, in whose veins probably ran the blood of the Bailie Nicol Jarvie, or some other noble ancestor, and in whose bosom the assumption of any shadow of authority over him raised quite a storm. "Nobbler! he's had a nobbler of brandy," and here the voice became slightly sarcastic, "a nobbler of brandy, a nip of gin, and a go of rum, already this morning, and now he says he won't move."

"Aye! what's that?" said Mr. Fraser, "three drinks gratis! I will not have these disorderly ways in the house, Mr. Forbes. I'm surprised at you—quite surprised at you! Start him on the wallaby track at once, if you please, neck and crop. Bundle him out, and set the dogs on him."

On this mild reproof, Mr. Nichol Forbes, like one of Ossian's heroes, "On his hill of storm arose in wrath." Then was heard a peremptory order to leave the house, and a rollicking refusal to comply with that request. A short scuffle ensued, one or two blows were heard, the trampling of boots on the floor, and a rattle of tumblers; a suppressed objurgation on one side, and an out-spoken drunken protest on the other; and the fly-blown party was violently ejected, and the door slammed in his face. How the junior partner, who seemed a good deal "raised," felt after his exertion is not known; but that he did join the senior member of the firm shortly after in the usual matutinal tumbler of rum and milk I understood to be the fact.

The next day I crossed the Sydney-road, which runs between the ranges and the flat country. On the east side of the road I found the mountainous district abounding in green grass and running streams—what a new chum would think the *beau ideal* of a sheep country; and in effect this neighbourhood was in high repute at the time, whilst the flat country to the west, which was noticeable for its dry, burnt-up appearance, and the prevalence of salsolaceous vegetation, was considered to be very inferior. On this head the mountaineers at that time plumed themselves not a little, rather looking down on the dwellers on the plains. Of course we all know now that the estimate formed on this subject was quite an erroneous one, and, as a fact, that those overlanders who took up country to the eastward of the Sydney-road, amidst abundance of water and green grass, met but with scant success as sheep-farmers; those whose fortune led them westward, or down the rivers, as a rule doing exceedingly well. Indeed, now-a-days, green-grass country and bad country are pretty generally synonymous terms.

However, causes had not yet produced their effects, and at Tallarook, where I was kindly received by the proprietor, I found a very pleasant hut, floored and well furnished: good

stabling, an excellent table, and a picturesque
look-out; in fact, all the necessaries, and most
of the luxuries, attainable in the bush. The
country in which I now found myself bore
the reputation of being in the hands of a
number of rather fast-going men, one of whose
favourite amusements was cards; and it used
to be said at the time that flocks of sheep
occasionally changed hands as the result of
an evening's unlimited loo. Whether these
reports were strictly accurate I cannot say ;
nor whether, at a later period, when over-drafts
were less common at the banks, the merry men of
those parts did, as was rumoured, actually settle
down quietly to whist, with sheep points and a
bullock on the rub. At all events, many a wild
prank of the Upper Goulburn and Devil's River
men furnished matter for gossip at the time ; and
so, for the rest, *se non e vero, e ben trovato.*

At Tallarook that evening I met a few choice
spirits. The Honourable G—— K——, a guest
stopping at the place, I remember, was there
when I arrived ; and, a little before sundown, two
neighbouring squatters, both sons of colonels,
one of whom was well known subsequently in
Victorian political circles, rode up to the door.
The company were all young men, and in high
spirits ; and being friendly, intimate, and of a
kidney, a good deal of very lively gossip ensued,
which gave one a pretty fair idea of the ways of

9

the neighbourhood. During dinner (which was a good one, and well served) it was related that a shepherd in the neighbourhood was said to have discovered gold; at all events, it was known that he was constantly digging in the gullies and creeks, and that when he had completed his term of service he purchased a small stock of provisions and started for some distant ranges with a spade and pickaxe. Of course, his success as a gold digger, if he had any, was kept to himself, as the precious metals, at that time, were held to be the property of the Crown. After dinner, and the post-prandial pipe in the verandah, the company sat down to loo, which was kept up with little intermission till three or four o'clock in the morning. Being sleepy, I retired comparatively early, and was awakened about sunrise by a piston-cornet with which our host was calling the sleepers to breakfast. There were two beds in the room in which I slept, on one of which (his Hessian boots and spurs still on) lay the future legislator, who regretted to me that he had not gone to bed when I did, as he said his head ached, and that his losses had been £30.

Next evening I arrived at the station where my brother was awaiting me. Like that which I had just left, I found everything very comfortable there—in fact, too comfortable under the circumstances; for the owner, like the other squatters

CHAPTER XIII.

CORROBOREES, AND GIVING IN MARRIAGE.

By February, 1842, or thereabouts—just a year after my arrival in Port Phillip—the little troubles incident to removal and settlement had been got over at Tongala, and having now my brother to assist me, I paid off my overseer, and so reduced my expenditure by £100 per annum.

At that date my clip of wool had been delivered in Melbourne; winter's stores carted up; sheep-yards, huts, and paddock completed; out-station huts put up, and the bushman, who had with the assistance of myself and the overseer finished these jobs, been paid off and got rid of, so that there remained on the ground, besides my brother and myself, three shepherds (whose flocks had been increased by a thousand lambs), a hut-keeper, and a bullock-driver. This staff of men, it is true, would have sufficed for a much larger number of sheep, and yet could not well have been reduced, as it is necessary for the proper manage-ment of sheep that there should be on a station, besides the ewe flock, one of weaners and year-lings, and a third of wethers and rams. As far as my brother and myself were concerned, we were now very much at a loss for something to do.

This was the first time we had to complain of what in after years we suffered a good deal from.

Persons who have not had experience of such situations will perhaps hardly realize how heavily time hung on our hands. We read a good deal, of course, but after one has done enough of that sort of work for the day, a weary portion of the twenty-four hours still remains to be got through. Besides, a hundred and fifty volumes do not constitute an inexhaustible supply of literary food. Conversation not unfrequently halted a good deal for want of fresh subjects. Nor could it be otherwise, cut off, as we were, from the outer world. Around us was nothing but the same everlasting gum-trees basking in changeless sunshine, whilst the rarely-varied meal of tea, mutton, and damper made its appearance on the table three times a day with such dyspeptic regularity that I used to loathe the sight of it. Of course, in self-defence, we did what we could with horses, dogs, and guns to relieve the monotony of our days, but our pastimes gradually lost their charms. However, something had to be done; so, like sailors snowed up in an Arctic winter, we cast about for fresh trifles to elevate into importance, and expend our surplus energies on. Unfortunately, of botany and bird-stuffing, and things of that sort, we were both ignorant; neither did it occur to us to take up the aboriginal languages, or grapple with the traditions of the ancient and singular race with which we had been brought in contact, or we might have found pleasant and unfailing occupa-

his orderly, a sergeant, three troopers, and a man in charge of the cart.

This latter proved to be a native of Africa, who, as he came in sight, sounded a call on the bugle, to the great edification of the whole of us, white and black, who had turned out to witness the approach of the cavalcade. This was the party which the blackfellow had described as consisting of "Towsan," which, all the country over, is the aboriginal English for any number over half-a-dozen. The police were armed with carbines and pistols, the sergeant carrying a cavalry sabre only. Their dress was the usual uniform of their corps; and their horses, with the exception of tether-ropes round their necks, were turned out in a decidedly military way, with inconvenient bits, peculiar saddle-cloths, awkward saddles, and sore backs. The Commissioner's horse was likewise accoutred much in the manner of the charger of a cavalry officer, and his dark green costume, fixed spurs, Hessian boots, blue cap with braided band, &c., were decidedly military in their effect, and might easily have passed for the uniform of an officer of some regiment of irregular mounted rifles. On dismounting, he threw the reins to his orderly, and accepted my invitation to take up his quarters with me for the night; his party proceeding to tether their horses and pitch their camp under a shady tree on the river bank.

The duties of a Commissioner in those days
were numerous and varied. The most important
of them had reference to the Crown lands of his
district, on which he issued licenses to squat.
He also settled disputes about boundaries.
Disagreements on this score, which in later
times would have taken a judge, with his jurors,
barristers, witnesses, and *attachés* of the court, a
week to dispose of—Bah! the Commissioner
settled them in half-an-hour, or less; sometimes
probably hearing only one of the claimants, and
sometimes neither. The Commissioner of the
district in which I had settled was not what one
would call a bright man, but he did such business
off hand, his jurisdiction in the matter being
possibly summary in more senses than one.
From what came under my own observation, I
should say that our particular Commissioner kept
few records of his official acts, if any; and never
caused any marks to be made on the trees or
land in connection with the boundaries of the
runs. Indeed, I fancy he considered things of
the sort mere red tape nuisances: his custom in
cases of disputes, as far as it came under my
notice, being to hear but short statements, give
his decision in few words, change the conversation, light his pipe and ride away. This style of
doing business, it is true, was called in question,
later on, by ill-disposed persons, and even spoken
of in a disparaging and jeering manner, and

some, no doubt, suffered inconveniences from it ;
but it used to be thought generally that, though
our Commissioner's method did not secure accuracy, it was well enough suited to the times, and
so gave satisfaction ; and possibly it might have
gone on giving satisfaction indefinitely, had not
malcontented individuals and busy-bodies got
attorneys and barristers to spy out little imperfections, make disturbances, and bring into court
matters which were never dealt with in expectation of such proceedings in any way. But if
our Commissioner's rule did give a fair amount of
satisfaction in the early days, it was mainly
owing to the confidence which the public had in
the impartiality and honour of the gentlemen
who filled the office. Besides, the squatters, I
think, generally held to the opinion that the
Commissioner, whilst decidedly more expeditious
than juries, displayed about the same appreciation
of fact as those time-honoured bodies, after
counsel on both sides has been heard and their
brains properly mystified with contradictory
swearing.

In addition to such matters, it was also one of
the functions of the Commissioner to adjust the
frequent differences which occurred between the
original lords of the soil and the Anglo-Saxon
parvenus. Now, though the reader may fancy
that this was easily done, it was not, in fact,
without difficulties. Disturbances were constantly

occurring. Generally the first intimation the
Commissioner got of a case was a letter from a
stock-owner complaining that after having treated
the Blacks with uniform kindness and consideration for a length of time, they had suddenly killed
one of his shepherds under circumstances of peculiar atrocity, and roasted and eaten two hundred
of his flock. On the receipt of reports of this
sort the Commissioner proceeded, as soon as he
was able, to the scene of the outrage, where he
heard the complaint repeated *viva voce*. Strange
to say, the Blacks habitually neglected to give
their version of the tale, though we know that
they had constantly very serious charges to advance against shepherds, in connection with their
conduct towards the females of the tribe. As the
Blacks, therefore, neglected to appear before the
Commissioner in what might be termed his judicial capacity, nothing was left for him as guardian
of the public peace but to appear before them,
which he did at a gallop, sabre in hand, surrounded by his troopers industriously loading and
discharging their carbines. Now, it may seem
strange to the reader that there were a few well-
intentioned visionaries, at the time, who made the
Government policy, as carried out by the Commissioner, a subject for unfavourable comment.
Some asserted there was no statute which authorized proceedings of the sort; that the Blacks
were unable to represent wrongs, which everyone

knew they suffered, from want of knowledge of
our language; that fire and sword were carried
into their camps, and death indiscriminately dealt
out amongst them, without any proper examination of the complainant having been made
or a single deposition taken. In fact, that less
evidence was required to condemn a tribe to
destruction than to consign an habitual drunkard
for four-and-twenty hours to the lock-up. Other
persons indulged in poetic flights, in the very
worst taste, in connection with the subject, and
describe John Bull as landing on foreign shores,
the Bible in his pocket, a blunderbus in one hand
and a rum-bottle in the other, leaving the savage
no alternative but to give up his land and die by
one instrument or the other, drunk or sober.
All this being as tedious to answer as it is
trifling in itself, we will pass on to another
complaint, which was, that the Commissioner and
his troopers occasionally *administered justice with
sword and carbine to the wrong tribe in mistake.*
In connection with this, veracity compels me to
admit that the aborigines, being a very homoge-
neous race, much alike in colour and features, with
but little variety of costume—there being also but
little evidence, and that purely circumstantial, as
to which of them had committed any particular
outrage—cases of mistaken identity would, and
did, occasionally occur.

But though one must always regret occurrences

of this sort, it is consolatory to remember now—
a fact of which we were ignorant at the time,
—that whilst our troopers were busily shooting
down in mistake individuals who had not injured
us in any way, but whose acquaintances had, that
we were absolutely acting—by a fluke, no doubt—
in accordance with a law in force in all our
tribes, which makes vengeance fall not only on
an offender, but equally on the first of his tribe
or kind who may come to hand. From this we
see how constantly our busybodies were in the
wrong.

But, besides duties of a composite judicial and
military character, the Commissioner had other
functions. For instance, he determined on the
issue and renewal of licenses for bush public-
houses in his district, and had his say as to the
rates chargeable at such places for refreshments
and fodder. If to the above we add that Commissioners were a good deal about town, active
on the subject of Assembly balls, took an
interest in club matters, mixed a good deal in
society, and were very constant in their attendance
on the Governor (or Superintendent, as he was
styled), it will easily be allowed that they did not
eat the bread of idleness.

As regards the Commissioner of our district,
he was popular and highly respected, and his
visits acceptable to the sheep-owners. Besides
the welcome novelty of having our solitude

broken in upon by a pleasant, chatty person, well up in current news, he generally carried with him a few newspapers, the perusal of which was, of course, quite a treat. That they were often dated several weeks back was of little consequence, as their contents were generally quite as new to us as if they had been only a day old.

On this occasion the Commissioner accepted my proposal to take a ride with me next day to the river Murray, which he had never seen, and which is only three miles from Tongala. On our way to it we crossed the Madowla Lagoon, now, and for many years past, a fine sheet of water, but at that time dry and full of saplings, several years old. On reaching the river, which was very low at the time, we forded it, and crossed into New South Wales proper, continuing our ride along the sandhills to the northward.

Amongst the pines and she-oaks scattered over the ridges the grass was so green, and looked so inviting, that the place quite took my fancy, and I applied on the spot for a block of five miles' frontage to the river by eight miles back, which was granted without difficulty, the Commissioner and myself both forgetting that we were actually in a district to which his authority did not extend. However, nothing was ever said on that point, and I occupied the country in question until it suited me to leave it. Later on it formed a portion of Sir John O'Shanassy's Moira station.

After several hours' riding we were again approaching the Murray, when my dogs got sight of an old man kangaroo. A halloo, as we started, giving him notice of our presence, he made tracks for the river, which was close at hand, taking the water with a magnificent bound from the top of a perpendicular bank some thirty feet high. The dogs, getting down as they could, dashed after him into the stream, and we stood on the bank to see him worried. A skirmish followed, in which several ugly claw-wounds were received, the dogs swimming in a circle around their prey, closing with him as opportunities offered; but as the water just there was too deep for the kangaroo to bottom, and the mode of warfare not suited to his nature, it was his fate to succumb, which he did nobly, making his final plunge head foremost, tail on high. As the sun disappeared, we, the first white men who had been in those parts, paused a moment to admire the scene. Whilst we stood in silence in the shade, gazing on the noble stream, a laughing-jackass, his serenity disturbed probably by the sight of our party, gave out his note from a branch overhead, and broke the stillness of the woods. Another and another of his kind, from the tall trees right and left along the river bank, took up the singular laugh, which, growing less and less distinct as it receded, gradually died away. A smart canter of twenty minutes brought us to our dinner at Tongala.

in that neighbourhood, was living beyond his income, as results shortly proved. Besides, generally, the jovial mountaineers paid but little attention to their stock; and then their bills in town, outlay in racehorses, loo, and so forth, must have been something considerable. Besides, there were the high rates of provisions and wages, and the depreciated state of the wool market; so that, even if they had from the beginning confined themselves strictly to whist and the economical stakes indicated, it seems very doubtful whether they would have got through the bad times.

After resting a few days at this station, I returned with my brother to Tongala, where I found the shearing had gone on swimmingly, and was nearly completed.

CHAPTER XII.

A VISIT FROM THE COMMISSIONER OF CROWN LANDS.

ONE evening in the beginning of 1842 I was startled by a sudden outcry from the Blacks' camp hard by, and on going to the door of my hut to ascertain the cause of the hubbub I was met by a blackfellow, evidently in a state of excitement. In the hurry of the moment he had

dropped his opossum-skin cloak and seized a
bundle of spears, which he held in his hand ; and
I noticed that the lubras were bundling their
picaninnies on to their backs and hurriedly preparing to decamp.

"Massa !" said the blackfellow, "you see ?
Policemen come up now. Towsan (thousand)
policemen ! I believe that fellow directly
shootum all about blackfellow !"

With some trouble I quieted the apprehensions
of my sable neighbours so far as to induce them
to sit down again in their camp, telling them that
the policemen (whom I could not yet make out)
never interfered with any but *wild Blacks*. Of
course the Bangerang (as the people of the
Tongala tribe were called), having learned a few
words of English, and acquired a relish for
tobacco, tea, and roast mutton, so far from sus-
pecting for a moment that they could be looked
on as wild Blacks, thought, no doubt, that they
had reached a very high stage of civilization, and
that they were not, therefore, after what I had
said, in any way concerned in the approach of
the police, who bore a villainous name amongst
them.

In a few moments I saw several horsemen,
with a spring-cart in their train, coming over the
sand hill. The *cortège* turned out to be that of
the Commissioner of Crown Lands, who led the
way on a magnificent chestnut horse, followed by

tion at once in a rich field for inquiry; so, in default of something better, we took to much swimming, throwing spears, climbing trees after the native fashion (by means of tomahawk-notches), in all of which exercises we became tolerably proficient, especially as regards the first and last of these accomplishments. Not that the spear-throwing was altogether a failure, as by dint of practice we not only arrived at such a stage of excellence as to be able to make the Blacks, at whom "we hurled the light Djreed," look out pretty sharply, but at last I actually succeeded, I recollect, in spearing one poor fellow through the foot, which of course was looked on as a grand success, though my brother, who I think was a little jealous, hinted that it was only a fluke. However, fortunately for us, incidents of one sort or another did turn up now and then to relieve our dull days a little, and we got used to making the most of them, such as they were. As no road passed Tongala, which was a sort of *ultima thule*, white strangers in those days scarcely ever found their way to the place, so that anything in the shape of novelty which reached us usually came by means of our black neighbours.

On one occasion, I remember, after the arrival of a pair of our sable friends from up the river, it became evident that something of interest had occurred. What this was did not at first appear. From the animated harangues at the camp that

night, it was evident that there was something in
the wind. Next morning, too, there was a decided
movement in the direction of the manufacture of
personal ornaments; so that reed necklaces, red
ochre, pipe-clay, armlets of fur, plumes, bones to
wear through the nose, and other adornments
began decidedly to look up in the aboriginal
market, and come into strong request amongst
the youthful of both sexes; and, in fact, not with
the young people only, as it was noticed that
several ladies who must long since have passed
the grand climacteric took to forcing combs
through their tangled locks and beautifying
their faces with a compound of ruddle and fat.
The doings of these ancient dames, indeed, we
found, were quite matters of amusement to some
half-dozen hearty young bachelors in the camp—
roystering blades, who, in greasy grandeur, slyly
watched their doings with much zest. Besides
the ladies of uncertain age, there was another
little class of individuals who were evidently
affected by the something—whatever it might be
—which was going to happen—I mean that portion of the maiden section of the community
which was considered to have reached the mar-
riageable age. Bangerang girls, the reader should
know, were promised in infancy to men of some
neighbouring tribe in exchange for other girls,
for none married within their own tribe; and as
such promises were almost invariably kept, these

aboriginal young ladies were, of course, spared the trouble of taking any steps on their own account in a matrimonial direction. Hence, at the juncture in question (for it leaked out, at last, that the Ngooraialum, a neighbouring tribe, were shortly expected down the river, to exchange betrothed females), these interesting young persons, who were about to be delivered over to their natural enemies—as, rightly or wrongly, they regarded their future husbands—not only took no part in the reed-necklace and ochre-and-fat movement, but absolutely relinquished their ordinary attentions to personal appearances, and sat in the camp in that discontented, pouting mood which they, as well as their civilized sisters, can occasionally assume. As a rule, these girls would be about twelve or fourteen years of age, and their husbands-elect some five and thirty years older, and already the lords of one or two spouses; for if the civilized man of our day is perhaps somewhat undecided as to the advantages of matrimony, the Australian savage is unmistakably an advocate for that state; so that not only do the influential men get as many wives as they can, but no lubra is allowed to remain single after the age which I have just mentioned, nor widow on the sunny side of forty-five to wear her weeds above a week. In this way it happened that one seldom saw a couple in which both the parties were young.

At first I had some little difficulty in entering into the spirit of what was going on, and the proposed exchange of girls, spears, and stone tomahawks, as well as the corroborees which I heard were to take place, interested me but slightly; but, on the principle, I presume, that strong feelings are infectious, I at last, from constantly hearing the matter discussed as a most important event, ended by becoming almost as anxious about the arrival of the Ngooraialum as my Bangerang neighbours themselves. Indeed, I entertained serious thoughts at last of asking to be allowed to give away the brides, and should probably have moved in that matter had not my very imperfect knowledge of aboriginal tongues prevented me.

At length, one evening, a low murmur in the camp, which somehow reminded me of the sound which proceeds from the poultry-yard when the shadow of a hawk sailing overhead is noticed by the feathered community, attracted my attention, when an excited blackfellow, his eyes adance, entered my hut in a very unceremonious manner, exclaiming, " Massa ! Old man Wong come up now ! Postman, that fellow belonging to Ngooraialum;" or, in other words, that old Wong (crow), the anxiously-expected *avant courier* of the Ngooraialum, was at hand. Of course I turned out to see what would occur. In due time old Wong approached the camp, whither I expected he would have bent his steps and received a hearty welcome. Such, however, it seemed was not the orthodox mode of procedure.

As to the Bangerang, after they had satisfied themselves by a glance that it was really Wong who was at hand, they continued each what he or she was engaged about, as if entirely unconcerned at his arrival; taking care, however, to keep their eyes averted from the direction in which he was coming. This little peculiarity, I may notice, is very characteristic of the Blacks, who never allow themselves to give way to any undue curiosity as regards their fellow-countrymen, and as a rule refrain from staring at anyone. Wong, when he arrived within twenty or thirty yards of the camp, slowly put his bag off his shoulder without saying a word, gazed around him for a moment in every direction except that of the Bangerang camp, and sat down with his side face towards his friends, and quietly stuck his spears one by one into the ground beside him, with the air of a man who was unconscious of anyone being within fifty miles of him; the Bangerang, in the meantime, smothering all signs of impatience, continued pegging out their opossum-skins, conversing with those near them, or whatever other matter they might be engaged in. Probably five minutes passed in this way, when an old lubra, on being directed in an undertone by her husband, took some fire and a few sticks, and,

approaching the messenger, laid them close before
him, and walked slowly away without addressing him. Old Wong, as if the matter hardly
interested him, very quietly arranged his little
fire, and, as the wood was dry, with one or two
breaths blew it into a blaze. Not long after an
old fellow got up in the camp, and, with his eyes
fixed on the distance, walked up majestically to
the new-comer and took his seat before his
fire. Though these men had known each other
from childhood, they sat face to face with averted
eyes, their conversation for some time being
constrained and distant, confined almost entirely
to monosyllables. At length, however, they
warmed up ; other men from the camp gradually
joined them ; the ice was broken, and complete
cordiality ensued ; and Wong having given the
message of which he was the bearer, that the
long-expected Ngooraialum were coming, the
conference broke up, the new-comer being at
liberty to take his seat at any camp-fire, at which
there was no women, which might suit his fancy.
As was generally the case, he selected the
bachelors' camp, at which no doubt he kept the
young men awake till a late hour with gossip of
all sorts, and odds and ends of native news.

The next evening, from amongst the branches
of a tree in which they were playing, some young
urchins announced the arrival of the Ngooraialum. As the Blacks usually hunt as they

travel, they seldom move in bodies, and hence the new-comers straggled up in twos and threes. The bachelors, being unencumbered, arrived first; next, perhaps, couples without children; then the old and decrepit; and, lastly, the families in which there was a large proportion of the juvenile element. As they arrived they formed their camps, each family having a fire of its own, some half-dozen yards from its neighbour's; that of the bachelors, perhaps, being rather further off, and somewhat isolated from the rest. On this occasion the Ngooraialum were accompanied by several Pimpandoor Blacks, a tribe from the Campaspe, their immediate neighbours, who spoke the same language as themselves, and were at that time friendly.

After the strangers had arranged their camps (which, as the weather was fine, consisted merely of a shelter of boughs to keep off the sun), and each group had kindled for itself the indispensable little fire, which the aboriginal always keeps up even in the warmest weather, they began to stroll about, and some of them came to my hut with the usual request for tobacco. Though displaying all the distinctive marks of the Australian race, the new-comers, as a lot, differed in some respects from the Bangerang. Besides, for instance, speaking a different language, and pitching their voices in a lower key, they were as a rule smaller and more muscular men, with a carriage which I have never seen surpassed in dignity. Byron proposes, as typical of this sort of thing—

"The Andalusian dame from mass returning,"

but though I have had, perhaps, more opportunities than his lordship of seeing and admiring the stately Andaluza, I can hardly give her the preference, in the point of erect and graceful bearing, over the Ngooraialum stalking forth from his camp wrapped in his opossum-rug. In Spain it was the women, and amongst the Ngooraialum the men, who excelled in this way; the muscular opossum-eaters of the male sex exhibiting a dignity of bearing which was not found amongst their women, nor in the same degree amongst the more loosely knit, semi-fishermen Bangerang septs.

Of these tribal meetings, one of the principal always, and sometimes the only object, used to be the performance of their corroborees, in which they took the greatest delight. On this evening the Bangerang corroboried, the Ngooraialum being the spectators; the character of the performance being rather that of an exhibition than a dance, as we understand it. From this cause, perhaps, tribes rarely corroboried unless they had another tribe as spectators, except for the purpose of practice. When a new corroboree was invented, neighbouring tribes were very anxious to see it, and took it up at once if it pleased them, so that a production of the sort which satisfied the aboriginal critic, both as to figure and melody, often found its way to very distant tribes, who, as I have frequently noticed, sang it without any idea of the meaning of the words.

On this occasion the men of the Bangerang withdrew after dark to a smooth piece of ground, shaded by towering river gums, two or three hundred yards from the camp, and after lighting a couple of large fires, in the space between which the performance was to take place, they sat down to what I suppose I must call dress for the evening. Between the blackfellow's evening costume on gala occasions, and those to which my town reader has been accustomed, it will readily be understood that some differences exist, and that the appearance of a blackfellow at a ball in corroboree costume would create quite as great a sensation among our countryfolk as would one of our carpet knights in orthodox evening costume indulging in a *balancé* in the front rank of a corroboree.

The blackfellow's mode of adorning himself, besides being picturesque and effective, is in excellent keeping with his surroundings, and, like everything else about him, fits his circumstances admirably. On the suit of well-fitting black with which nature sent him into the world (his opossum-rug being discarded for the occasion) he smudges on forehead, cheeks, arms, chest, and

thighs a groundwork of rouge made from a sort
of clay which is burnt for the purpose. On this
he inscribes lines or draws figures with pipe-clay;
and though the get-up of no two men is exactly
the same, they all have a decided family resemblance, and harmonize well. Around the eyes, for
instance, there are often streaks of pipe-clay, some
of which enclose both eyes, whilst others sepa-
rately encircle each eye. The hair of the head, in
every case on this occasion, was confined either by
a netted fillet or a narrow band of twisted
opossum skin, which was tied behind, the ends of
the strings hanging down between the shoulders:
a plume of emu or cockatoo feathers being frequently inserted in it. The chest also was
adorned with some device in pipe-clay, a favourite
one being the tortoise ; others drew white streaks
along the ribs, which gave the individual the look
of a skeleton, and so on. In all cases the performers wore a belt round the loins, from which
depended, both before and behind, a thick bunch
of opossum-skin thongs, which hung half-way
down to the knee. In addition, tufts of green
leaves were bound tightly round each ankle, and
rolls of fur around the thick part of the arm.
There were, besides, strong lines of pipe-clay
which extended from the ankle upwards, along
the leg, both inside and out. The aim proposed
in the get-up seemed to be to produce as savage
and terrible an effect as possible, which probably

was the style which found favour with the weaker sex. In great measure the object of these exhibitions seemed to be the portrayal of battle or hunting scenes—generally the former.

When the men had completed their preliminary arrangements, the women of the tribe came to the ground, and were stationed by an old blackfellow, who acted as master of ceremonies, all huddled closely together a little on one side of the spot which was to be occupied by the dancers. They were a good deal in the shade, so as to be but little seen, their part of the performance being to supply the music, which consisted of wild and peculiar airs sung in chorus, to which they kept time with a sort of rude drum, extemporized by rolling up their opossum-rugs—which they held between their knees—into hard lumps, and beat with their hands, the fingers being open and extended. It is exceedingly curious to notice how very closely all this resembles our theatrical arrangements, which could not by any possibility have been known to the Blacks for many years after. Indeed, practically, they are still unknown to them at this moment, after a lapse of forty years.

Preparations being in this advanced stage, the occasional clash of shield and boomerang, snatches of song in female voices, or the wild yell of delight of some warrior, who, as he rose from his toilet, executed a short *pas-seul* to test the

security of his trappings, and his vigour for the
dance, warned the Ngooraialum, who had begun
to gather about the point of attraction, and seat
themselves on the ground, about ten yards in
front of where the performance was to take place,
that all was ready.   Suddenly, as the last of the
spectators were seated, some light fuel was thrown
on to the burning logs; the fire shot up into a
blaze; the master of ceremonies struck together
the two short sticks with which he marked the
time, and the shrill voices of the lubras (women)
burst into song.   At the same moment the sable
performers, until now unseen, one by one issuing
from the outside gloom with the silence of shadows,
if we except the rustling of the boughs round their
ankles, took up their position in a row between
the fires; each man, as he came into line, extending his arms and legs into that peculiar attitude
which makes one of the marked singularities of
the corroboree.   The effect of the whole scene
was startling enough; the impression produced on
my mind being, that I had before me what might
not be a bad scene for a *diablerie* comedy of a lot
of fiends escaped from their dungeons, and intent
on a hell-dance in celebration of the event.   This
was the first time my brother and I witnessed a
corroboree, and we sat on the ground in a somewhat prominent position on the left side of the
dancers, three or four yards from them, a good
deal in advance of the Ngooraialum spectators,

who, just visible by the reflection of the fire, might be seen to watch the show, motionless as statues cut in ebony. Never on any succeeding occasion did I see the corroboree danced more successfully. The Blacks themselves, as yet uninfluenced by civilization, and wrapped up in their own customs, were in a highly excited state, and thoroughly in the humour; the night, though fine, was dark; not a breath of air was stirring; so that the whole of the surroundings were precisely what suited the performance.

Without troubling the reader with the details of an exhibition which has been so frequently described, I may remark that I was strongly impressed with the scene on this occasion. The extraordinary energy displayed by the dancers; their singular attitude; the quivering thigh; the poised spear; the whitened shield borne in the left hand; the peculiar thur! thur! thur! which their lips emitted in unison with the measured tramp of their feet; their ghastly countenances; the sinister manner in which the apparition had noiselessly stolen from the surrounding darkness into the flaming foreground, and executed—now in open order, now in a compact body, to the sound of wild voices, and the clash of savage arms—their *can-can diabolique*, made up a picture thrilling from its novelty, its threatening character, and its entire strangeness. Then, when the tumult grew hotter, and heavier the tramp of

naked feet, and the voices of the women trem-
bling with emotion waxed shriller and shriller,
these wild warriors, worked up apparently to
uncontrollable fury, with heaving chest and
glaring eyes, their heads turned to their left
shoulder, and their savage eyes fixed on my
brother and myself, suddenly as one man threw
back their right arms and brought their right
shoulders forward, as if to plant in our breasts
their spears which now converged on us,—the
display seemed to have passed from the theatrical
to the real. The idea that all was over with us,
and an intense longing for my pistols, flashed
through my brain. But before I could attempt
to move, the climax had been reached, and the
performers, dropping their spear-points to the
ground, burst into one simultaneous yell, which
made the old woods ring again, and then hurried
at once out of sight, a laughing mob, into the
forest's gloom. Was that yell, fancy suggested,
the farewell cry to pleasant earth of a rabble-rout
of fiends hurrying back to subterranean prisons in
obedience to some mysterious power ?

This might be termed the first act of a play
which was gone through in a very different spirit
from the tame exhibitions got up by our broken-
spirited tribes during the last thirty years or
more, there being but a faint resemblance between
the corroborees danced by the savage in his wild
and subdued state.

To pass on from the corroboree, the reader will remember that the chief object of the meeting of the two tribes was the delivery of the betrothed girls to their husbands. These young persons were now to quit their relatives and the scenes of childhood, and take their places in a strange camp amongst another people. On this occasion two or three Bangerang girls found husbands amongst the Ngooraialum, who returned the compliment by making as many Bangerang men happy. In every instance it was noticeable that the husband was considerably older than the wife, there being generally twenty years—often much more—between them; indeed, as I frequently noticed, few men under thirty years of age had lubras, whilst the men from forty to fifty had frequently two, and occasionally three, better halves. The day before the young ladies were given in marriage, the Blacks, for some reason or other, perhaps because they desired to be alone, removed their camp across the river, so that I did not witness what occurred on the occasion; but the following account, which a blackfellow who was present gave me of the proceedings, is, I have no doubt, pretty accurate.

The girl about whom he spoke was called Kilbangaroo. A couple of hours after nightfall she was directed by her father to go to the camp of Wawgroot, the man to whom she had been promised years before. Wawgroot had already a lubra of some twenty-two years of age as his wife, who was decidedly a belle amongst the Blacks ; a sprightly, arch-spoken, laughing young lady. At this particular time, my informant said that Polly—as Mrs. Wawgroot No. 1 was called— was sitting beside her husband in the mia-mia, looking a thought sulky, and as though some outburst of feeling on her part was imminent. Whether the fact of her being likely to give her husband a little of her mind on the occasion did not make her as much a person of interest to the camp at large as the bride is doubtful. In the meantime Polly's lord and master sat before the fire, smoking his pipe in silence. Probably he was at a loss for some subject of conversation which would be welcome to Polly at that particular time. Altogether, it was said that he was a little bashful as regards the young wife, and a good deal in awe of the coquettish young lady sitting at his elbow, who he knew was quite capable of making a scene which would be particularly amusing to the camp, and, of course, correspondingly disagreeable to himself.

As it grew later, however, Kilbangaroo's father began to urge on her that it was time she went to the camp of her husband-elect. At first he spoke in a low tone of voice, and suggestively as it were, and as though the matter was not to his liking ; then, as he got no answer, in a half angry key. In the meantime the bride was lying at the camp fire enveloped in her opossum-rug and pretending to be asleep. She was, of course, keenly alive to what was being said to her, and well knew what she was expected, and what she would be made, to do; but whether her hesitancy in going to Wawgroot's mia-mia proceeded from shyness, or whether she was reluctant to give up all ideas of a certain young bachelor of a neighbouring tribe who was said to be far advanced in her good graces, or whether, as I suspect, it was considered the proper thing to give as much trouble as possible on such occasions, it would be difficult to say. At all events, for the present she neither stirred nor spoke.

After some delay the father again took up the theme, and this time he reasoned a little with his daughter—"Why are you stupid, Kilbangaroo? Were you not promised to him long ago? Are not all the young girls sent to their husbands' camps?" Still the obdurate maiden lay motionless and gave no sign. The father, at this juncture, my informant mentioned, gave one of his dogs an unmerciful blow with his nulla-nulla (or club) for some trifling offence, and sent the animal howling lustily through the camp. This, I surmise, might have been to remind the bride, through the instrumentality of the dog, of what might happen to herself if she tried his patience too far. About an hour passed in this sort of way, the girl still pretending to be asleep, when

the father's endurance began to waver; so, having
given vent probably to one or two of those
untranslatable phrases with which the Bangerang
were wont to ease their minds when strongly
exercised, he gave his daughter a rude thrust
with the point of his nulla-nulla. Of course
Kilbangaroo could no longer feign sleep—she
knew that matters were growing serious; so she
sat up, her dishevelled and dusty hair shading a
face expressive, I have no doubt, of the most
sublime sulkiness. "Go," said the father,
following up his advantage, "Be off"—and here
he let fly such a string of expletives, and grew
so hot, that he was likely soon to strike—so the
mother interfered, and called on her daughter to
go. "Make haste," said the father; still the
maiden budged not. So he raised his nulla-nulla
—"Will you go?" said he; and, receiving no reply,
was about to bring down the heavy weapon on
her head, she in no way seeking to avoid it, when
the mother caught his arm, as she opened in
vociferous abuse of her daughter, and, raising her
by the shoulders from the ground, lifted her on to
her feet. By this time, I presume, what was
held to be the proper amount of unwillingness
had been acted; so Kilbangaroo, with her bag
containing her few trifling personal effects slung
over her shoulder, walked noiselessly to Wawgroot's camp, at about a yard from which she lay
down, completely enveloped in her opossum-rug;

and in this way, like her *antepasados*, was she given in marriage.

Having interested myself in this phase of aboriginal life, there was one individual connected with it whom I thought myself bound to see, and that was the youth who was said to have lost his heart to the bride; so I went to the bachelors' camp, and, after chatting to the lot for some time, I said, as if accidentally, to the *desdichado*, "So Kilbangaroo's gone; is it not a good job? In the Ngooraialum country she will always have fat *ürip* opossums to eat and a fine warm rug to sleep in, and that is more than she would have in this part of the country." The poor fellow tried to smile, but I saw he was hurt. He merely said, "She will eat fat *ürip* opossum, but I shan't see her." This touch of nature was brought to my mind, not long since, by some verses of a troubadour ditty, which set me thinking of how little real difference there is in the feelings of men, civilized or savage, and how near akin we all are. The lines are these :—

> " Mais voil que sia castellana
> E qu'ieu la veia la semana
> O'l mes, o l'an una vegada,
> Que si fas reina coronada,
> Per tal que no la vis jamais."

The next day, as I heard, whilst Wawgroot was out hunting, his domestic troubles began to

crop up, as the first wife, after abusing the younger
one in the choicest Billingsgate, took the opportunity of beating her soundly with her yamstick,
no one offering to interfere, and as a consequence
the injured young lady left the camp and took
refuge in the bush. When the husband came
home and found what had occurred, he proceeded
at once to admonish the lady of his early affections
with his nulla-nulla, in a style which would
probably have killed most white women, reducing
her temporarily to complete obedience, after which
he set off with Kilbangaroo's father in search of
the fugitive, who in due time was seen following
them back to the camp. Interrupted occasionally
with outbursts of jealousy, I heard afterwards that
matters on the whole, from that time, went on
tolerably well in Wawgroot's camp, as the good-
man was known to have a heavy nulla-nulla, and
to use it freely if provoked; otherwise he was
naturally a quiet person, and a great valuer of
peace in his domestic circle.

As far as I could learn, what took place at the
nuptials of the bold Wawgroot and the juvenile
Kilbangaroo was an average instance of what
occurred in these tribes when girls were given in
marriage. To be sure, it was hinted that when
the bridegroom happened to be a bachelor there
was less reluctance to be overcome; but generally
I noticed that it was not until a year or so had
elapsed, and the young wife had received two or

three severe beatings, that obedience became
habitual, and quiet thoroughly established in the
family. As a proof of the general prevalence
of such wooden admonitions, it may be noticed
that most women bore about their persons proofs
of savage treatment at the hands of their husbands; but, putting aside occasional ill-usage, it
always seemed to me that the women were happy
enough, and got on very comfortably with their
lords.

The next time I saw Wawgroot was about
two years after the epoch of his marriage. I had
been wild-dog hunting near Toonaiba, and was
making my way home, when I heard a shrill
cooey, which, on looking round, I found to proceed from a camp on the edge of the plain.
Riding up to it, I found its tenants were
my old friend Wawgroot and his family,
so I dismounted to light my pipe and ask the
news. I then noticed that Kilbangaroo's sulkiness had been replaced by her constitutional
good-humour; her cheeks were red with *noro-
noro*; her well-greased hair was neatly combed
and tied up; she had on quite a showy opossum-
rug, elaborately scored with approved aboriginal
designs, enveloped in which, peeping over her
shoulder, was a little black thing, which seemed
the delight of its mother. Even Mrs. Wawgroot
No. 1 appeared to have got reconciled to her
presence, and to be fond of the baby.

CHAPTER XIV.

THE DESERTED CAMP.

ONE morning, a few days after the young lady of whom I have spoken in the last chapter had been disposed of, I awoke rather later than usual, and, on proceeding to the river to take my matutinal plunge, I found that my black neighbours had decamped without leave-taking; and hence the stillness which had led me to oversleep myself. However, I took my bath and was soon dressed, our costume in those days being of a very simple character—shirt, boots, breeches, belt, spurs, and a cabbage-tree hat being the principal matters; collars, coats, razors, studs, braces, buttons, and abominations of the sort not having yet taken possession of us. After breakfast, having nothing to do, I took up my gun and canoed myself across the river, with the object of getting a brace of ducks for dinner, as well as of seeing whether any of the Blacks had remained behind at the camp. On approaching it, however, I found that the flitting had been general. The fires which still smouldered sent up their blue smoke, in shadow and sunlight, amongst the trees. Of the mia-mias, some were standing; others had, wholly or in part, been thrown down by their late occupants, the more easily to collect their effects at starting. About them were lying some discarded odds and ends; a broken shield, the toy-spears belonging to the picaninnies, the remnants of an old net, a scrap or two of opossum-rugs, and similar objects. There were some bones, too, on the ground, covered with flies; whilst a solitary hawk and a bevy of crows seemed to have taken possession of the spot. The former, indeed, had not yet entered on active measures; but, surveying the scene from an overhanging branch, seemed to meditate in grave uncertainty the course which he should pursue. The crows, on the other hand, with their usual impertinence, hopped smartly about with half-loosened wing, picking up some scraps of food, but avoiding rags and other sus-picious-looking articles. As I leaned unseen against a tree, cogitating over the wandering ways of my black friends, admiring a certain picturesqueness which attaches to all their belong-ings, and debating with myself whether the time had come for knocking over one or two of the crows—with whom I was constantly at feud, in consequence of their depredations on my young lambs—I noticed a dog, evidently the lost property of some blackfellow, skulking noiselessly among the deserted mia-mias. He was of the breed indigenous to the continent, his growth stunted by the starvation which he had endured with his thriftless master, for whom, apparently, with pricked ears, he was smelling about. Not finding him, after a little the animal jumped on to the trunk of a fallen tree and sat down, his tail gathered carefully under him. The *dingo sejant*, as a herald might call him, was, poor brute, bereft of hair from back to foot, being, as is common with Blacks' dogs, in an advanced state of mange. After looking about him for some time, and giving utterance to a few plaintive whines, he raised his nose towards the sky and broke into the dreary howl common to his kind. The crows hopped off a little at the sound, evidently suspicious that something was wrong; the meditations of the hawk apparently remaining undisturbed. Again and again beginning at his lowest and ascending to his highest note, Pokka gave out his melancholy cry, reminding me of Campbell's melodious line—

"The wolf's long howl from Oonalaska's shore."

I did not wait for him to finish his solo. A shot from my gun rolled him over in the midst of his melody, the contents of the other barrel going to the crows; terminating at once misery and mange, as well as some danger to my flocks.

CHAPTER XV.

STEELE'S CREEK.

I HAVE already mentioned that the district of Port Phillip, now the colony of Victoria, originally formed a portion of New South Wales, better known in England in those days as Botany Bay. Like other colonies, it had its youthful trials, being from its cradlehood treated by its elder sister as a future rival, and put upon accordingly. The principal complaint of the Port Phillipians was that the revenue derived from their Customs and the sale of their Crown lands, instead of being disbursed on local wants, was, in spite of every remonstrance, expended on the public works of Sydney, six hundred miles away, or on the roads and bridges of New South Wales proper, a tract of country in which the people of Port Phillip had about the same amount of interest as the citizens of Manchester might be supposed to have in the roads and bridges of Moscow. This unworthy treatment was, of course, keenly felt by the rising settlement, and my father, a resident in Tasmania, whom business used to bring here occasionally, even at that time sympathized very warmly with the young colonists in the matter. Early in 1842 he left Tasmania, where he had lived for some twenty years, and came to reside in Port Phillip, bring-

ing with him considerable experience in public
business, and what was in those days a large
capital. What his intentions were when he left
Tasmania I cannot say, but what he did was to
devote himself from the first to the public
business of the young settlement, and especially
to the object of obtaining from the home Government its separation from New South Wales ; and
with this in view he took up his residence in
Melbourne, to the great detriment of his personal
interests.

As it was his intention to invest still further
in pastoral property, the management of which
would no doubt have been his occupation had it
not been for public matters, he sent for me soon
after his arrival, and directed me to look out for
the purchase of another station ; and finally, in
July, 1842, he bought one with four thousand
sheep and a small herd of cattle on it, for which
he paid, if I recollect right, about £2,000. The
run was known as Steele's Creek, and was situated
some four miles to the westward of Kilmore. On
this new purchase I took up my residence as
manager, having a younger brother to live with
me as a companion. Though Steele's Creek was
in the centre of a comparatively well peopled
neighbourhood, and in every way much better provided with comforts and appliances than Tongala,
somehow it was not to my fancy. In the first
place, as regards my neighbours, though I was on

amicable terms with those around me, except in one instance there was no intimacy, so that I did not reap much advantage on that score. Besides, the hunting and shooting were indifferent; and during my residence at Tongala I had got so accustomed to roaming over large tracts of unoccupied country, that I felt myself disagreeably straightened in a place which was only twenty, or five-and-twenty miles round at most. The solitude, too, of Tongala, sooth to say, suited me pretty well on the whole, and the characteristics of the country were more congenial to me than those of Steele's Creek. Particularly I missed the pleasant river, about which much of my idle time was spent in swimming, shooting, or canoeing.

As an investment Steele's Creek turned out well; though, had its purchase been delayed for some months, it might have been had probably for a third of the price, so great was the fall which took place in all property. Shortly after taking charge I marked two thousand lambs, which brought the flocks up to six thousand; whilst the shearing produced a very satisfactory clip of wool, both as regards quality and quantity. Of this period of my squatting experiences comparatively few incidents remain in my memory. As a rule I had even less to do than at Tongala, and, with the exception of reading Corneille's and Racine's Tragedies, which were almost the

only books I had, my chief sources of amusement
were my visits to the hut of two brothers, my
near neighbours, who had lately arrived from
England. These gentlemen—stark new-chums,
who knew nothing of bush life, and were but ill
provided with station requisites—had purchased a
small run, with a thousand ewes, close to my
father's, just after my arrival at Steele's Creek;
and as we got on well together, I used to pass a
good deal of my leisure time with them, and was
able to help them with the loan of a team
of bullocks now and then, and things of
the sort; as well as with the result of my experience in bush matters, such as it was. The
youngest of the brothers was hardly out of his
teens; the other a man of about thirty, who, as he
termed it, with evident and mysterious satisfaction, had "seen a great deal of the world;" in
which process, it appeared, he had also, as sometimes happens, pretty well seen the end of his
cash, and had come to Australia for the purpose
of retrieving his position. He was a genial
companion, full of energy: a good smoker, an
interminable yarner, and well up on the subjects
of guns, pointers, hounds, horses, pigeons, &c.;
having likewise some smattering of rat-catching
lore. He was not what one would call a reading
man: and, if not very intellectual, his talk at all
events was amusing; and I was of course glad,
whilst we smoked and drank coffee, to avail

myself of the opportunity of acquiring some information on his subjects, concerning which I was in lamentable ignorance. On the occasions of my frequent visits to the hut of my neighbours, and of theirs to mine, conversation often reverted to some of the matters just enumerated, when my friend not unfrequently indulged in somewhat tall statements. That he had come to believe his yarns of nine-feet walls and mouths of coal-pits leaped by astonishing hunters, and covies of partridge shot down with marvellous precision with guns which must have had the range of field pieces, I think there can be no doubt.

Whilst on the subject of *mon ami véridique*, I may relate one of the only occurrences which took place during my residence of eight months at Steele's Creek which has impressed itself with much vividness on my recollection; a narration which, though given in all seriousness and good faith, my friend of the leaping horses and long-range fowling-pieces could never be brought to look on as anything but a joke on my part. The matter in question was the appearance of a ghost, and the facts are these :—

One cold, starry, winter's night my younger brother Charles and I were sitting beside the fire in our comfortable little hut, chatting and smoking as usual. He was about sixteen years of age, and had not long returned from college in the old country; was of great physical strength, and of decidedly good health, courage, and nerve. In other respects there is little to be said about him. He is dead long since, poor fellow; was well read for his years, unimaginative, and altogether, I should think, a very unlikely subject to conjure up "spirits from the vasty deep." As has been said, he and I were leading a very humdrum sort of life, riding a little now and then, now and then doing a little work amongst the sheep, and so on. Our evenings were divided between reading and conversation; we both smoked a good deal, and drank nothing stronger than tea—circumstances which I think it right to mention, as the *esprits forts*, I believe, have made up their minds that the only ghosts seen in the nineteenth century are those begot of bad nerves and disordered brains: neither of which explanations, it seems to me, are in the least available in this instance.

On the fine, starry, winter's night in question, then, my brother and I were sitting quietly in our hut, one on each side of the fire which glowed in the capacious chimney. We had been talking about the business of the station, and every-day matters of that sort: the fire had burnt low, and it was getting on towards bed-time; so my brother, like Corporal Trim, knocked the ashes out of his pipe, stood up and stretched himself, saying that he would go to bed. Replying that I would follow him in a few minutes, I continued to smoke, my eyes fixed on the embers. In the meantime my brother did not go direct to the bedroom, but to the front door, which led out of the room in which we were sitting; opened it and went out. The door shut behind him, and not long after I heard him speak, as I thought, to a pair of kangaroo dogs, which were always about the place, when I sank into a reverie as I gazed on the flickering flames on the hearth before me. I had passed a few moments in this abstracted state, when I became conscious that my brother, instead of going to bed, had returned to his seat by the fire.

"I thought you were off to bed," said I; and receiving no answer, I looked up at him. For a moment I was completely staggered. Instead of the smooth face untouched with emotion and somewhat sleepy, which I had just before looked on, I saw one so ghastly, so startled, so horror-stricken, that for the moment I could hardly believe it to be that of my brother. After gazing on him for a moment, I asked him what was the matter—whether he was ill? He opened his mouth to reply, but, unable to utter a word, cast an apprehensive glance in the direction of the front door, towards which he pointed faintly with his hand. Considering for a moment, I thought it might relieve him to be left alone, so I walked to the door and went out, without being able in the least to conjecture what was the matter with him. In the bright starlight nothing unusual met my eyes. The lamp in the shepherd's hut I could see was out, and my kangaroo dogs were not there, but everything seemed quiet. Above, the lamp of heaven was

" Riding near the highest noon,"

and around everything was as cold and crisp as might be, so I paced backwards and forwards for a while, thinking of my brother, and perhaps, as I looked up to the sky, recalling Shelley's verses—

" Tell me, moon, thou pale and gray
Pilgrim of heaven's homeless way,
In what depth of night or day
Seekest thou repose now ? "

After a few moments passed in this way, I returned to the hut and resumed my seat at the fire.

The short time that had elapsed had, I found, been sufficient for my brother to recover his self-possession, and though the traces of disturbance were still visible in his countenance, they were hardly such as a chance observer would have noticed. After I had taken my seat, he proceeded to relate what had happened to him. " You will remember," said he, " that a few minutes ago I wished you good-night. As I passed the front door, I thought I would see how the weather

was, so I went outside and was walking in the
direction of the fallen tree before the place,
looking towards the sky, when I noticed suddenly,
some fifty paces off, a person wrapped in a sheet
advancing to meet me. Who it was I could
not make out. The size of the person did not
agree either with that of the old shepherd or his
wife, and so I concluded that it must be the
smaller of the two men who are working amongst
the sheep. Whoever it was, however, the whole
affair seemed to me so stupid and commonplace
that, notwithstanding the liberty that the man
was taking, I felt inclined to be amused at the
very absurdity of the thing. At first I had
intended to say something cross, but as I was
sure the person in white was aware of my having
noticed his presence, I turned somewhat out of
his path and again looked up at the sky, not
doubting that the joke would end, and that the
ghost would pass on without subjecting himself to
a rebuke. Contrary to my expectations, however,
he did not pass on, but continued to advance,
took his stand within a yard of me, and seemed as
if looking at me through the sheet, which, with
the exception of his feet, which I noticed were
naked, covered the whole of his person. I still
felt quite certain that it was the individual I have
mentioned, and began to feel annoyed at his
presuming to amuse himself with me in such a
way, so I said to him, 'You are quite mistaken,

my man, if you think pranks of this sort will be tolerated here ; go to your hut, and don't repeat such tricks.' Perhaps you heard me speak ?" I replied that I had—as I thought, to the dogs. "Instead, however," he continued, "of complying with my directions, the man stood his ground, and, with his eyes apparently fixed on me from behind the sheet, began to rock himself from right to left on his feet. This was too much for my patience, and, determined to muzzle the offender, I sprung quickly forward. All this time I saw him as distinctly as I see you. The moon gave us as much light outside as our candle does in this room ; there are no trees to intercept the view. I was under no apprehension, and was certain that I should lay hold of my man, who made no attempt to escape. In fine, I was in the act of grasping his throat, when—judge of my horror, if you can—*my hand passed through the man*, the impalpable thing in white, whatever it was—which, on the instant, disappeared and was gone."

After discussing the matter for some time we went to bed. My brother, to the day of his death, continued to believe firmly that what he saw that night was a ghost—in which I am inclined to agree with him. The reader will of course take his own view of the case, and is welcome to smile if he likes ; and yet, though I know pretty well what is said on the other side, I hold the reasons

given as of small weight when contrasted with
what I am convinced is the fact, that the belief in
apparitions is constant and general amongst persons
of every age and country. Indeed, observation
has led me to doubt whether anyone has ever
succeeded in emancipating himself from the feeling
that such things have happened to others, and may
happen to himself. In health, no doubt, much
may be done to overcome feelings of the sort, but
in sickness and the decay of the physical powers
the feeling is apt to revive, as it certainly
reappears with every generation. Perhaps a
belief in the supernatural is as constant in the
human mind as the instinct of self-preservation.

As Steele's Creek was rather overstocked with
six thousand sheep, according to the notions of those
times (when people entertained somewhat princely
ideas on the subject of feed for their flocks), it
was decided to reduce their numbers, and I
accordingly started for Tongala with two thousand
of the ewes. My road was by what we now
know as Pyalong, Egan's Creek, Redcastle, and
Colbinabbin. The summer—for it was the month
of December—was hot and dry, and at Mount
Camel, or, as the Blacks call it, Yiberithoop, my
sheep got their last drink, the distance from
Tongala being about fifty-five miles. From
Yiberithoop down the Colbinabbin Creek, and
across the plains to Tymering, took me, I remember, two days and a half of tedious driving, the

12

sheep being in one lot with two shepherds. As a
matter of course I had a bullock-dray with me, on
which we carried, amongst other things, a cask of
water for ourselves and the sheep dogs, in connection with which arose a dispute between the men
which resulted in a serious loss to my father. It
happened in this way. As the shepherds toiled
over the heated plain, painfully driving before
them the thirsty flock, which, accustomed to the
green grass of the cool hilly country, could ill
support the heat of the plains, the bullock-driver,
who was a cantankerous, bad-tempered fellow,
overtook them, and refused to allow the men to
get a drink from the cask. This of course irritated
them not a little, and occasioned a row at our
mid-day camp, which ended in my interfering
and finally sending the bullock-driver about his
business, a step which turned out to be as unfortunate as it was hasty and imprudent. Of course, as
the first consequence, I had to tie up my horse
behind the dray and drive the team myself, which,
however, did not trouble me much. Towards
sundown that evening we arrived at Tymering,
and camped amongst the she-oaks, and so far
everything went on well.

The whole party, however, was a good deal
fagged, as our drive of eight miles, which was all
we could accomplish, was over treeless plains,
under a burning sun, so that nothing but the
most constant efforts on our part could keep the

sheep moving. It was Christmas-eve, I remember, and a furious hot wind had been blowing the whole day in our faces. Weary, begrimed and half-choked with dust, with blood-shot eyes and sunburnt faces, the three of us sat at the camp, after having had a pot of tea and something to eat, our thirst but half-quenched, each one by himself, with his back against the leeward side of a tree. The mournful wailing of the wind as it streamed through the she-oak scrub, and our fatigue together, made us disinclined to talk; so we sat in silence, each, I suppose, occupied with his own thoughts. The fierce sirocco was driving before it sticks and leaves; and, in the distance, quantities of peculiar red-coloured bushes were rolling away to the southward, tumbling over and over before the gale. The horizon had that singular wavy appearance which is common to the plains in such weather; no birds were to be seen, but here and there moving columns of dust, grass, and leaves, the result of whirlwinds, towered high in the air; whilst, close at hand, covered with ashes from the small fire, which, though lately kindled, had already burnt itself out, lay our kettle, frying-pan, and pannikins, and the bag containing our gritty meat and damper. To complete the scene, there were the panting sheep, and bullocks with protruding tongues; the close-on-setting sun bathing the landscape in a dull red light, suggestive of an eclipse. Altogether it was a melancholy camp that night, and the more so from the reduction in our little party.

The next morning, however, as we took the road at day dawn, we were enjoying all the exhilaration of a change of weather and a light southerly breeze, so that we accomplished about six miles to our day camp before the great heat came on. It being only nine o'clock when we arrived, no probability of being able to get the sheep to move till three, and the distance from Tongala but thirteen miles, I unfortunately determined, being a little sick of the work, and short-handed, to let the bullocks out of the dray, and on my horse drive them into the station to water; having no doubt that a fresh team, with men and dogs, might be back early to bring on the sheep, which were now beginning to get knocked up from thirst. However, though I arrived in good time, and sent out a fresh team with such directions as would have secured satisfactory results if they had been followed, it so happened that the driver allowed his bullocks to give him the slip, went after them, and never returned: there being no doubt that the poor fellow, who was a one-eyed man, lost himself and perished miserably from want of water; whilst, from the delay thus occasioned, five hundred of the flock died the next day, before reaching the river, or shortly after.

CHAPTER XVI.

THE MOIRA.*

In the early days of the colony, as the reader is already aware, the possession of sheep constituted practically the right of their owner to occupy, under a yearly £10 license, sufficient land to graze them and their two years' increase. Whether the flock amounted to five hundred or fifty thousand, the license fee was the same; and as regards its duration, it was generally understood that it would be renewed annually, on the original terms, until purchasers of the fee simple of the land, at £1 per acre, were forthcoming; a contingency which, in remote situations, fancy put off for a century or two. Besides the license fee, however, there was payable to the Treasury a half-yearly assessment of a halfpenny a head on the sheep, and this was the only additional charge. Touching the issuing of licenses, the Commissioner of Crown Lands, so far as I had experience, was usually guided by the applicant's estimate of the quantity to which he was entitled; which, as a rule, turned out in the sequel to be considerably in excess of what was contemplated. When, therefore, I reached Tongala with the fifteen hundred

---

* In Australia it is not unusual to prefix the definite article to the names of places; as, *the* Moira, *the* Terricks, *the* Wee-waa, &c.

ewes referred to in the last chapter, my
first care, as a matter of course, was to
obtain a proportionate increased area of run.
As the neighbouring country, with the exception of the Goulburn frontage, was entirely
unoccupied, the direction in which I should
extend the run was a matter for consideration. It so happened, however, that my brother
Richard, who resided at Tongala in my absence,
had seen and taken a fancy to a tract of country
on the south side of the Murray, which was
known to the Blacks by the name of Moira. In
a flying visit made to it some short time previous,
he had found that, under water for several
months of the winter and spring, it abounded
in summer in excellent sheep feed, in the shape
of couch grass, young reeds, and so on, and
was usually as green as an emerald from
November till March, when other pastures were
withered and dry; whilst there was quite high
land enough about it to ensure a retreat for the
sheep in case of any sudden inundation. As
characteristic of the Moira, he mentioned that
it abounded beyond all belief in unusually fat
fish, swarmed with leeches and snakes, and the
ducks were so numerous that I cannot tell now
how many he bowled over at one shot. As we
learned afterwards, its extensive reed-beds were
the great stronghold of the Bangerang Blacks,
whom, as will be told presently, my brother had

found somewhat troublesome during my absence at Steele's Creek; and owing to the plentiful food supply, it was a favourite place of meeting for all the tribes in the neighbourhood. Hence, it had advantages and disadvantages. Since those days it may be noticed that the Moira has contributed largely to the fish supply of Melbourne and Sandhurst, and that a considerable export of its leeches has been made to London.

In consequence of my brother's representation he and I started before sunrise one morning to make a thorough examination of this country, and decide whether or not we should take it up. Mounted, I remember, on two vigorous rowdy horses, we trotted merrily along the Towro sandhill, which leads from Tongala station to Madowla lagoon. When within a quarter of a mile or so of the water, our attention was arrested by some one singing. The notes rang clear and silvery on the still morning air; the songstress, for it was evidently a woman's voice, infusing into her lay the vivacity and *abandon* of life's springtime. On arriving at the spot we paused for a moment to listen, advancing through the tall trees on the banks of the lagoon as the last notes of the song died away. I had seen Madowla a hundred times before, but its deep waters and emerald margin somehow never appeared to me so cool and fresh as on this particular occasion.

Beneath us, as we reined up on its high banks, standing in the sunshine on the green mossy plants which fringed the water's edge, was the young Waringulum lubra whom we had just been listening to. She had been singing, it appeared, to her first-born, a chubby urchin, who, half hid by the dewy herbage, lay snugly wrapped in furs at her feet. The mother and her baby were alone, the sparkling black eyes of the child fixed on its parent. She was not wanting in good looks of a sort, and had evidently just come out of the water. Her opossum-rug was drawn tightly round her, the uncovered portions of her skin showing a light copper-colour. Her black hair, which glistened with water drops, was confined by the fillet commonly worn round the brow, and in it was inserted a plume of white feathers. In fact, altogether she might just then have been considered a decidedly favourable specimen of an aboriginal belle. At hand, by the water's edge, a fish was roasting on a fire, which sent up its slender column of smoke to linger awhile amongst the arched boughs of the overhanging eucalypti; the dripping net which had served for the finny capture hanging on a bush at hand.

"Good morning, Mellapurning!" said my brother. "Good morning, Massa!" replied the young lady in fur, a little surprised at our appearance.

" What for you sing to-day ? "

" Alonga Kotoopka (baby)," said she, smiling.
" That pella plenty laup now ! "

" Where kooli (husband) belonging to you ? "

" Look out 'possum. You air-im tomahawk ?
Mine yait-im pish alonga Kotoopka."

" Te ! te ! borak Kotoopka yait-im pish."

Here the mother, turning her head to one side,
with an arch expression of face, made with her
tongue a sound much resembling the drawing of
a cork from a bottle, which did duty as an
exclamation of surprise. " No yait-im fish ?
Top-a-bit you mikalite. Tungooga Kotoopka
thaichimiac mungi ! "

" Well, good-bye, Mellapurning; can't stop
now : we are off to the Moira," said my brother,
who did not care to see young omnivorous perform. So we cantered on, crossed the Tiia
Creek at its mouth, and sped along the Blacks'
track to Pama, and thence, keeping on the edge
of the fine old red gums (off which we noticed
many a canoe had been stripped in old days),
to the Moira itself, at the mouth of the Baala
Creek, some fourteen miles from home. After
wading the creek, we dismounted to light our
pipes and rub off numberless leeches which had
attached themselves to our horses' legs and bellies
as we passed through the water. On this, my
first visit to the Moira, I thought the place had
a very pleasant aspect, of a mixed Australian and

semi-tropical character. It happened that there were no Blacks there at the moment; but some camp fires smouldering under the shade of a spreading tree, and the bags and nets which hung from its branches, showed that they were not far away. Looking around, on one side of us we saw extensive reed-beds intersected by the Murray, which (an unusual feature in colonial rivers) flowed here almost without banks, and on the level of the plain. The other half of the circle was occupied by open, grassy, forest land, which extended we did not know how far. The grass under foot, as yet undefiled by flock or herd, was as green and fresh as Eden, and the landscape generally bathed in a soft, hazy, sunlight, such as Monsieur Buvelot would love to depict. But we were just then intent on sheep-feed, and not on scenery; so, after a brief delay, we remounted and rode over a plain of green couch grass of some length, and on through a narrow opening in the reeds into what proved to be a charming little savannah of perhaps half a square mile in extent. The grass in it was about a foot high, and so thick that the tread of our horses was as noiseless as that of the camel.

Through the reeds, which stood considerably higher than our heads, a light breeze was playing intermittently, with a sound which reminded one of the gentle wash of the ocean in a sandy bay. The isolated meadow, into which we had found

our way, proved, as I have said, of but trifling
extent, so that in less than a mile we found ourselves confronted by a wall of old reeds. They
were about ten feet high and grew only a few
inches apart, the interstices being occupied by the
débris of those which had fallen, couch-grass, and
numerous convolvuli. Some fifty yards off,
amongst the reeds, however, was a gnarled and
spreading gum-tree, from the branches of which
a view of the neighbouring country might be
obtained. To this solitary old giant we accordingly forced our horses, with considerable
difficulty, and clambering up its short trunk took
our seats amongst its branches some forty feet
from the ground, whence we were enabled to
overlook the country for a considerable distance
round, and discuss its capabilities at our leisure.
A sea of reeds, of several miles in extent, as far
in fact as the eye could reach, met our view on
two sides, flanked by some grand old trees,
amongst whose branches, no doubt, long genera-
tions of Blacks had hunted the opossum and
flying-squirrel, the Murray, broad and bright,
coming into view here and there. The reeds
were by patches and strips of different hues and
growth, in accordance with their ages and the
periods at which they had been last burnt; and
in the distance we could make out, by the reflection of the sun, a flight of white cockatoos,
which, probably disturbed by some solitary

savage prowling along the river's banks, had
sought safety in flight, and after surging backwards and forwards for a few minutes, now
flashing in the brilliant sunlight, now disappear-
ing beneath the shadows, had settled not far from
where they had risen, on a tree, to which their
white plumage gave the appearance of being
covered with blossom. On a closer examination
we also noticed several patches of good open
country, such as we had just left, and that the
whole could be made available, with little trouble,
by burning. As from our elevated seats we
watched the smoke, which curled here and there
from the distant camps of the Ngarimowro, my
brother, I remember, drew my attention to a reed
at hand, which, more lofty than the rest, bowed
gently to the breeze. A convolvulus encircled
its slender shaft, opening a hundred azure chalices
to the south wind, whilst about its feathery top,
probably feeding on its seed, a fire-tail fluttered.
Bathed in the argent light of an Australian
sun, the bird, leaf, and flowers seemed to us a
charming object, fit, indeed, for an artist's pencil.

Having delayed some time, and satisfied ourselves that the Moira would suit our purpose, we
retraced our steps to the mouth of the Baala,
where we found some Blacks who had returned
to camp, and were grilling fresh caught fish, in
the disposal of which we gladly assisted them,
giving them a little tobacco in return. As I

wished to see the river frontage between the Baala Creek and Pama, which appeared too rough for riding, and might contain a reed-bed, I persuaded one of these Blacks, with whom I was acquainted, to take me in his canoe to the latter place, where my brother agreed to meet me with the nags.

The canoe in which Tommy and I embarked, like those commonly in use at the Moira, of which there were about thirty, was of very thick redgum bark, something over twenty feet long, with a small fire—on which a fish or a duck might be grilled—burning on a hearth of clay in the bows. The craft being baled out, and a heap of fresh couch-grass put on board for my accommodation, I seated myself on it, gun in hand, whilst Tommy, a rather civilized Black, who had often been at the head station, and spoke English pretty well, shoved her off, and sent her merrily along with his rowing-pole. There is always something pleasant in gliding down a broad tree-shadowed river in hot weather, doubly so when it is unexplored, and novelty lends an additional charm; and so I found on this occasion. We had scarcely turned the point which hid the camp from view, when the stillness so characteristic of Australian scenes, closed round us, hardly broken by the light plash of the rower's pole, the gentle ripple of the water against the sides of the canoe, and the disturbed frogs, which leaped into the stream, as now and then we rounded a promontory. Stately and hushed, old Tongala * flowed on through his trackless woods! For myself I was inclined to be silent, but my boatman took up the cicerone's part, drawing my attention as we passed to spots which one way or another were of interest to himself and his tribe. The country on the right bank, he informed me, belonged to the Moi-theriban, that on the left to his own tribe, the Wangatpan. The Moitheriban (literally, Moira people) were a numerous tribe, and had plenty of fish and thousands of spears. They had pro-mised him a girl to wife, in exchange for his sister, whom he had given to one of them some time ago; but his intended was not old enough yet, he said, with a sigh, but was to come to his camp when next the manna was on the trees. Then there was a fishing weir, rather an exten-sive affair, at the mouth of a creek we were passing, which, he told me, belonged to some old man whose name I have forgotten; another, a little further on, was the property of quite a youth, a Kogomoolga, indeed, whose front tooth had only just been knocked out, his father being lately dead. Then there was a little creek, which was bringing back the last of the flood-water into the river, the fish in which I learnt

* Tongala is the aboriginal name for the river Murray in this portion of its course.

belonged to an uncle of Mellapurning. All these were evidently very important matters with Tommy.

"By and by," he continued, "you see ole man blackpella. No gammon that pella; pather belonging to Warri. You look out now!" Nor had I long to wait for the sight of the promised patriarch, for, on rounding a point, a long reach of the stream came into view, about the middle of which was a fishing party engaged at their work. The majority of these people, at least the elders, I learned from my guide, had not only never had the curiosity to have a look at my party, not fourteen miles off, at Tongala, but had never yet seen a white man, and I soon found that they were both surprised and displeased at finding a pale-faced stranger invading their fastnesses without having sent them word. It so happened that the party was rather a defenceless one, consisting principally of women, old men, and children, the young men being out hunting, so that on seeing us, a general stampede took place for the shore; whilst yells of every variety of shrillness, from voices of every age, burst on our ears. Tommy laughed heartily at the scamper, and tried to reassure his kinsfolk, shouting to them at the top of his voice "to sit down; that I was friendly and would not injure them," and so on. But his assurances were without avail. The *sauve qui peut* was general, all paddling their canoes in hot haste to a point at

which the banks, which were of some height,
sloped gradually to the water's edge. To give
them time to get out of the way, Tommy slackened
the speed of our canoe, allowing her to drift broad-
side on, whilst our sable friends, big and little,
stepped on to the grass, as their canoes, one by
one, touched the shore, hurrying to the cover of
some friendly trees near the bank. Old men and
women, as they fled, might be seen picking up the
children who were very numerous, whilst some
little urchins, who had probably been amusing
themselves spearing frogs and tadpoles at the
water's edge, mounted lesser urchins on their backs
and bore them to shelter in the most gallant
manner.

To this precipitate retreat, however, there was
one exception, in the person of a very old man—
the identical Warri's father, of whom Tommy
had spoken. From what I afterwards knew of
him, I should think he must have scored his
ninety summers. This poor wreck of humanity,
disregarding the many and vociferous entreaties
of his friends, refused to retire. Somewhat
emaciated and bent, with bald head and long
white beard, he stood naked and defiant by the
stream on whose banks he had seen the best part
of a century pass by. He had never before seen
a white man. His fishing spear quivered in his
hand, and, after an abortive attempt at a war-
like caper, he howled, abused, and spat at me.

in senile fury, asking, as Tommy afterwards explained, why I came to the Moira? What I wanted? That I was a demon from the grave! That the water, the fish, and the ducks belonged to his tribe. That he spat at me and hated me. That I was Pekka (a ghost), but that man or devil he would spear me!

Whilst the poor old fellow was thus giving vent to his fury, every soul who had found shelter was yelling at the top of his or her voice for him to come away and join them, as I fancy they expected to see me raise the gun which I held in my hands (of which weapon they well knew the use) and put a stop at once to his abuse and his life.

In the meantime we were drawing gradually nearer to him, when I noticed amongst the trees a middle-aged man who seemed to have grown desperate, jumping about with his spear shipped in the yoolwa. This fellow dragged a girl of some ten years from behind a tree, and, with a sharp, angry exclamation, pushed her towards us, clear of the cover. Until forced on to the open ground, the child hung back and resisted. When she found that course useless, however, her manner altered, and she walked steadily towards the old man with a quiet and resolute step. Every cry now ceased. No doubt her people had heard that white men did not war with children, and it was on this ground that she, and

13

not a man, was sent to bring back the tribal grandsire ; but still they could have had no certainty of what I might do, and the moment must have been one of anxious suspense. Curious to test the temper of the people, I whispered to Tommy to be silent, that I should not hurt her, and raised my gun to my shoulder. The child, now not many yards off, noticed the action, looked me full in the face, and without altering her course, gathered her opossum-rug tightly about her, and with somewhat stately step, passed close before the gun to the gibbering old savage. Addressing him in a low soft tone, without further notice of me, she took his hand in hers. The simple act somehow seemed to bring back the old man to his accustomed state of dependence, and, as if all recollection of myself and the scene he had been enacting had suddenly left him, he lowered his spear, his head sank down, and in silence the girl led him back to his descendants.

"Push, Tommy!" said I, unwilling to annoy these people further. One vigorous shove cleared us of the bank, and the stream soon swept us round a point, and out of sight of the camp. "Well, well!" said Tommy, "big one stupid ole man! no gammon!" "What name belong to young girl?" said I. "Undyārning," replied Tommy. Good nerves, Undyārning, thought I, and a good representative of her race in that particular; and we again floated silently down our liquid road, between grand old gum trees, abundance of couch-grass, and clumps of reeds, up which climbed convolvuli in waste luxuriance. Here and there crowds of ducks, and swans occasionally, took wing at our approach; the white crane, the blue crane, and the nankeen-bird, with out-stretched necks, looking at us inquisitively from many a branch a hundred and fifty feet overhead. At times, too, wigilōpka (the laughing-jackass) saluted us from his leafy arbour, whilst here and there, in spots which seemed to have special attractions for the bell-birds, their silvery notes were always ringing. Being satisfied with what I had seen, I shortly after applied for, and obtained about eighty square miles of Moira country, which turned out very valuable.

Since that day, some five-and-thirty years only have passed, and Blacks, reeds, and bell-birds are gone. Of the first scarce one remains; his cooey is heard no more in those parts, whilst the old forest itself is fast being converted by steam sawmills into railway sleepers. In our go-ahead days people of course are jubilant about such things, and I suppose I ought to be so too; but as a fact, the saws and the steam engines do not fill me with any particular delight, and I may as well out with the truth, that when the subject occurs to me it is to remember with regret

the primitive scene, the Black with his fishing
canoe, the silence, and the gum trees.

CHAPTER XVII.

CHANGES IN CONNECTION WITH FLORA AND FAUNA.

I HAVE just alluded to some changes which have
occurred in connection with the *flora* and *fauna*
of the Moira country, and it may not be out of
place to glance at others which commonly present
themselves in those portions of Australia which
have for a quarter of a century been in our
occupation. Beginning with our pastures, it is of
interest to recall for a moment the opinions of our
early explorers as to their value, were it merely
to remind us how wide they were of the reality.
The most superficial examination of their pages
shows that they habitally denounced as unprofit-
able wastes, which owners of stock would never
occupy, large tracts of country, the grazing capabilities of which, and capacity for rearing prime
stock, experience has proved to be equal perhaps
to anything in any part of the world; and that
this country possessed from the first, over a great
portion of its area, the inestimable advantage of
being ready for immediate use without the outlay

of a sixpence. This absence of preliminary outlay will be particularly noticed by those who
remember that many lands in Tasmania cost the
early colonists, with prison-labour, as high as £40
an acre to clear, before they could be thoroughly
fitted for the plough. In the category of prime
country ready to hand, and formerly condemned
as useless, must be included much of the district
now known as Riverina, and in extolling its
pastures it must be understood that I refer, not
to the quantity of forage they produce per acre,
which is low, but to the quality, which is super-
excellent.

The explorers who first entered Riverina were
Oxley and Sturt. Oxley's was what might be
called a trial trip, and a very gallant one, and no
old hand forgets that "*Sturt's furthest*" held the
post of honour on our maps for nearly twenty
years, and that he was a most energetic explorer.
But though I value highly the labours of these
leaders and their results, I may remark that the
records of their travels produce the impression that
they suffered a good deal from despondency as
they wended their way through the woods at the
heads of their small parties. Brought up in the
old country, where the features of nature are on
a small scale and the presence of man everywhere
visible, they appear never to have been able to
overcome early associations, or to reconcile themselves to the bush. Transplanted from an island,

continental features affected them unpleasantly.
Forests which took weeks to traverse ; plains, like
the ocean, horizon bounded ; the vast length of
our rivers when compared to those of England,
often flowing immense distances without change
or tributary, now all but dry for hundreds of
miles, at other times flooding the countries on
their banks to the extent of inland seas, wearied
them more in the contemplation than by travel.

Then we know that our cloudless skies, the
mirage, the long-sustained high range of the
thermometer in the central portion of the continent, troubled them a good deal more than they
do us, and helped to make them look on the dark
side of things. Hence, as a rule, their reports
were unfavourable. If the reader has any doubt
on this head, let him read, as an instance, Sturt's
account of his detention at Depôt Glen, and then
remember that the locality described as so horrible proved in time to be a very good sheep run,
differing in nothing from others around it ; and
eventually was found to be a gold field, and got
extensively worked. The garb of romance with
which Sturt cloaked it, wore off. Hence, in
connection with early mis-judgment and de-
spondencies, the funny outcome has often
presented itself of persons buying in fee simple.
allotments on Mount Miseries at £2 or £4 an
acre, and of others determined, at all hazards, to
locate themselves for life, if possible, at some

Mount Desolation or place with an equally objectionable name.

Referring particularly to Sturt's estimates of country, the reader will be amused if he contrast them with those of the Melbourne auctioneer of 1882, by finding now and then that a tract of country which the explorer had passed over during a day or two's march, and described as little better than genuine desert, is now covered with immense flocks of sheep in prime condition, and is valued, with stock, at perhaps from £50,000 to £100,000. In fact a great portion of the land which Oxley and Sturt described as useless is now worth, on an average, at least twenty shillings per acre. But all explorers were not constituted like Sturt and Oxley. Though a far more desolate country fell to Eyre than to any other explorer, country which, though bordered by the sea and comparatively near at hand, is still unoccupied, the Bayard of Australian explorers never faltered. Even three consecutive stages, each of one hundred and fifty miles, without finding a drop of water, were insufficient either to turn him back or extract a sigh; and it was not until his only white companion was butchered by the Blacks of his party, and he found himself in the desert, with a single black boy for a mate, horses drooping from thirst, the whereabouts of water unknown, and provisions all but exhausted, that

"some natural tears he shed"—not for himself,
but for his lost companion, and then kept on his
way. As for Mitchell, Leichardt, and other
explorers, they had imbibed a good deal of the
knowledge and ideas of persons born and brought
up in the bush; and, instead of suffering from
despondent views, we find them, on the contrary,
with a fresh paradise to report at the end of each
exploration.

But to return from this digression. After the
aborigines and the wild dog (originally the meat
consumers of the continent) had been got rid of,
the animals on which they preyed increased
enormously in many localities. As regards the
kangaroo, indeed, matters became very serious.
On an average, these animals, it is thought, consume as much grass as a sheep, and where a few
score had originally existed there soon came to be
a thousand; so that, in some places, they threatened to jostle the sheep and his master out of the
land; and, in consequence, energetic and costly
steps had to be taken to reduce their numbers.
As an instance of the proportions to which the
kangaroo plague attained in Victoria—not to
speak of Queensland, where the evil has become
much more serious—I may mention a property of
some 60,000 or 80,000 acres, on which ten
thousand of these animals were killed and skinned
annually for six consecutive years, their numbers
still remaining very formidable in the locality. In

other places, by means of long lines of fencing and high yards, specially erected for the purpose, as many as two thousand have sometimes been destroyed in a single day. The opossum, also, in the neighourhood of gardens and cultivation paddocks became very troublesome in some parts. As regards insect life, it still remains to be seen what the result of our colonization may be, bearing in mind that, of some sorts, Blacks and bush-fires used to constantly destroy large numbers.

Turning to the vegetable kingdom, we find the changes more marked than in the animal. As regards the grasses for instance. In the greater portion of Australia, indeed nearly all over it, the grass originally grew in large tussocks, standing from two to twenty feet apart, according to circumstances. It bore no resemblance to a sward, and when one drove over it in a dog-cart, a succession of bumps was experienced from its lumpy way of growing. Gradually, as the tussocks got fed down by sheep and cattle, they stooled out; and the seed got trampled into the ground around them, and in the absence of bush fires grew, so that presently a sward more or less close resulted, such as we see at present. Constant feeding has now cultivated this propensity, and year by year the grass is more inclined to stool. Originally also, in conjunction with a little grass, large portions of the continent were covered with salt-bush and pigs'-face. In places, as for

instance around Mount Hope and the Terricks, in
Victoria, the salt-bushes occasionally attained
the height of twelve feet, standing twenty or
thirty feet apart; in other localities a dwarf
variety of this plant prevailed, and grew so close
as almost to crowd out the grass entirely. With
this class of vegetation great changes have
occurred, and at Mount Hope (as in country
generally in which it grew), stocking has almost
entirely destroyed it. The pigs'-face, once general
in that country, has also disappeared, a luxuriant
growth of grass having taken its place. The same
may be said of cotton bush and other plants.
Then again, throughout the continent the most
nutritious grasses were originally the most common; but in consequence of constant over-stocking
and scourging the pastures, these, where not
eradicated, have very much decreased, their places
being taken by inferior sorts and weeds introduced
from Europe and Africa. Thus the capacity of
our pasturage has increased, whilst its quality has
decidedly been lowered. As regards our trees too,
it may be noticed that considerable tracts of
eucalyptus forest in Victoria have succumbed to
the attacks of parasitical insects, from whose
inroads, as far as I am aware, our forests do not
seem to have suffered prior to the arrival of the
white man.

In short, the state of this continent when we
took possession of it was, as regards *flora* and

fauna, as well as the conditions of soil and water, in the midst of which they existed, in many important particulars attributable to the ways of the people in whose hands we found it, as I shall presently endeavour to show.

Of this primary state of things—if I may so call it—the advent of the Englishman has been the disturbing cause, and the changes which have followed his coming are already distinguishable. Passing over the importation of cereals and weeds, a certain amount of ploughing, harrowing, and draining, and also the destruction of a good deal of forest as minor disturbances, we come to the introduction of sheep, cattle, and horses from Europe; for this introduction has in effect constituted the engine by which the Englishman has, to some extent, insensibly modified a few of the great features of nature in Australia. By their means also, there is little doubt that much greater changes will be brought about in the future. Those to which the introduction of live stock have led up to the present time are—an increase in our water supply, alterations in our creeks and rivers, and an increase in the productiveness of the soil. These results have been brought about in this way. By the trampling of stock the ground has been hardened and drainage increased; the beds of rivers, creeks, and lagoons by the same means have also been rendered more impervious to soakage, and their banks a little less precipitous, so that our watercourses are more easily filled than they used to be, and retain water longer; from the same cause floods are no doubt rather more extensive and frequent than in the past. As regards an increase in the productiveness of our soil, I have noticed not only that crops now grow where formerly they would not, and that grass is much more plentiful, but that one begins of late to miss on our clayey plains the calcined and barren appearance of thirty years ago, the result no doubt of the grass being fed off by stock, instead of being periodically burnt, as it used to be.

As the state of this continent is gradually undergoing some changes consequent on our introduction of the domestic animals of Europe, so, as I have already said, it seems to me that its condition, when we took possession of it, was largely attributable to the customs of its aboriginal inhabitants. Small in numbers—a few hundred thousands — their existence, at first glance, would seem to have been most inconsequential. Mere hunters, who absolutely cultivated nothing—the spear, the net, and the tomahawk—could have produced no appreciable effect on the natural products of a large continent. Nor did they; but there was another instrument in the hands of these savages which must be credited with results which it would be difficult to over-estimate. I refer to the *fire-stick*; for the blackfellow was constantly setting fire to the grass and trees, both accidentally, and systematically for hunting purposes. Living principally on wild roots and animals, he tilled his land and cultivated his pastures with fire ; and we shall not, perhaps, be far from the truth if we conclude that almost every part of New Holland was swept over by a fierce fire, on an average, once in every five years. That such constant and extensive conflagrations could have occurred without something more than temporary consequences seems impossible, and I am disposed to attribute to them many important features of Nature here ; for instance, the baked, calcined, indurated condition of the ground so common to many parts of the continent, the remarkable absence of mould which should have resulted from the accumulation of decayed vegetation, the comparative unproductiveness of our soils, the character of our vegetation and its scantiness, the retention within bounds of insect life (notably of the locust, grasshopper, caterpillar, ant and moth), a most important function, and the comparative scarcity of insectivorous birds and birds of prey. They must also have had an influence on the thermometrical range, and probably affected the rainfall and atmospheric and electrical conditions.

When these circumstances are weighed, it may perhaps be doubted whether any section of the human race has exercised a greater influence on the physical condition of any large portion of the globe than the wandering savages of Australia.

Referring once more to the deterioration of our pastures in respect to quality, it is to be remarked as a consequence that our horses of to-day, though on the average decidedly superior in appearance and breeding to those of forty years back, have not the same stamina. In cattle and sheep a falling off of the sort is not so readily detected, though it probably exists. In both cases, however, the periodical scarcity of fodder, as compared with the abundance of the past must in fairness be taken into the reckoning.

CHAPTER XVIII.

A VISIT TO THE MOIRA IN COMPANY WITH THE POLICE.

AFTER the return of my brother and myself from the Moira, we set to work to make preparations for occupying a block of country in that locality. Whilst so engaged, however, the solitude of Tongala was broken in upon by the arrival of several troopers, headed by the officer in charge of the native mounted police. The detachment, rather a larger one than usual, consisted, besides

the officer, of four black and four white troopers.
Such a visitation from the outer world, as a
matter of course, somewhat fluttered us Volscians
in Corioli. The station hands all turned out to
gaze on the strange men and horses, as if such a
sight had never met their eyes before, and
bestowed on the removal of cloaks, unslinging of
carbines, watering of chargers, &c., their un-
divided attention ; whilst the uniformity practised
in such matters by the troopers, and their
systematic clock-work-like mode of managing
matters which civilians are apt to look on as
trifles, did not fail to elicit, *sotto voce*, uncomplimentary remarks from some of my men, to whom
such methodical ways brought back unpleasant
reminiscences of prison days. The officer, who
accompanied me to my hut after he had seen his
men disposed of, carelessly unbuckled his sabre
and pitched it and his foraging cap on to the
sofa, and taking a chair, amused me a good deal
as he rattled out, in the most *dégagé* manner, that
he had received instructions " to put himself at
the head of his present force, apprehend all
troublesome Blacks, and restore quiet to the
disaffected district; that a reinforcement in the
person of Corporal Rolfe, a non-commissioned
officer in whom he placed the greatest confidence,
was momentarily expected ; that his fellows were
all of the right sort, specially trained indeed by
himself ; and that the service was thoroughly to

his liking, however he might otherwise regret his temporary absence from Melbourne and the ladies."

The effect of this unexpected gush was not a little heightened by the jaunty ways of my guest, who, having got rid of his buckskin gloves, and propitiated his moustache with some little caresses, sauntered up and down the room in all the fascinations of a preternaturally erect carriage, shell-jacket, fixed spurs, and red stripes down the side seams of his breeches. In fact the *tout ensemble* of the thing tickled my fancy so much, occurring in the midst of monotonous days, that I have not yet forgotten it.

Another of the little peculiarities of my guest (a pleasant and genial person), and one which I found exceedingly comical, was his habitual use of military phraseology; so that shepherds' huts and places of the sort figured as *positions* in his conversation, men riding abreast were said to be *in line;* a camp in the bush took rank as a *bivouac,* and so on. In addition it was charming also to notice on a short acquaintance, not only that the estimate in which this warrior (long since, poor fellow, a pilgrim to the happy hunting grounds) held civilians was, in the main, a low one; but that, unknown to himself probably, he looked on them as a very unimportant portion of the community, whose *raison d'être* might have been

the erection of towns in which the military in
times of peace might enjoy the usual *agréments*
of society, of which the daughters of civilians to
flirt with formed a prominent feature; whilst, of
course, in times of war, such places would be
put to their proper purposes, and be defended,
battered, and sacked in the orthodox way—as we
always read in history.

To pass on, however, to the cause of what, in
compliment to the manes of my military friend,
let us call this armed intervention at Tongala.
A few weeks previously, a shepherd of an altogether unwarlike spirit was tending a flock of
weaned lambs on the trans-Murray portion of our
run, the right to depasture which, the reader
may remember, had been granted by the wrong
Commissioner of Crown Lands on the occasion
of his visit to Tongala. Whilst seated on a fallen
tree in true Arcadian style, *sub tegmine Eucalypti*,
watching his woolly charge crop the tender
herbage, or rather " 'eving a smoke," as he himself
related, his cogitations were suddenly disturbed
by a loud " *Waugh!* " and a blackfellow tapping
him on the shoulder. The intruder, it appears,
was naked, in full war-paint, and armed with
spear and waddy. What the original intentions of
this child of nature were on the occasion it would
be difficult to determine, though possibly the
circumstances, duly weighed, might lead persons
used to such cattle to the inference that they

14

were to knock out the brains of our Australian
Corydon.   But, at all events, from some cause or
other the gentle savage did not proceed to such
extremities, as it appears that he only asked in a
quiet way for some tobacco; and the shepherd
gave him some, with which, *and the carbine,*
which was lying against a tree at hand, he
hurriedly decamped.

The shepherd being thus disarmed, about
seventy Blacks issued from a neighbouring scrub,
where they had lain concealed, and each speared
and carried off a sheep; the abstracted carbine
being finally laid down for the shepherd to take
possession of.   The whole proceeding was very
original, no doubt, and in the minds of the Blacks,
I suspect, there lurked an idea that the restora-
tion of the carbine would be held partially to
excuse the abstraction of the sheep; probably a
trivial matter in their estimation, as no doubt it
would appear to them that we white men had far
more live mutton than we were able to make use
of.   The shepherd, in the meantime, a good deal
flustered, drove his sheep to the yards, and
informed his hutkeeper of what had occurred,
whilst no doubt the Blacks proceeded, with the
ladies and children of their establishments, to cook
mutton chops on a large scale.   As, moreover, the
Murray's wide stream intervened between the
shepherd and Tongala, my brother did not hear of
what had happened for some days, by which time,

of course, our mutton-loving children of nature had made a pretty long trail.

This rather costly *déjeuner à la fourchette*, in which my father had compulsorily played the part of absentee host, was followed, as it happened, a few days subsequently, by the arrival of two troopers making the usual patrol, a circumstance which my brother thought particularly fortunate. They belonged to the border police, a body quite *au fait* at preserving order in the bush ; and the first act of its representatives on this occasion, when they learnt what had occurred, was to seize a solitary blackfellow who happened to be at Tongala, and secure him with a bullock-chain, one end of which was padlocked round his ankle, and the other passed through the slabs of the kitchen and made fast within. Next morning these two trooping worthies, with their *détenu* as a guide, set off in search of the Blacks, for the purpose of " setting them right." It so happened, however, that when they got within a hundred yards of the Murray, their prisoner, who well knew what was in store for his tribe should he discover their retreat, made a bolt for the stream, when one of the troopers galloped after him, and, before he could reach the water, shot him down. The poor savage, I heard, dropped at once mortally wounded, close to the river bank ; looked up at his slayers, and, drawing his opossum-rug round him, died shortly afterwards without a word or a groan.

The troopers then went on and continued the
search for some short time, which proving ineffectual, they returned to the corpse, which was
now cold and stiff. The friends of the deceased
never exactly knew, I believe, what had become
of him, for the troopers placed the body in a canoe
which happened to be at hand, which, pushed
into the current, conveyed its ghastly freight
down the stream. Who knows what conjectures
perchance occurred to distant tribes as they saw
drifting through their ancient domain this victim
of the white man? I always regretted this
catastrophe.

This proceeding of the police, however, it was
hoped would put an end to further aggressions
of the sort, when, unfortunately, a hundred and
twenty lambs were allowed by another shepherd
to wander off unperceived from his flock. After
straying some distance, this mob was observed by
a party of Blacks, who, unable to withstand the
temptation of fat meat *à discrétion*, drove the
lambs to a secluded spot, where they killed and
ate them. A large number, I afterwards heard
from the Blacks themselves, were killed and
roasted at once, whilst they broke the fore legs of
the rest to prevent them straying, a message
being sent to the absent part of the tribe
"bidding them to the feast." In due time they
arrived, to the number of a hundred or so, and
ate up the lot in three days. Such feasting and

greasing of heads had never probably been known in the history of the Bangerang, and no doubt the tribe was merry and witty at the expense of the "white-pella." This further outrage on the part of our sable neighbours being discovered a few days after its occurrence, was reported to the authorities in Melbourne, and hence the present appearance of the police on the war-path at Tongala.

As the Blacks, who were now to be taught manners, would probably be found at the Moira, on the bank of the Murray, across which they would certainly swim on the first appearance of the police, it was agreed that the sheep and dray which I was despatching to the Moira should be sent on ahead and halted at some distance from the river, the tribe being decoyed to the encampment, so that the white troopers might be enabled to close with them away from the water. As regards the black portion of the "force" it was decided by the officer, for various urgent reasons, that it should be left at Tongala. This reduction of his forces, I noticed, seemed to prey a good deal on the military mind of the leader (a man of well-known pluck, however), and produced an uneasiness which even the timely arrival of Corporal Rolfe did not entirely remove. Why it should have been so I never could exactly understand. Danger (except to the enemy) there could be little or none, the result being substantially the same, in respect to fire-arms, whether they be opposed to spears or pop-guns.

Measures having been thus concerted, a flock of sheep in charge of several men, and accompanied by a dray and bullocks, was despatched to the Moira with the requisites for forming an out-station, the time of its arrival being so arranged as to be shortly antecedent to that of the police. This "combined movement," as the officer pointed out to me afterwards with some satisfaction, was managed more successfully than sometimes happens in war on a larger scale; for shortly before the police "debouched" from the timber which skirted the proposed scene of action, the other party had arrived in the proper quarter, and, as could be seen, had gathered round them the Blacks, whom it was so desirable to entice from the vicinity of the river and the reed-beds. The result of this was an immediate charge on the part of the troopers; a movement executed, as it seemed to my inexperienced eye, with more *élan* than regularity. Being myself with the party, and armed with sword and pistols, I received a friendly hint from the officer, before charging, to abstain from the use of weapons unless called upon by him to act: an injunction which, being of a peaceful tendency, was quite in accordance with my feelings. And here I regret, for the reader's sake, that I am unable to describe the evolutions which

ensued, for though I have a perfect recollection
of what occurred, I am destitute of the knowledge necessary to enable me to set down the
circumstances in the proper relations of cause
and effect, as the officer did in a report (bulletin!) on the subject, which he read to me
prior to forwarding it to the authorities. That
there were, however, some points concerning the
matter in which we did not completely agree,
truth requires me to confess, as he omitted some
incidents which I thought should have been
mentioned. On my hinting something to that
effect, however, he laughed good-humouredly,
saying, that "persons unconnected with the
public service know nothing of reports; indeed
civilians from first to last are ill fitted to
describe collisions of the sort, being apt to blurt
out statements more properly held in reserve,"
which it has since occurred to me might probably be the case.

However, *lo cierto e*, that one of the police
horses bolted at the outset and carried his rider
almost out of sight, whilst another trooper, lodged
by his charger in the fork of a tree, very provi-
dentially escaped getting his neck broken, the
chargers generally being, as the officer stated in
his report, "somewhat unsteady." The Blacks in
the meantime passed through or round our "line"
and fled to the river, followed by the remaining
horsemen, no shots having been fired so far, or

spears thrown; when, as the last aboriginal was
in the very act of leaping from the bank into his
native stream, someone at hand, not connected
with the "force," on being called upon by the
officer, discharged two barrels, putting one ball
through the fugitive's arm, and the other through
an old cap which he had on. This proceeding, however, appears to have been irregular in some way,
as it found no place in the bulletin. At this
juncture, I recollect, the officer, who was leisurely
scanning the opposite bank of the river, across
which he had driven the enemy in such masterly
style, received a slight wound in his sword arm
from a spear hurled by a blackfellow from the
opposite side. "Hit at last!" was his laughing
exclamation, as he handed me a white handkerchief, the corner of which I had noticed peeping
from the pocket of his shell-jacket, to bind up
what he termed the "scratch."

The Blacks having retreated across the Murray,
and the troopers being assembled again round
their leader, that indefatigable officer, after a few
moments spent in reviewing the battle-field, turned
his attention towards my sheep camp in quest of
stragglers. Fortunately one blackfellow still
remained there, who, having been promised the
head of a sheep, which was being butchered for
supper, waited quietly for the expected prize, in
spite of the firing and galloping which had been
going on. This unfortunate was accordingly

seized by our party and at once placed in hand-cuffs, which, being found too large for his hands, were transferred, at the suggestion of Corporal Rolfe, to his ankles.   Thus secured, whilst the force refreshed itself with tea and damper, I could not behold this poor savage without pity.   Left to himself with his manacles on, his first idea was to run; this, of course, he found to be impossible, and nearly fell in making the attempt, so he stooped down hurriedly and made a desperate effort with his hands to burst the shining little links which held him.   Whilst doing so, I noticed he cast a hurried glance at us, seemingly of wonder that no one moved to prevent his escape, for as yet he had not realized the fact that the little bright bands would perform that service unaided.   Then he made another trial to run, and another great final effort to break the links, when his real position burst on him for the first time.   He now knew that he was a captive, a thing without a name in his language.   For a moment there was a look between terror and despair, when the savage, with heaving chest and inflated nostril, turned his face towards where, half-a-mile off, stood the mia-mias of his tribe, and gave utterance to a long wild cry for assistance.   But his yell was unanswered, and no doubt he considered his fate fixed beyond the possibility of hope.

The name of our prisoner was Warri.   His wife, who was present at his capture, was allowed

to escape unmolested, and when dinner was over
we set out for Tongala, the troopers securing
their captive by a rope, one end of which was
round his neck and the other made fast to a
trooper's horse. Once secured, and the hope of
escape gone, the prisoner accepted his fate in a
manly enough way, and marched stoutly along
with his captors, so that we reached Tongala
without accident. As Warri and I were well
acquainted, we had several conversations during
the two or three days the police remained at the
station, he making frequent inquiries of me as to
why he had been captured and what was to be
done with him. During this time, as escape was
impossible with the handcuffs round his ankles,
he was allowed to wander from one hut to
another during the daytime pretty much as he
liked, the police of course having an eye to him,
his style of progression under the circumstances
being wonderfully grotesque. Though suffering
somewhat from anxiety and uncertainty, however, poor Warri struggled manfully to keep
up his spirits. Indeed, he smoked and yarned,
and begged for tea and sugar, as if he had a
century to live. Sometimes, too, he would come
and seat himself before the door of my hut,
when little dialogues like the following would
ensue :—

Warri.—" Well, massa !"

A.—" Well ! Warri, my boy, sit down."

W.—"Give me smoke? (I gave him some tobacco). Where police take me now?"

A.—" I believe to Melbourne."

W.—"Melbourne, eh? What will the white-fellows in Melbourne do to me?"

A.—" Well! can't say. I don't know."

W.—" I believe they'll hang me—eh?"

A.—" I believe so."

W.—" Well! (with a loud cluck) well! why are you stupid? Why do you get your own blackfellows hung?"

A.—" Well! why do the Blacks eat up my sheep?"

W.—"Stupid! Stupid! Blackfellow."

Warri would then hobble off in the most comical way, with shortened stride, his pipe in his mouth, to seek sympathy elsewhere. My object in frightening the poor fellow was, of course, to impress on him thoroughly, and eventually through him on his tribe, the disagreeable consequences of sheep-stealing.

In due time Warri, in charge of a couple of troopers, was hoisted on top of a loaded wool-dray, which I was despatching to Melbourne, my men indulging in a good deal of coarse jeering on the occasion, the poor fellow's face looking blacker than ever. Probably he had little hopes of again seeing his native woods or his tribe, his idea being, I fancy, that he was to be executed in public for the special delectation of the Governor

and white people of Melbourne. On his arrival
in town, he was committed in due form by the
Police Magistrate to take his trial for sheep-
stealing, which, however, was brought abruptly to
an end by Judge Willis (who then occupied the
bench) declining to allow the trial to proceed
until an interpreter could be found, on the ground
that the prisoner was unable to understand the
proceedings, or cross-question the witnesses. The
expression of the prisoner's face whilst this point
was being discussed was certainly strongly corro-
borative of the judge's view, as he answered none
of the questions put to him, the only matter
which appeared to arrest his attention being the
barristers' wigs, which seemed to puzzle him a
good deal. What he expected, I believe, was to
see a strong man make a rope fast to one of
the beams overhead, from which he was to be
suspended before the judge, whom he no doubt
took for the Governor.

Seeing that nothing was done, and that Warri
had become a law-point incarnate, and was neither
to be tried nor set at liberty, I lost all interest in
the matter and returned to Tongala. Being in Melbourne again, however, some three months later, I
visited the prisoner in his cell, and found him in
bad spirits and ill-health. He was delighted to
see me. Indeed, though he had assisted to
devour my father's sheep, and I had got him
imprisoned in return, a sort of friendly feeling

had always existed between us, as for my part I
never could view either him or his countrymen,
on such occasions, as worse than naughty children, who should have been well flogged and
locked up for a month. So, as I pitied the poor
fellow, thought he had been punished enough,
and was of opinion that his return to Tongala
would add to the security of property there, I
bestirred myself to get him released. After some
little delay this course was determined upon by
the authorities, who, I fancy, hardly knew what to
do with the prisoner. Upon learning that this
decision had been arrived at, I visited Warri
once more in his cell, and, after a little delicate
badinage on the subject of hanging, informed him
that he was to be set free : and at my suggestion,
to prevent the Melbourne Blacks from killing
him, that he would the next day after dark be
driven in a spring-cart well outside the limits of
the town, and there be set at liberty. Poor Warri
stared at me with all his eyes, and was some time
before he could believe that I was in earnest, and
that his difficulties were to come to so pleasing an
end ; and it was only after I had shown him a
blanket, tomahawk, and small supply of food,
which I had brought for him, that he allowed
himself to believe that what I said was the fact.

When I returned to Tongala, a fortnight later,
I found Warri and his lubra (wife), Mirandola,
already there, and had from him a long account

of his adventures on the road up, and of how he passed through the country of some hostile tribes. Ever after he and I were the best of friends, as he ascribed his release entirely to me; whilst the sage Bangerang, who firmly believed that unnumbered police troopers and officers in shell-jackets would be sent to the Moira to punish any undue indulgence in mutton on their part, became henceforth quite reclaimed characters.

CHAPTER XIX.

A SUMMONS.

SHORTLY after Warri's release, I gave over Steele's Creek station to one of my brothers to manage, and again took charge of Tongala. In those jolly days *du temps jadis*, most things in the colony, as the reader is aware, were in rather a primitive state. Amongst other conveniences, common in civilized lands, with which we were all but unprovided, was a postal service. In such matters it was our stone period. The stage-coach or Cobb and Co. era had not yet arrived; indeed, even its fore-runner, the postal tax-cart, with a pair of horses yoked out-rigger fashion, had not yet commenced to jolt over the crab-holes at the

regulation pace of seven miles an hour, so that
persons requiring to send a letter, or go to any
place, had to find their own messenger or means
of transit. As a consequence, all the principal
roads were much frequented by horsemen, either
going to Melbourne or returning to their stations,
or to country business of some sort; and as people
were glad to beguile the otherwise lonely road
with conversation, like some of Sir Walter Scott's
heroes, they were not generally over fastidious
with respect to the temporary acquaintances made
on the way. Indeed, there was a novelty in such
haphazard companionships which lent them a
certain zest. Of course there were exceptional
individuals, to whom the onus of venturing into
conversation with an unintroduced person was a
responsibility too grave to be incurred.

Men of this sort, it was remarked, usually sailed
by at a canter on the opposite side of the road,
with averted eyes, on discovering that the person
overtaken was not one of those who enjoyed the
advantage of their acquaintance. As horses were
scarce, and dear also, it was not unusual to
despatch important letters, law notices, &c., by
messengers on foot, engaged for the trip. On
one occasion my serenity at Tongala was disturbed
by the advent of a pedestrian of this class, who
put into my hands a legal notice, which made me
conversant with the facts that Messrs. A. B. C.
and Co. had filed their schedule, and that it

appeared I was indebted to them to the amount
of about £300, for which, if I remember right, I
was to be held liable if I failed to reach Melbourne
before a certain specified day.   From the firm in
question, I may remark, my father had usually
obtained his station supplies up to that time; and
though, strictly speaking, I had nothing to do
with the matter, the station account being merely
by arrangement kept in my name so that it might
be distinct from another account which my father
had with the same firm (on which it appeared
that it was indebted to him some £500), I was
nevertheless a good deal startled by the receipt
of the half-printed, half-written notification in
question; the more so when I discovered that
only three days of the term allowed for my
putting in an appearance remained unexpired.
My perturbation arose, no doubt, from my ignorance of courts, as well as from impressions I had
received concerning them on the occasion of
Warri's appearance before Judge Willis.   My
idea, however, of the law and its limbs was of
little moment.   The matter on hand was, that
there were a hundred and fifty miles between
Tongala and town, which I had to get over in
three days.   This could have been accomplished
comfortably enough, had it not been that a week
or two before I had turned all my horses into the
bush to get fat, with the exception of a well-bred
stripling, recently broken, which I had in the

paddock. After breakfast I saddled this animal and proceeded to look up the mob; but though I continued the search all day, visiting every spot at which I thought them likely to be, I was unable to fall in either with the animals or their recent tracks. This was annoying; but as they had evidently left their usual haunts, and it might take some days to find them, I thought it best to start next morning for town, and trust to fortune to get a fresh mount at some station on the road.

In consequence of the day wasted, the 150 miles, or thereabouts, had to be done in two days, and long before daylight I was on the colt. The poor brute, I remember, was in low condition, suffering from lampas, tucked up with the previous day's ride, and altogether in sorry plight. However, by patiently husbanding his strength, giving him time, and leading him a great part of the way, I succeeded in getting him over some forty miles by about two o'clock, at which hour I reached Cooma, or Ardpatrick, the first station at which I had any hopes of being able to borrow something better calculated to carry me. The owner of the station—who, fortunately, was at home—had, as I was aware, only one nag, a little black mare, which held a foremost place in his affections, and which he used to speak of as the "wee bit beastie." This he kindly lent me—not, however, I fancy, without some qualms, as he cautioned me not to override her. At starting I pressed him to use my colt, which would have recovered from his fatigue in a day or two. Riding away from the door, I did not feel very sanguine of reaching town within the specified time, as little more than twenty hours remained to accomplish the hundred and odd miles which had still to be done. However, on getting fairly away, I found the " wee bit beastie," at all events, was right enough for her share of the business, which was to get over some forty miles in three hours, as it was indispensable that I should reach Baileston, the next station at which I might hope for a fresh mount, with daylight enough left to get up the horses. The pace which I required to go to effect this would not, I was aware, have quite found favour in the eyes of the owner of the mare, but I felt myself excused by recollecting that my case was urgent ; that the gallop would in all probability do her no harm ; and that, in the event of anything going wrong, I could pay for her. The animal, I remember, was a six-year-old, of Valparaiso blood for the most part, standing fourteen hands and a half high, with muscular legs, short pasterns, round barrel, straight shoulders, head like a soap-box, unpleasant to sit, slow, and of villainous action, but withal used to work, in fair condition, fresh, very stuffy, and as sound as a bell.

With a nag of such a description, the reader will easily understand that my second stage, if an improvement on the first, was not altogether a luxury; but, at all events, I was not long over it, as, with attention to pace, and the exercise of a little judgment, I not only got through the forty miles pretty well at a hand-gallop, reaching Baileston before sundown, but landed the mare "comparatively fresh," as the jockeys have it. This was so far so good; and when, on my road back, I restored the mare to her owner, none the worse for her trip, with some encomiastic remarks I thought myself bound to tell him of the spirit we had gone on the road down, I was much amused to notice his conflicting sensations on the occasion; some displeasure at the mare having been made to go faster than a jog-trot—his own accustomed pace—and pride in what he thought the "beastie's" grand performance. However, the latter feeling prevailed eventually, and he passed the matter off with a sort of good-humoured growl, declaring that I was "ane o' they tearing chiels wha's gate o' ganging wad fairly brak doon a steam-engine; though, nae doubt, the beastie wad hae galloped on to Melbourne itself if necessary."

The circumstances under which I dropped on my neighbour on this occasion of my returning the mare were, I remember, highly characteristic of the man, who, it may as well be said, was no

other than the rough diamond before spoken of,
who, but for "Prince Chairlie," would have been
Lord Oliphant. On riding up to the door and
asking for him, I was informed by the hut-keeper,
who was kneading a damper on the dinner table,
that "he was inside," and to "walk in." So I
walked "inside," and into what proved to be the
bedroom. Coming out of the bright sunlight, I
could not, for the moment, distinguish objects
very well; but when I did, it was to find my
friend in bed, leaning on his elbow, smoking, and
gazing into space, his face a little flushed and
delicate-looking. For an instant he did not
notice me, but when he did he exclaimed slowly,
" Aye ! it's a gran' book that Puckwuck !" From
the surroundings it was clear that he had spent
the day in bed reading.

But to return to my ride. At Baileston, as I
have said, I expected to be able to borrow a fresh
horse should I be so fortunate as to find the
owner of the station at home, so that I was particularly pleased, not only to meet him at his door,
but, after the usual greetings, to learn that my
favourite chestnut mare had been found on his
run, evidently on her way back to the Devil's
River, where she was bred, and was safe in his
horse-paddock close at hand. This, of course,
partly explained how it was that I had been
unable to find my horses at Tongala.

After thanking my neighbour for his kindness

in taking care of my mare, I explained to him that I was on urgent business and unable to accept his invitation to stop the night, so he directed the chestnut to be got up. In the meantime we sat down to dinner, which over, I lit my pipe, shook hands with my friend, and got into the saddle. My horse-riding reader will understand the relief I felt in a fresh mount, especially as instead of the rolling gait, stubby action, beer-barrel-shaped back and short neck of the " beastie," the exchange brought straight-stepping, strong, springy legs, elastic pasterns, long sloping shoulders, good middle piece, a light mouth, and plenty of rein. What with the change of horses and dinner together, I remember even now the sense of comfort which came over me as I rode away from the door. As regards the seventy or eighty miles which remained to be done, they might now have been got over by sunrise, if necessary, but for a circumstance which made it desirable that the mare should not, if it could be avoided, be ridden too fast or too far. This, however, was of no moment, as by diverging a few miles from the road I should be able to get a fresh mount from my brother at Steele's Creek, which was about midway between Baileston and Melbourne. The consequence was that I rode on leisurely through the night, as Steele's Creek lay off the road and was difficult to find in the dark. Notwithstanding the pleasant style in which the mare carried me, however, the hours seemed long and tedious, as young people cannot well keep their eyes open all night. A sharp frost, too, increased the sense of drowsiness, and I thought once or twice of throwing myself on the ground and taking a nap, which I was only restrained from doing by the reflection that I might probably sleep too long, or the mare give me the slip. So, to keep myself awake I took to singing, listening to the cries of the night birds and flying squirrels, and looking for opossums, whose pricked ears and furry tails one could see now and then amongst the leaves of the box trees.

In this way I managed to keep awake: but I have often thought since, what different thoughts would have occupied me that night could I have foreseen what was about to occur in the colony. That the very insolvency which was then hurrying me to town—that of the then leading mercantile firm in Melbourne—was the first of a long series shortly to follow, which were to end in a general crash; that the results of the extravagance of the colonists as a body were at hand; that the general bottled beer and champagne bill of the community was about to be settled; that in clearing off the score a very wide-spread ruin would result, so that properties which had cost thousands not long since, would shortly be sold at auction for a few hundreds; that sheep, two or three years back

worth 30s. to 40s. a head, would be sold at 1s. per
head; and that such sales would occur when the
animals absolutely had one and sixpence worth of
wool on their backs.   That of such mares as I was
then riding (for which I remember I had paid
nearly £40) it would take the selling value of one,
if not two, to realize the invoice price of a common
saddle; and that this state of things would continue
until Mr. O'Brien, of Yass, should make the happy
discovery that a fat sheep might be melted down
so as to be made to yield tallow to the value of
6s. or 8s. in the London market, by which means
stability would be given to the great industry of
the colony.   But, like others, reflections of the
sort did not disturb me then, so I pushed on in
a drowsy manner to Steele's Creek, and there
exchanged my pleasant mare for a disagreeable, fat,
short-backed, short-winded, under-bred cob, whom
I coaxed into Melbourne, with a liberal allowance
of spur, by about nine o'clock, having been the
best part of thirty hours in the saddle.   The habit
of constant saddle-work prevented me, however,
from feeling fatigued with my ride, so that, after
seeing the lawyers with my father, I passed the
rest of the day in town in the usual way.   Indeed,
I used to say about that time, and later, that with
relays of good horses it would be possible enough
to ride five hundred miles at a sitting.

CHAPTER XX.

CORAGORAG.

THE country of the lower Goulburn is to the eye an almost perfect level, broken here and there by sand-hills, which in some cases attain a height of fifty or sixty feet, varying in extent from an isolated hillock to continuous ridges three hundred yards wide, and several miles in length. How they came there I never could make out, but they always struck me as a singular feature, not unlike the sand-hummocks of the sea-shore. With the exception of the sand-hills, the soil which prevails is to a considerable depth a stiff clay with an admixture of sand.

On one occasion, whilst strolling near the banks of the river, my brother noticed a large log of wood which hung in the fork of a tree some six feet from the ground. The position of this log caused us, I remember, a good deal of surprise; was sometimes a subject of conversation, and was examined by us more than once. The log was old and charred by fire, and must have weighed two or three tons. The indentation which it had made on the bark of the tree showed that it must have hung where we saw it for several years. That it had never formed a part of the tree in which it lay was evident; so that the question was, as with the apple in the dumpling, how it got into the position it then occupied. That it had not been placed there by human hands was certain, and yet how else could it have got there? On talking to our sable friends, the Bangerang, about it, they said at once that the log had been floated by the flood waters of the river, and so left suspended where we saw it. As this explanation, however, in a neighbourhood such as I have described, pointed to the inundation of a large tract of flat, and, just then, arid country, which to our inexperience seemed unlikely, we set down the matter of the suspended log as akin to that of Mahomet's coffin, and entirely beyond our comprehension. A solution of the puzzle came, however, and that before long, for the winter of— I think—1843 was so unusually rainy that the greater portion of our *(entre rios)* run became inundated, much of it to the depth of several feet.

This altogether new aspect of affairs resulted from the overflow of the rivers Goulburn and Murray, and fully explained, amongst other things which had caused us some surprise, how our log came to be suspended in the fork of the tree. The consequences of the flood were, of course, unpleasant, for it circumscribed our pasture, and rendered the management of our flocks difficult and inconvenient; added to which,

the ground became boggy, and the use of horses
out of the question, so that my brother and myself
had not only to visit our out-stations on foot—a
matter of some hardship to persons who had
pretty well given up walking for the saddle—but
frequently to carry out the shepherds' rations on
our shoulders. When Blacks could be had, of
course we availed ourselves of their services; but
when such was not the case, there remained no
alternative but to do the pack-horse business ourselves. The number of men at an out-station
being three, their weekly rations of flour, tea, and
sugar weighed about forty pounds, which, on such
occasions, we used to carry in two flour-bags, of
which we each took one. The ground being
boggy, and, here and there, knee-deep with water
for a mile or two together, our march of ten or
fifteen miles was, of course, a fatiguing one.
Very nearly at the start, I remember, we had to
face a mile or more of continuous water, from
ankle to thigh-deep, which extended through the
forest—with the exception of the Towro sand-
hill—as far as the eye could see in every direction. Across this space, the road or track
being quite obliterated, we had to plod our
way amidst grass, sticks, and crab-holes, sink-
ing at times deep in the mud. And yet I
recollect, though the labour of travelling, encum-
bered as we were, was considerable, that for a
short time, whilst the novelty of the thing lasted.

the numerous ducks and waders, busy on what had been dry land, and the green trees and flowery sand-hill reflected in the watery mirror, was a sight which gave me pleasure.

Besides these flooded flats, we had also four or five creeks to cross, which were cold enough at that season. These we used to swim, with the few clothes we had on, and the rations rolled in bundles on our heads, a proceeding which rendered the former somewhat damp, and did not improve the other, though flour is not so easily damaged in this way as one would expect. Occasionally, however, at the wider creeks we stripped a bark canoe large enough to carry the impedimenta, which one of us pushed before him as he swam. On our return we had to bring meat for our table in the same way, so that our goings and comings on these occasions were laborious enough, not to speak of the undesirability of a dozen baths or so on a winter's day. After some weeks, however, we became so disgusted with this sort of work, especially as the flocks began to show the ill-effects of short-commons, that I determined to look out for country in the neighbourhood more suitable for winter, and to apply to the Com- missioner for an extension of run, reserving that between the rivers for summer feeding. With this object I saddled my chestnut mare one morning in August, strapping on an opossum-rug, in which were rolled up some mutton and damper,

and a little tea and sugar (the bushman's usual
fare in those days), and started to examine the
plains which I had traversed in my several
journeys between Wolfscrag and Tongala. This
tract of undulating and sparsely-timbered country
extends from Yellamigoloro, six or eight miles
south of Colbinabbin, to Echuca, a distance of
about forty miles, and was, as the reader is aware,
at that time entirely unoccupied. Heretofore I
had only known it as a waterless land, and consequently no better than a desert for squatting
purposes, though well grassed and handsome; but
on this occasion the difficulty was—not to get a
drink, but to find dry land enough for the sheep.
However, after a day spent in reaching and
examining the country, in the course of which
I must have passed close to Conneilla Creek
without seeing it, I fixed upon that portion of
the plains which was known to the Blacks as
Coragorag, as best suited to my purpose. in
which locality I found a good-sized patch of
timber and several sound, well-grassed ridges, with
swamps only here and there in the intermediate
spaces. *Apropos* of the name Coragorag, I may
remark that the aboriginal nomenclature of the
colony was much more minute than one would
suppose from what has been preserved of it, so
that even spots possessing little of a noticeable
character had their distinguishing appellations.
In some neighbourhoods a few of the aboriginal

names, which are frequently very euphonious, have been retained by the whites, though generally in a mutilated condition, as we usually leave out a syllable or two, accentuate incorrectly, and otherwise travesty them. In the sister colony of New South Wales aboriginal names are very common, and a few of our early settlers named Victorian runs after those which they had originally occupied in the former colony. The principal natural features round Coragorag (a sonorous appellation in the mouth of the Pinpandoor, which has now dwindled into Crag-crag) bore the names of Tai-mer-ing, Ariogo-barning, Ullumbubil, and Chirathabel.

On the occasion of this visit to Coragorag, the ground, then untrampled by stock, was so soft, and riding such slow work, that I had barely time to see what was necessary, and determine on the country I should appropriate, when night began to draw nigh. Getting home being, as I had anticipated, out of the question, I pulled up and unsaddled, the site of my camp that night being a ridge about a mile to the north of the spot on which the Messrs. Winter subsequently erected an extensive dam across the creek which supplies the Baangyoobine swamp. Why the position and circumstances of this particular camp have been so distinctly remembered I am at a loss to say; but we all know that things of a very trivial nature do occasionally fix themselves in our memories. If,

however, my recollections of the night I passed on
that hillside are vivid, they are not altogether of
a pleasant description. The chops of course were
delicious, and champagne now-a-days is not the
nectar that quart-pot tea was at twenty; but still
it was not agreeable to unsaddle for the night in a
spot up to one's ankles in mud, haphazard, as I
may say, on the centre of a large uninhabited
plain. Indeed it seems natural, to black and
white man alike, to choose for resting-places spots
which form, as it were, features in the landscape;
so in open country one seeks the patch of timber,
and in woody districts the edge of the plain;
whilst in permanent settlements the white man
surrounds his cottage with plantation or clearing,
according to the circumstances of the place; and
it was upon this principle, I suppose, that my
camp that night seemed particularly miserable to
me.

There was, indeed, a pleasant warm scrub
within two miles of me, on which I cast wistful
eyes; but, then, it was so late, and everything so
wet, that I was afraid I should be unable to light
a fire in the dark, having nothing but a tinder-
box with me for the purpose. In addition to
other discomforts, the wind was cold and boisterous, and there was nothing out of which to
make even a breakwind, much less a shelter
against the rain which was evidently impending.
As I looked round from my hillside, a wide

waste of undulating country was before me, bounded by ranges to the west, and on every other side by forest; being dotted here and there with numerous swamps and sheets of water, from one to another of which immense flights of ducks, of several sorts, constantly winged their way. The scene, as a painter might say, was in neutral tint, and wore altogether a sombre, desolate aspect, which somehow or other had a depressing effect on my spirits. Of course I was young then, and my being unaccustomed to solitude and loneliness had something to do with it; and I stood awhile, I remember, after I had hobbled my mare, bridle in hand, taking stock of the surroundings—of the wild clouded sky, of the dimly-seen native-companions and other waders stalking through the shallow waters; of the thousands of ducks which with a strong whir of wings swept overhead at a frantic pace, as if in alarm, to alight again at no great distance in one of the many sheets of water, whence perhaps another lot of waterfowl, disturbed by their arrival, or rendered uneasy by the instinct which leads them to forecast the coming storm, rose to make a circular flight of a mile or two.

Whilst surveying this scene—so desolate and dank just then, so handsome and cheery at other times—I cast also many an anxious glance around in quest of the smoke of Blacks' camps, and failing, after some time, to discover any, set to work to make my preparations for the night. I had dismounted near a solitary dead tree, under which lay some broken branches, which I collected for my fire. The supply would have been scarcely sufficient for a white man's necessities in a general way, but I had adopted the Blacks' fashion of a small fire made with the ends only of the sticks, as more comfortable and convenient, and for this it was abundant. When my fire, which cost me some trouble to light, had burnt up, and I had pulled a few tussocks of old grass, on which I might lie to some extent free from mud, I unrolled my 'possum-rug and set my quart-pot to boil. Having eaten nothing since breakfast, I was naturally in excellent trim for dinner, and soon very satisfactorily engaged with grilled chops, tea, and damper; so that between the genial glow of the fire, the disappearance in darkness of the dreary landscape, and the inspiration of a good feed, a wonderful change of mind came over me. The remembrance that Blacks might pay me a visit when asleep, and that their visits under such circumstances meant death, left me; and as I lit my pipe and stretched myself out on my opossum-rug, I felt a loaded horse-pistol better than half-an-hour before, especially when I reflected that from the minute examination I had made of the ground during the day, Blacks could hardly be about, without my having seen them or their tracks. Smoking and sipping my tea, looking at the fire burn, and listening to the clink of the mare's hobbles, or to the note of swans high over head, possibly winging their way to some distant water as yet unknown to the white man, and now and then indulging in a reverie on one subject or another, I got on as far as I could judge until nine o'clock, when, Blacks notwithstanding, drowsiness began to creep over me. Before turning in, however, I got up to make my final arrangements for the night, such as they were, that is, to mend the fire, short hobble the mare, and cut off with my knife the clay which had adhered to my boots and breeches, which completed, and having noticed that the wind had dropped, and that the sky was starless, and dark as Erebus, I betook myself to the comforts of my rug, and with my head on the saddle, and my back to the fire, soon fell asleep, probably only delayed by the pleasant sensations which one used to experience when camped out just before dropping off; the result, I presume, of the warmth of the fire and of getting out of the wind.

I slept soundly and comfortably until about midnight, when in a gradual sort of a way I became sensible that rain was falling in torrents. A moment later a clap of thunder induced me to peep out of the folds of my rug, a brilliant flash of lightning revealing to me an inky sky, water streaming in sheets down the hill-side, and

16

my mare standing still not far off, the ground
being too soft for her to move much in her short
hobbles. As yet I was not wet, the rain probably
not having long set in, but I knew of course that
I soon should be, so as there was nothing to be
done to improve matters, I shut my eyes again
and turned the cold side to the fire for another
nap. When I again awoke, which was in a couple
of hours, I was in anything but a comfortable
plight, for my opossum rug, the worst of all
covering for a rainy night, was completely satur-
ated and clung to my clothes like a wet shroud,
the side on which I lay being cold and stiff. The
rain too was coming down steadily, and the
sputtering fire getting low. In fact, my hillside
had become very miserable. Sleep being now out
of the question, I got up, threw aside my dripping
opossum rug, mended the fire, put on my quart-
pot to boil, and lit my pipe. Of course I was
soon completely wet through, and had nothing
else to do but sit or stand by turns before the fire,
and steam first one side and then the other till
daylight, when, having breakfasted in readiness,
I saddled my mare and made tracks home. This
was but one of many scores of rough nights on
which I have camped out at one time or another,
and if my recollections of it are exceptionally
vivid, I attribute it rather to the impression which
the lonely, desolate, and diluvian aspect of the
winter's scene left on my mind, than to any

special inconvenience I experienced from the weather.

Being fully satisfied with the desirability of Coragorag as a winter's run, my brother and I took two flocks of sheep there a few days after my return, the extent of country, for which in due time I obtained a license, being about fifty square miles, or thirty-two thousand acres, as I have since learnt—for in those days we knew nothing about acres in the bush. Whilst on the road to Coragorag, my brother first saw an emu stalked by a blackfellow, of which operation he gave me a graphic account as we sat by the camp-fire that night. Accompanied by a Ngooraialum Black, and an excellent kangaroo dog which always followed him, he had walked on ahead of the sheep, with the object of lighting a fire and otherwise preparing for the arrival of the party. On reaching the top of one of the undulations of the plain, the quick eye of the savage caught sight of an emu feeding about a mile off. On the instant he and my brother came to a stand, and seeing that the bird had not noticed them, they retreated a few steps to be out of sight, and arrange what should be done. This was quickly decided, it being agreed that Mr. Tom, in default of spears, gun, or hunting gear of any kind, should take the dog in leash, and, before slipping him, stalk as close as possible to the emu. On occasions of this sort, when there

is no natural cover, birds or animals are usually
approached by means of an *impromptu* screen of
boughs, which the Blackfellow carries before him
in his hand. In the centre of the screen a hole
is left through which the hunter watches his
quarry, advancing quickly whilst the animal is
feeding, and stopping instantly he raises his head
to look about him, the noticeable feature of the
matter being that the kangaroo, emu, turkey, or
whatever the animal may be, never observes that,
what to him must appear to be a bush, gets
constantly nearer and nearer, or in fact notices it
at all, *so long as he does not see it move;* should
that occur, of course the game is up at once, and
the beast takes to flight; otherwise a skilful
hunter with good sight will often approach his
prey to within a few yards. On this occasion, no
boughs were at hand of which to make a screen,
so Mr. Tom determined to go hunting in the
character of a *black stump*, just as one of our
city magnates might go to a fancy ball in the
character of a noble of Louis the Fourteenth's
time; the savage, however, being admirably
fitted for his part by nature. This course being
decided on, Mr. Tom put a strap round the dog's
neck, and dropping his opossum rug, stood up in
puris naturalibus. Cautioning my brother not to
show himself, and grasping the dog's collar with
his right hand, he raised his left arm so as to look
like the branch of a small burnt tree, of which

his body represented the stump, bringing his head close to his left shoulder. In this attitude, watching an opportunity when the bird was feeding, he commenced his advance, my brother wriggling himself cautiously through the grass to the top of the rise, whence he had a full view of what went on.

The Black's mode of proceeding was, whilst preserving the posture originally assumed, to press quickly on towards the bird as long as he was feeding, keeping his head close to his shoulder, and the whole of his person, with the exception of his legs, rigidly still. The moment the emu looked up, the hunter, who had his eye keenly fixed on him, became instantly immovable, holding the dog—which was hidden from the emu, partly by the man's body, and partly by the grass —pressed closely to his thigh. After a couple of hundred yards had been got over in this way, my brother said that Mr. Tom's likeness to a black stump became perfect. Advancing and halting, as occasion served, the Black was not long in getting within a couple of hundred yards of Baraimal (as the Ngooraialum call the emu), when the bird showed signs of not being altogether satisfied about the "stump," probably because the dog began to be visible. Another advance of some score or two of yards was effected, however, when the emu suddenly raised his head, drew himself up to his full height, and took to his heels. Then

came Smoker's turn. He had seen the emu, Mr.
Tom said, for some time, and evidently understood what was being done. He was now let go,
and started with a yell, my brother and Mr. Tom
following on foot. The ground, however, was soft,
which left the noble bird but little chance, so
Master Smoker soon had the emu's long neck
between his fangs.

CHAPTER XXI.

THE BANGERANG TRIBE

I HAVE seen the name of this tribe written Pan-
draing, Pandurang, Pinegorine, and in other
ways. The Ngooraialum pronounced the name
Baingeraing, but the tribe called themselves as
I have written the word. A residence of ten
years at Tongala gave me excellent opportunities
of noticing the ways of my Bangerang neighbours,
as well as those of several other tribes which
dwelt on, or frequented, my father's run. In fact,
I knew well every member of the tribe, besides
something of their language, wars, alliances, and
ways of thinking on most subjects, but still it is a
matter of regret with me now that I did not,
when I had the opportunity, make myself

acquainted with several matters concerning which science of late years has become interested.

What was properly called the Bangerang was a tribe composed of two sections, named respectively Wongatpan and Towroonban. Collectively they spoke of themselves as, and were called, Bangerang. When I first settled at Tongala, the Wongatpan numbered certainly not less than one hundred and fifty souls. Their head-quarters were at Wongat, as they called the country just at the junction of the river Murray and the Baala or Broken Creek. The spot is three or four miles higher up the river than Barmah as it is, and Paama as it should be spelt. Hence, Wongat is a small portion of the Moira, or Lake Moira country; is mostly under water in winter, the river just thereabouts being crowded with fish to a remarkable degree. The Towroonban were much less numerous than the Wongatpan, for they only mustered some fifty persons, big and little. They took their name from a sandhill called Towro at that particular place, which is between the Madowla lagoon and the Murray. This sandhill, of which Towro is only a small portion, is of considerable length, and is intersected by the Goulburn, the Madowla lagoon, and the Murray, and is sufficiently peculiar to have furnished us at Tongala, in those days, with food for discussion as to the circumstances to which it owes its formation, with which, however, it is not my intention to trouble the reader.

Adjoining the Bangerang there were two tribes
which numbered about fifty individuals each, and
spoke the Bangerang language, with some slight
difference in, I believe, half-a-dozen words only.
They called themselves respectively Wollithiga
(or occasionally Wollithigan) and Kailtheban, and
had no doubt seceded from the Bangerang at a
comparatively recent epoch; indeed the Bangerang occasionally spoke of their neighbours in a
hesitating sort of way as Bangerang Blacks. The
country occupied by the Wollithiga was at and
about the junctions of the Goulburn and
Campaspe rivers with the Murray. The country
of the Kailtheban was principally on the south
side of the Goulburn, extending from Tongala to
Toolamba, at which point they came in contact
with the Ngooraialum tribe, which they called
Ooraialum. Concerning the boundaries of the
countries of the Ngooraialum and Bangerang
tribes, which were not marked, or even determined
with any precision, it was noticed that these people,
being indifferent friends at best, kept each well
within its limits, so that there was a strip of
country on the outskirts of about four miles wide,
which formed a sort of neutral ground, over which
both parties hunted occasionally, but on which the
Ngooraialum never camped at night.

Of the origin of the name Wollithiga I know
nothing positive, but have little doubt that it is
derived from Wolla (water), a portion of their

country being much subject to inundation. The Kailtheban derived their name from the river Goulburn, which is Kaiela in the Bangerang language, so that the appellation of this tribe signifies *People of the Kaiela*. Occasionally too, a Kailtheban would speak of himself as a Waaringulum, a name given him by the Ngooraialum, of which I shall have something to say further on. Hence the reader will notice that the Ngooraialum and Bangerang were so far foreign, that neither pronounced correctly the name of the other, Ngooraialum becoming Ooaialum, and Bangerang becoming Baingeraing; their languages, in fact, being different.

Between the Ngooraialum, on one hand, and the Bangerang, Wollithiga, and Kailtheban on the other, though intermarriages took place, feeling was far from being of a friendly character; in fact, it was not difficult to see that the Ngooraialum looked with contempt and dislike on the whole of the Bangerang-speaking tribes, with which, prior to the coming of the whites, they had been almost constantly at deadly feud. For this reason, when a Ngooraialum was irritated with a Wollithiga or Kailtheban Black, he would speak of him disdainfully as a *Baingeraing*.

The Kailtheban and Wollithiga, on the other hand, if no Bangerang were present, objected in a quiet way to be called Bangerang, though most friendly with that people, and, as we have seen, speaking the same language, saying, " The Bangerang are Murray Blacks, and our country is on the Goulburn."

Besides the tribes above enumerated, there also dwelt near the Bāngerang, the Boongātpan, Pikko-lātpan, Angootheraban, Ngarrimowro, Moitheri-ban and Toolinyāgan tribes, of the whole of which the Ngooraialum always spoke as Bangerang, whose languages, I am in a position to state, were clearly of Bangerang origin, *and readily under-stood by any Bangerang Black*. Of these tribes and their languages I knew something personally, but more from the accounts of the Bangerang and some of our old settlers, from whom I have learnt that the Moitheriban numbered three hundred souls, or more; and that the whole of these six tribes might be set down at the lowest compu-tation as averaging one hundred and fifty indivi-duals all round, so that in the year 1841 the whole Bangerang race numbered not less than twelve hundred souls. In making this estimate, I have considered the matter carefully and am in accord with several gentlemen, who had much better opportunities of knowing their numbers, and were more interested in the matter than the Commis-sioners of Crown Lands, who upon being called upon, furnished government with reports on the subject, which though founded on the merest guesses, have since been received as statements of weight.

During my residence among the Bangerang, a large and steady decrease took place in their numbers, so that at the end of ten years, I doubt whether as many as eighty of the original two hundred were left. This falling off I attribute to diseases—which had originated with the whites, and been passed on from tribe to tribe—having made their appearance amongst the Bangerang a year or two prior to my squatting in their country. I may add that but two individuals fell by the gun (one of the deaths being the result of a very singular accident), and that spirituous liquors were not in use at all amongst them, so that these common exterminators of savage races were absent on this occasion. There was, however, no doubt, a tendency to disease consequent on the partial abandonment of their traditional ways of life for others less healthy, for, after my settlement in their country, the Bangerang gave up in great measure their wholesome and exhilarating practices of hunting and fishing, and took to hanging about our huts in a miserable objectless frame of mind and underfed condition, begging and doing trifling services of any sort. To this course they were mainly led by their desire to obtain from the new-comers various commodities, such as iron toma-hawks, tobacco, and especially flour, mutton, sugar and other articles of food, for which they quickly acquired a keen relish, and preferred to the game, fish and roots, on which they and their ancestors had subsisted. Besides these causes of decrease it must also be stated that infanticide increased, whilst a certain listlessness and want of interest in life which sprung up under the pressure of our occupation had perhaps something to do with the reduction of the tribe.

Speaking of this subject brings to mind a circumstance (and there were possibly others now forgotten) which led me, in those days, to suspect that the Bangerang and neighbouring tribes had greatly fallen off in numbers some time prior to the settlement of the whites in Port Phillip.*

At Colbinabbin and Coragorag, in the country of the Pinpandoor, one met with strong evidence of such having been the case. I refer to the ovens found in their country, which were out of all proportion numerous when compared with the wants of the tribe as it then existed. The prominent feature in connection with these ovens, many of which, at the time of which I write, had been long disused, was, not that their capacity for cooking as regards size was in excess of what the tribe would require (as this would at last inevitably result from the constant addition

* The writer believes that he has seen all the published estimates of our black population which have been made from time to time since 1843, and, with larger information than they were based on, feels convinced that the aboriginal inhabitants of Port Phillip (now Victoria) could not have numbered less than fifteen thousand souls when our occupancy of the colony began in 1835.

of material), but that very commonly two or three large ovens existed in close proximity, which, in view of the customs of the tribe, I can only account for on the supposition of much larger numbers of Blacks than we ever saw, having in former days habitually assembled at these places—numbers whose food it would be inconvenient to cook in one oven. This seems the more probable when it is borne in mind that these ovens, which are mere heaps of cinders and calcined clay, are efficient and convenient in proportion to their size, and that it is hardly likely that a second would have grown up close to one which already existed, had one been found sufficient. Now, when I resided in that country, one always was found sufficient, nor did I ever see two adjacent ones in use at the same time. Indeed, many were never used. It should also be noticed that two were never found together except at very favourite camping places. These ash and clay accumulations, many of which have been used as a makeshift for gravel, are amongst the few traces which the Blacks have left behind them. The largest which I have seen are some fifty yards in circumference, and three or four feet high in the middle; very frequently a tree of considerable size grows out of them, which, of course, could only have sprung up during a protracted period of disuse. What I have said concerning the ovens of the Pinpandoor, applies also, if I mistake not, to those found on Kanbowro, or as the whites call it, the Gunbower Creek.*

The way in which these ovens were used was as follows :—When there was food to be baked, the women, with their hands and yamsticks, scooped a hole in the mound; if in doing so they came upon any lumps of clay (for there was no stone in those parts), they roughly lined the bottom of the hole with them. If none were met with, they quickly dug up a quantity for the purpose with their yamsticks, from somewhere near at hand. These lumps were about twice the size of a man's fist. The bottom of the hole being lined with them, a fire was made on top of them, and on the fire were thrown more lumps of clay. When the fire had burnt down, these last lumps were removed to one side, and the hot embers to the other. The hole being thus cleared of everything except its flooring of hot lumps of clay, the latter were strewn thinly with grass, or with the leaves of a herb called pennyroyal, green if possible, and well damped with water. On this

* Since the above was penned, the writer has measured roughly some ovens close to Paiāngil head station, on the Murray, of which the dimensions are :—Two ovens, sixty yards in circumference and four feet in height; another, sixty yards in circumference and five feet in height; another, eighty yards in circumference and four feet in height. There were several others within 300 yards of these which were not measured.

were laid. neatly packed, the animals or roots to be cooked; then came another coating of wet grass, next the remaining lumps of heated clay, and then the burning embers. These were often covered with a sheet of bark, and on top of all these was a quantity of earth. In an hour or two the food was taken out well-cooked and clean.

The conclusions to which the facts connected with these ovens seem to lead are, first, that in 1841 the Blacks in the neighbourhood in which I lived, were not so numerous as they had been; and second, to judge by the trees growing out of the ovens, that the reduction in their numbers had taken place some fifty years or so antecedent to that date. As to the cause of such reduction, there are strong reasons for assigning it to small-pox, of which disease, in its most virulent form, many individuals amongst the Pinpandoor, Ngoo-raialum, Bangerang, and other neighbouring tribes bore the marks. Indeed, I and several others, two of whom are still alive, saw at Tongala, in 1843, or thereabouts, a Bangerang child absolutely suffering from this complaint. It may not be out of place to mention here that I never heard of, or noticed, consumption being amongst the natives until after several years' residence at Tongala, and even then there was very little of it.

I have already mentioned that of the two sections into which Bangerang was divided, the Wongatpan was the most numerous. Between

them and the Towroonban several little distinc-
tions, mental and physical, existed, as well as some
differences in their way of life. The Towroonban
were to a considerable extent an opossum-hunting
people, whilst the Wongatpan lived chiefly on fish
and roots. The principal habitat of the Wongatpan was the Moira, which is (or was) a reedy
miasmatic locality, particularly that portion of it
known as Wongat. In those days the Wongatpan
loved fish, more especially fat fish, and to lubri-
cate their persons with its oily exudation. The
supply of their favourite food existed in such
abundance, and was so easily procured that I
often wondered how that sage people managed
to pass their time before my party came and
taught them to smoke. That accomplishment
fairly acquired, however, matters went on flowingly,
their leisure hours being divided between putting
the pipe to its legitimate purpose and begging my
tobacco. When they were not doing one, they
were pretty sure to be doing the other, so that the
words, terrible from constant repetition, *i inyanook
bakka, mitta Cowel, inyarnica!* (give little tobacco,
Mr. Curr, smallest!) rang for ever in my ears.
The ladies, it is true, in their persuasive way,
prefaced their requests with "thoma ngieni" (dear
you) one of the few terms of affection they had;
but it all ended in "i inyanook bakka."

Besides catching fish and waterfowl in weirs
and nets of divers forms and descriptions, it was

the custom of the Bangerang in all weathers, when the river was not discoloured by floods, to enter the water with short barbed spears in their hands, with which they dived, and speared their finny prey in its own element.   In this way they took large quantities of fish, of from half-a-pound to sixty pounds weight.   They were, of course, all excellent swimmers, and dived *à merveille*. This sort of life was no doubt agreeable enough as long as summer lasted—a man enjoying a delicious bath whilst in pursuit of his supper—but when winter set in, and the water got cold, it was miserable enough.   The fish at that season were also difficult to spear, and the custom was for a number of men to form a line across the river, and dive in concert at a given signal, and swim down stream spearing what they could.   After repeating this operation several times, they would rush, bitterly cold, to a big fire which had been prepared on the bank, and warm themselves in the blaze and smoke, and, after restoring circulation a little, plunge again into the cold river.

Occasionally, too, the Bangerang obtained fish by poisoning the water of some small lagoon. This was effected by throwing into it a quantity of fresh gum-tree boughs, as the result of which, in a few hours, the fish died and came to the surface.   It is singular that amongst these fishing tribes hooks and lines were unknown.

It was a custom of the Wongatpan when there

17

were only a few of them at the Moira, and when hostile visits, which always occurred at night, were apprehended, to withdraw after dark to the reed-beds in their canoes, on board of which they slept on such occasions. This, though an effectual, must have been a truly wretched expedient, as it would be hard to imagine anything more miserable than a family passing a night in a damp canoe in the fœtid atmosphere of a reed-bed—not, as the poet says,

" Hushed with buzzing night-flies to their slumbers,"

but stung to madness by villainous mosquitos, which generally abounded in the locality.

In consequence of the rather stationary life led by the Wongatpan, who seldom left the banks of the Murray and the swamps and reed-beds in its immediate vicinity, the rearing of children was comparatively an easy matter amongst them, so that, as the Blacks are fond of children, infanticide was less common than with other tribes, and picaninnies more numerous in their camps. From the ease with which fish was obtained, old people of both sexes, who cannot live where food is scarce, abounded at the Moira; many, as far as I could judge, being seventy years of age, and some very much more. In their persons the individuals of this section of the tribe were less vigorous, slighter, and taller than those of the other; their hair was also decidedly shorter, wavy, and sometimes had a curl in it which reminded me a little of the negro. These circumstances seem to point to the fact that an amphibious mode of life affects the person, and particularly the hair; and that the Bangerang must have long dwelt where I found them, to allow time for such differences to develop themselves. They also form portion of a series of facts which go to show that the black race inhabited this continent for a long period prior to our discovery. The Wongatpan were also less decent in their habits than their opossum-eating relatives, probably from their amphibious mode of life so constantly requiring them to be naked. Altogether they were inferior to, and to some extent looked down on by, the Towroonban, their more stalwart kinsfolk.

Besides the fact that the Bangerang territory was parcelled out between the two sub-tribes, and that fishing weirs on the numerous channels which conducted the flood-waters back into the Murray were owned by individuals, and descended to their heirs, I recollect, on one occasion, a certain portion of country being pointed out to me as belonging exclusively to a boy who formed one of the party with which I was out hunting at the time. As the announcement was made to me with some little pride and ceremony by the boy's elder brother, a man of five-and-twenty, I not only complimented the proprietor on his estate, *on which my sheep were daily feeding*, but, as I was always prone to fall in with the views of my sable neighbours when possible, I offered him on the spot, with the most serious face, a stick of tobacco for the fee-simple of his patrimonial property, which, after a short consultation with his elders, was accepted and paid. On two other occasions, also, if I remember right, some Blacks objected to hunt with me over certain land, on the plea that it did not belong to them. That both individuals and families amongst the Bangerang had particular rights to certain lands I have no doubt. but practically they were little insisted on. Had, however, anyone not of the tribe attempted encroachments, it would have been an instant *casus belli.*

Amongst the Bangerang there was not, as far as could be observed, anything resembling government; nor was any authority, outside of the family circle, existent. Within the family the father was absolute. The female left the paternal family when she became a wife, and the male when he took rank as a *young man.* The adult male of the Bangerang recognized no authority in anyone, under any circumstances. though he was thoroughly submissive to custom. Offences against custom had sometimes a foreign aspect, and brought about wars with other tribes. Within the tribe they usually amounted to wrongs of some individuals, and for every substantial wrong custom appointed a penalty.

Anyone who had suffered a wrong complained of it, if at all, at night aloud to the camp, which was silent and attentive. Then the accused was heard. Afterwards those who chose, men or women, expressed their views on the subject; and if general opinion pronounced the grievance a good one, the accused accepted the penalty sanctioned by custom. Had an offender refused satisfaction, he would probably have been murdered by the injured party, and no one would have avenged his death. In the absence of the least show of constituted authority or rank, some members of the tribe had more influence in public matters than others; and when several of this sort took up any question in concert, I believe it invariably happened that the tribe was guided by them. This influence was enjoyed by men of mature age, as well as by younger men of marked ability; also by such as had a reputation as sorcerers or warriors, or were the husbands of several wives, especially if they had large families. These brought the consideration which riches secure with us. On the serious decline of a man's bodily or mental vigour his influence grew less. But, though there was no government, there were certain important practices among the Bangerang which deserve to be called laws. Some of the principal of these had reference to the transfer of the young from one class to another (particularized hereafter), the knocking out of their teeth, making

the ornamental scars on their backs, breasts, and
arms, and restrictions with respect to food.
There were also others which had reference to
females. In the latter case only did infractions
occur with some frequency, on which occasions,
as I have already noticed, the persons aggrieved,
when they chose, made their complaints publicly
in the camp, and publicly vindicated their rights,
the offender being often constrained by custom to
go through the ordeal of having a certain number
of spears thrown at him, and so run the risk of
death or wounds in satisfaction for the injury
done.

Though each section of the Bangerang was
thoroughly independent within the limits of its
own territory, they were virtually one for the
purposes of war. As regards war, however, as in
other matters, there was no attempt to coerce any
individual to join in an onslaught, or to adopt any
course to which he was disinclined. A common
danger or a common desire led to meetings and
consultations, and so simple and uniform were
interests generally that measures were usually
proposed which met with the approval of all ; but
if anyone did dissent from them, he was at
liberty to take his own course, and there was no
attempt at coercion ; and as there was no government, or attempt to govern, so there was no
opposition. With the Wollithiga and Kailtheban the Bangerang were on very intimate terms,

so that for war purposes they might almost be said to be one people. In addition, they were bound in a lesser, though a stout, friendship with the other six Bangerang-speaking septs, which, together with themselves, were surrounded by a number of tribes which looked on them as foreigners, and hated them in common; spoke a language different from theirs, and cut off stray members as opportunity offered, each tribe on its own account. Nor were these Bangerang intimacies barren of effect, for, besides a good deal of intermarriage, they did not resort to witchcraft against each other, and in the hour of need one tribe was at liberty to seek refuge in the territory of the other. At the same time, suspicion was not entirely absent amongst themselves; and had a few Bangerang men been found on the territory of any of the six tribes without some feasible explanation to offer, they would, as likely as not, have lost their lives. However, I remember, in the very early days, several of these tribes meeting together and sending a strong body of fighting men to meet the Ngooraialum at the Protectorate Station, which occupied the present site of Murchison, and I am under the impression that alliances of the sort were frequent before the coming of the white man interfered with native policy.

In domestic life the man was despotic in his own mia-mia or hut; that is, over his wife, or

wives, and such of his children as had not relinquished parental protection. Over the girls his
authority ceased when they became wives, and
after his twelfth year or so the boy was very
little subject to the father, though parental affection always endured. As regards his wife, he
might ill-treat her, give her away, do as he liked
with her, or kill her, and no one in the tribe
interfered; though, had he proceeded to the last
extremity, her death would have been avenged by
her brothers or kindred. I once heard a Black
say, who had obtained a wife by exchange of
sisters with a Ngooraialum, "If he beats my
sister, I'll beat my wife." On the death of the
husband, his widow and children become the
property of his heir, who would be his brother, or
some other male relative of the same generation
as himself who had gone through the ceremonies
by which the rights of manhood were conferred.
No man married a woman born in the tribe.
Wives were obtained by the exchange of females
with any other tribe; so that the man who had a
daughter exchanged her for a wife, for himself or
his son, as he thought proper.

Concerning marriage I have already said something in a previous chapter. The reader has
learnt that there was no ceremony connected with
it; that the bride had no voice in the matter, but
was simply required to go to the hut of the man
to whom her father, brother, or uncle, as the case

might be, had given her. Girls were promised in marriage at a very early age—indeed, sometimes provisionally before their birth. Aunts and uncles spoke of their nephews and nieces by terms significant of such relationships, but addressed them as son or daughter. The idea of marriage between relatives, or even between men and women of the same tribe, was held in abhorrence. The Bangerang were unwilling even to speak of such a thing. I know an instance—a solitary one—in which a Kailtheban youth ran off with a Ngooraialum girl, a proceeding which for some reason the two tribes overlooked and confirmed. This was the only instance of a love match I ever knew. Few men under thirty years had wives; the exceptions as a rule had widows as wives: and the old men, young girls as second wives. Individuals had occasionally two, and even three wives, but only one as a rule. As the result of infanticide, the males in the tribe exceeded the females, in the proportion perhaps of three to two, so that a number of young and middle-aged bachelors on the look-out for wives always existed. Children belonged to the tribe of the husband.

It sometimes occurred that a man who had two or three wives gave away one of them. Prior to the coming of the whites, the Bangerang, as a a rule, enforced constancy on the part of their wives, and chastity on their unmarried daughters. A number of well-established customs lent their aid to this purpose ; thus a woman never sat in a mia-mia in which there was a man, save her husband ; she neither conversed nor exchanged words with any man, except in the absence of her husband, and in reply to some necessary question. If a man required to ask a woman a question, he did so from a distance, and in a loud voice which could be heard by everyone. In the case of old people, however, customs of this sort were relaxed to some extent. There were also men and women in neighbouring tribes who took the greatest care to avoid each other's presence. Whether, as I have read, it was because they stood in the relation of mother-in-law and son-in-law I never inquired. Girls, as a rule, were promised in marriage in infancy, espoused at twelve years of age, and became mothers at sixteen. Until married they lived in their father's mia-mia, from which their brothers of eight or ten years of age were excluded at night. They had no communication with persons of the opposite sex, except little boys. The women were considerably smaller in proportion to the men than amongst Europeans. They were not unmindful of personal adornment, using red ochre on the cheeks, and, occasionally, feathers in the hair for this purpose. They never adorned themselves with flowers. They wore their hair falling down on their shoulders; were generally chatty and merry, and often well formed and graceful. The unmarried girls wore a fringe, which depended from a girdle round the waist, and their opossum-rugs very closely wrapped about them. This latter peculiarity in unmarried and lately married girls was always noticeable. In youth they had feelings of delicacy. Females differed from males in their way of standing, their feet being always a little apart, and the toes slightly turned in and the heels out. Sir Thomas Mitchell, in the second volume of his " Exploration," pp. 69 and 212, in his portraits of two aboriginal women, has hit off these peculiarities nearly accurately; but in his portraits of men (see vignette to vol. i. and p. 92 vol. ii.), which on the whole are excellent, I think he draws the toes more turned out than they should be. Like the men, the women had the septum of the nose pierced, and the arms and chest ornamented to some extent with raised scars. The principal duties which fell to the share of the women in domestic life were to provide the daily supply of wild roots and vegetables, of which the food of the Bangerang in great measure consisted. It was their business also to transport the children and some portion of the *impedimenta* from place to place in their constant wanderings. The men carried their arms and personal effects. Frogs, and the small fish caught in nets, were provided by the women and elder children.

The number of children borne, on the average,

by Bangerang women I estimate at six, or perhaps eight, of whom nearly one-half fell victims to infanticide, a practice which resulted principally from the difficulty, if not impossibility, of transporting several children of tender age from place to place on their frequent marches. They also suckled their children for at least three years, much of their food being hard. Originally halfcastes were destroyed at birth. Parents were much attached to their children, and rarely punished or corrected them. Far, indeed, from controlling them in any way (though on rare occasions, when specially annoying, a child was brought to order by a not too gentle tap of the paternal tomahawk), they were habitually indulged in every whim; and as a consequence, in case of the boys at least, grew up as self-willed, thorough little tyrants as can well be imagined. On the march, for instance, it was common to see a mother, in addition to the household effects, which were often pretty heavy, carrying a stout young urchin who was too lazy to walk, and who insisted on being conveyed in that way. Indeed, I am persuaded that the complete selfishness and want of self-control which this mode of bringing up fostered would have gone far to have rendered tribal life impossible, had it not been for the subsequent training which custom made imperative; and that in fact a number of customs prevalent amongst the aborigines, which at first sight we are apt

to consider trivial and meaningless, were in reality
the foundation upon which principally reposed the
superstructure of tribal life in this continent.   The
Bangerang curriculum was as follows :—The
yarka, or male infant up to two years of age, and
subsequently the *maddiga*, or boy, was allowed to
grow up with the least amount of control possible,
as we have seen.   When eight or ten years of age
he was sent to sleep in the bachelors' camp, when
there was one at hand, with the young men and
boys of various ages, his parents still supplying
him with food.   In his new home, though no
violence was used, its inmates being all his
relatives, the child gradually became to some
extent the fag of everyone older or stronger than
himself, getting the worst place at the fire, instead
of the best, and being required at any moment to
render a hundred little services.   In his father's
camp he had been accustomed to handle whatever
was in it, but he was now taught to keep his
hands off whatever was not his own.   At ten or
eleven years of age the boy was made a *logo-
moolga*, gave up the name which he had hitherto
borne, and began to learn to endure pain and
restraint.   One of his front teeth was knocked out;
his arms, chest, and back had those long gashes
made in them, which, so painful at the time, were
subsequently to become his ornament and pride ;
the septum of his nose was pierced, and a bone
stuck through it by way of ornament ; he had in

great measure to supply himself with food; was
entirely forbidden the use of the most savoury
sorts of meats; was prohibited from going to his
father's camp, and discountenanced in conversing
with his mother, sisters, and other females.

At about sixteen years of age the *kogomoolga*
underwent a secret ceremony (which I never witnessed), and became a *panoopka*, or young man.
This was the great turning point in his life, and
he seemed thoroughly to appreciate the dignity
conferred upon him. In conjunction with a certain
shyness (which occurred at no other period of his
life), his bearing now became staid and dignified.
The games in which he used to join were indulged
in less frequently, and, in their place, he began to
devote himself to the vanities of dress. He now
affected the use of red ochre, adorned his head
with plumes, and made himself an opossum-rug,
which he scored and coloured in the approved
way. At the camp-fire at night he might now
occasionally be heard chanting his corroboree.
To please the ladies was evidently the chief
object of his solicitude. He also laboured at the
fabrication of spears and shields; kept his *kogomoolga* friends at a proper distance; was specially
imperative with the *mdddigas*; very sensitive of
ridicule; somewhat nice on the point of honour
(*pundonoroso*, as the Spaniards say), and occasionally got into fights with his elders, out of which
he generally came second best off. In his twen-

tieth year, or thereabouts, the *panoopka* became *yeyir* (a man), at which period some of the food restrictions, to which he had been so long subject, were removed, and he was at liberty to contract marriage if he could get a wife. Such was Bangerang education.

When several families were camped together at a spot at which they proposed to remain for a few days, the custom was for the women to leave camp an hour or two after sunrise for the purpose of getting roots and vegetables, catching shrimps or prawns, digging out rats, and carrying on other avocations of the sort. On their backs they carried their babies, and were followed by some or all of their children. Their start, yam-stick in hand, in long-extended Indian file, followed by numbers of half-starved dogs, was characteristic and peculiar enough. Generally their absence from the camp was about six hours, half of the time being loitered away in the shade or by the fire, according to the season, when they returned with a heavy load of food. It was when camped in this way for several days at a place that weapons and ornaments were manufactured, and games played. The men used to start out to hunt in threes and fours shortly after the women had left the camp, and returned about the same time. The ordinary business of the married men was to see to the safety of the family, procure meat or fish, and opossum skins enough to keep them clad.

Returned to the camp, both men and women would rest for a short time, and probably smoke a pipe. Then came preparations for the evening meal. The bachelors, in their camp, cooked each for himself, and at the family fires the father generally cooked the animals which he brought home, and the woman the roots, which were her contribution. In cooking meat a few hot coals were withdrawn from the fire, and the animal, if a small one, laid upon them, whilst, with two bits of stick in his right hand, the cook took up other coals, and laid them one by one on the meat. In the use of these bits of stick, which, from the mode of holding them, were made to act like tongs, the Bangerang and their neighbours were most expert. Any little sticks eight inches long and as thick as one's finger did; they were their only cooking utensils: enabled them to do with ease everything they required: saved them burning their fingers: and were quite characteristic of the camp. Whilst the carcasses were roasting, the first pangs of hunger—the husband's hunger —were allayed by the liver, heart, kidneys, blood cooked in an intestine, and trifles of the sort, which were hurriedly grilled, and swallowed with much gusto. In the meantime the opossums were laid on the coals and slowly roasted.

Sometimes, however, the husband would allow the wife to cook everthing: and occasionally an oven was brought into requisition, or a *woolum-*

bara, or large fire common to all at the camp,
was made by the women, in the ashes of which
were baked in a heap all the animals which had
been obtained that day by the various persons at
the camp. Then about dusk, or a little after,
ensued the aboriginal's principal meal, which took
him some time to despatch, as your Black is
eminently a leisurely feeder when he is at liberty
to choose the pace. After dinner came the pipe
and conversation, whilst the children dropped off
to sleep as they felt inclined; and it was invariably at this time that personal complaints,
and what we may call public affairs, were discussed, when there happened to be anything of
the kind on hand. As regards such discussions,
writers *who have not lived in the bush,* and
acquired a personal knowledge of the Blacks and
their manners, frequently describe in a very circumstantial way, and as a thing well known, a
council of old men, somewhat on the *Patres
conscripti* pattern, who deliberate in company, and
indeed govern the tribe. As a fact, however, as
far as I could learn, nothing of the sort existed
amongst the Bangerang. Usually, when matters
of general interest were pending, it was the
custom for anyone who chose, to harangue the
camp. This the orator generally did standing
beside his own fire, after the evening meal, when
everyone of the party was sure to be present and
awake. He was often wrapped in his opossum-

18

rug, and generally held in his hand a club or a spear. Young men could speak if they chose, but did so less often than the aged. Now and then one of them would make some observations, and a woman interject a remark, but the burden of discussion was generally borne by men of forty and upwards. When the first speaker had done, another, sitting or standing at his own fire, took up the theme. When morning came the subject was not renewed, and each took the course which seemed best to him, though they were generally pretty well agreed. If, however, an attack on some tribe had been decided upon, those who intended to be of the party, and others, would get together next day, probably at the bachelors' camp, and quietly talk over and arrange the details of the expedition.

To return to the subject of food. Meat before all was the Bangerang's favourite article of diet, and with it the husband gorged himself before he thought of giving any to his wife. Indeed, the children were usually preferred before her in this particular, and occasionally perhaps a favourite dog; for in savage life community of interest between man and wife is much less the rule than amongst civilized people; and as a husband is a constant check on the inclinations and free will of his wife, who has to perform the drudgeries of his camp, eat his leavings, and submit to occasional acts of barbarity on his part, it is not to be wondered at if she looks on him not as a mate so much as a master, and to some extent as an enemy. Her nature, however, is not very sensitive, and she has been educated to her lot, so that, as I believe I have already remarked, family life amongst the Bangerang, especially after the first year or two, was on the whole happy enough.

Amongst the Bangerang and the other tribes which I have known, each married couple had their own mia-mia or hut; the bachelors had one in common, and occasionally some widowed ladies beyond the age of wedlock kept house together. As regards the Bangerang bill of fare, it was varied—somewhat poor, but not insufficient. The standing dishes were roots of several sorts, opossums, and fish. Emu and kangaroo were scarce and but rarely obtained, whilst among the minor *plats* may be mentioned manna, eggs, kangaroo-rats, field-rats, birds of every sort, tadpoles, grubs, snakes, the larvæ of ants, and one or two wild fruits of an inferior description. The only edible substance they did not eat was the mushroom. Their food, if of indifferent quality, was at least wholesome and readily procurable, six hours a day abundantly sufficing for that purpose, so that hunger was little known. A craving for fat of any sort was very noticeable amongst them, for which reason the emu, when in "the pride of grease," was their most esteemed article of food. The Bangerang

country would have supported twice the number
of Blacks we found in it.

The animal on which the Bangerang and the
Blacks of the southern portion of the continent
generally were chiefly dependent for their supply
of meat was the opossum, a nocturnal creature,
weighing six or seven pounds, which hides himself by day in the hollow branches of the various
eucalypti. The mode adopted by the Bangerang
in ascending these trees, which often measured
a hundred feet to the first branch, was as follows :—The hunter, standing on the ground, cut
with his tomahawk a horizontal notch, four inches
long, deep into, or quite through the bark of the
tree, a little below his right hip, and another
opposite his left shoulder. Taking the handle
of the tomahawk between his teeth, or holding
it in his half-closed hand, the climber inserted
his right toe sideways into the notch first cut,
and, with his arms embracing the tree, raised
himself up by the strength of his leg so as to
stand on his right toe ; he then put the big toe
of his left foot into the second notch, and again
raised himself. Standing erect on the big toe of
his left foot, and maintaining his balance by
means of his left hand and right heel, which
he passed somewhat round the tree, he again
proceeded to cut with his tomahawk, which he
always held in his right hand, two notches as
before, one a little lower than his right hip, and

the other opposite his left shoulder, when he made two more steps. Repeating this process again and again, the tree was soon ascended, and, by those accustomed to the operation, without much fatigue. This mode of ascending trees I amused myself with practising at Tongala, but owing to the skin of my feet not being thick and indurated like that of my black friends, the pain I suffered prevented me from being able to cut more than six or eight notches without descending to rest. I and my brothers found that even a little use hardened and strengthened our feet considerably, and enabled us, besides climbing, to lift objects with our toes nearly as well as the Blacks. Since that time I have read ridiculous statements of the feet of savages being like those of monkeys; but the truth is, they resemble exactly those of white persons unaccustomed to shoes.

There were amongst the Bangerang many restrictions concerning particular articles of food, so that children, girls, young men and women were forbidden the use of some of the choicer sorts; nor did I ever know any of them (except in the case of a lad half-starved, and on my persuasion) break through this tribal custom. The reasons assigned by the Blacks for their abstinence always seemed to me so inadequate and *bizarre*, even from their own point of view, that I thought they were deceiving me in the matter,

until I found that the explanation given was
confirmed on all hands. One of the alleged ill-
consequences of eating food of the forbidden sorts
was, I remember, that a high wind would arise;
and yet I never heard that high winds were
disagreeable or injurious, or objected to by the
Blacks when they did occur. In fact, for stalking
emu or kangaroo a high wind was most desirable, as the waving of the grass and the boughs
in motion caused the hunter's approach to be less
noticeable. As an instance of how their ideas
ran in such matters, I remember, in early days,
the Bangerang attributing the death of an infant
at the breast to the circumstance of its father
having eaten some beef.

It is a noteworthy fact connected with the
Bangerang, and indeed, as far as I am aware, with
the whole aboriginal population (notwithstanding what Captain Gray asserts to the contrary
in connection with the Blacks of Western Australia), that as they neither sowed nor reaped, so
they never abstained from eating the whole of any
food they had got with a view to the wants of
the morrow. If anything was left for Tuesday, it
was merely that they had been unable to consume
it on Monday. In this they were like the beasts
of the forest. To-day they would feast—aye,
gorge—no matter about the morrow. So, also,
they never spared a young animal with a view to
its growing bigger.

Infanticide was common amongst the Bangerang, as amongst other tribes, and particularly in
the case of female children, and, I have no doubt,
had been practised from time immemorial. They
themselves gave as their reason for it the impossibility of the women carrying more than one
infant in their constant ramblings. Besides, they
suckled their children until they were fully three
years old.

Writers often allege want of food or a dread of
over-population as the excuse, but in this there is
no truth in the case of the Bangerang, for food
was plentiful, and they were very wasteful of it.
I have often seen them, as an instance, land large
quantities of fish with their nets and leave all the
small ones to die within a yard of the water. I
have often spoken to them on the subject, and I
am sure the idea of over-population never entered
their heads.

In their wild state they never used salt or
other condiments, and, except a sweet drink
which they manufactured in the season by dis-
solving manna in water, water was their only
drink. Their mode of drinking was also somewhat curious, for they commonly walked into the
stream up to their knees, bent down their heads
and threw the water into the mouth with the
right hand. At the camp they drank from the
calabash. As regards cannibalism, which is well
known to exist to a great extent in Northern

Australia, it cannot be said to have been practised amongst the tribes of which I write,
though on rare occasions a morsel of the fat
of a slaughtered foe was devoured as an act of
triumph; a proceeding, moreover, of which the
perpetrators, when spoken to by white men,
were thoroughly ashamed. Usually a piece of
the kidney fat was taken from the slain,
wrapped up carefully in many folds of opossum
skin, and so preserved for months, perhaps, by
the victor.

A very noticeable feature of Bangerang
economy was the harmonious way in which the
individuals composing the tribe lived together.
A simple sort of etiquette and precise customs
regulated their bearing towards each other, and
usually prevented any difficulty arising, so that
I rarely knew of a fight between members of
the tribe, and seldom heard anyone speak disparagingly of another. As the result of restraint
in many things connected with his savage life,
the Black very easily accommodated himself to
the routine of stations; discipline, if not too
severe, rather meeting with his approval. It
should be remarked that aboriginal restraints
were, in the majority of cases, though not altogether, of a negative character; an individual
might not do this, and might not eat that, and
might not say the other. What he should do
under any circumstances, or that he should do

anything, were matters with which custom interfered less frequently.

When out hunting, the game captured by each was his own property. If one of the party returned unsuccessful, he rarely asked for a share of another's game, nor did he take it ill if none were given him; but, if a bachelor, he would get some roots from any female relative he might have in the camp. If an individual killed a kangaroo without assistance, it belonged to him, though it would certainly be shared with many others; but if several assisted in the capture, the animal was divided amongst the party, the man who first drew blood, I believe, receiving the skin (which was valuable) in addition to his share of the meat.

It used to seem singular to me, when I first knew the Bangerang, that, except in the performance of incantations, which were only practised by a few, very little was known of experts in any of these accomplishments. Each Black was master of everything known or performed by his tribe; no one addicted himself specially to any particular accomplishment, except witchcraft; and no one ever got another to make a shield, climb a tree, or spear a fish for him. Whatever tools, arms, or implements were made, belonged to the maker and not to the tribe. They used often to joke me and say that I could make neither a gun, nor a tomahawk, nor sugar, nor flour, nor anything else. With respect to the aged and infirm, the

customs of the Blacks were very unamiable. As
they were simply tolerated, and not well able to
help themselves, little but the poorest food and
worn-out opossum cloaks fell to their share. To
the last, however, there was much more consideration for a man than for a woman; nor would
it be easy to picture to oneself anything more
repulsive than one of these poor females, reduced
by age to little better than a skeleton, imbecile
in mind, and hideous and squalid in person—
allowed to follow the tribe it is true, but meeting with scant assistance; she, on the other hand,
patient and uncomplaining, with an interest in
the children, and a civil word for all. As a
rule these old ladies had little to eat but roots,
save perhaps when a lizard, a snake, or a wild-
dog too lean to suit those who were more fortunate, was given up to them. On one occasion
I remember active steps being taken to get rid
of an old woman. The circumstances were these,
and they exhibit an amount of brutality rarely
witnessed amongst the Bangerang. A few families had camped on the opposite side of the river.
They were a good deal about the station during
the day, and the cause of their camping where
they did was, I believe, to prevent their dogs
getting into mischief about the huts, as I used to
visit all canine indiscretions with a charge of shot.
In the camp was an old woman reduced to the
last stage of decrepitude. She was unable to

walk, and life was evidently fast ebbing away. At length one morning I heard that she had grown so weak that she was unable to move, and that her complaints and groans were very distressing. Towards evening, noticing that the Blacks had left, and being anxious to know what had been done with the dying person, I crossed the river and went to the camp, where a horrible sight met my eyes; for the Blacks, I found, before they left, had gathered together a considerable pile of dry wood, laid the dying woman on it and set it on fire. The perfect skeleton of the deceased, entirely denuded of flesh, now lay before me on top of the flaming logs. A considerable time elapsed before the individuals implicated in this barbarity made their appearance again at Tongala, and when they did, they seemed conscience-stricken and sheepish enough. They pleaded in excuse that nothing could save the woman; that she must soon have died; that her groans frightened them; and that if deserted the wild dogs would have eaten her.

The Bangerang had very faint ideas of beauty. *Beautiful* and *pretty* were expressed in their language by the word *kalinya* (το καλον !) which also meant *good*. As applied to women, *youth* and *beauty* were, to a considerable extent, esteemed the same thing, so that young wives were always in request. On one occasion I heard a man say, when extolling the charms of a young woman, that her skin was smooth and bright as the wood of the box-tree off which the bark has been newly stripped. Neither kissing, shaking hands, nor any other salutation of the kind was in use amongst the tribe, though frequently men of different tribes made exchanges of arms or articles of dress in token of good-will; and women, in like manner, exchanged ornaments. In connection with the *names* borne by the males there existed amongst the Ban-gerang some matters of interest. In the first instance the names given to the children were the result of the whim of the parents. They were named after an ancestor long dead, or after a habit, or a skin disease, or some part of the body, or a personal peculiarity, or an animal or locality. After boyhood, however, no male could be said to have a name, as subsequently they invariably addressed each other either by a term of relation-ship, or by the name of the class in the tribe (*Yarka*, *Panoopka*, &c.) to which each person belonged. When several boys had arrived at ten or twelve years of age they underwent, in company, the operation of having an upper front tooth knocked out, after which they dropped the name hitherto borne, and were henceforth spoken of or to as *Kogomoolya*, or *Wonga* if the operation had been purposely omitted. I never knew but one Wonga, and on what grounds he had been allowed to retain his tooth I am not aware; but

I have no doubt it was the result of some precise custom, as the Bangerang were very punctilious in such matters. After some four years we heard those whom we had known as Kogomoolga or Wonga called Panoopka. Later on this last appellation was dropped, and the youth became a nameless man. Once a Kogomoolga, the name borne in infancy was never heard again, nor without extreme difficulty could any individual be induced to tell what had been another's name; as for his own, it was out of the question. In fact, they seemed embarrassed when the subject was mentioned. To a certain extent a fidgety feeling existed with them, even as regards the names received from the whites, to which their custom avowedly did not extend; so that if, as often happened, a man changed his "*white*" name, he was apt to be disconcerted if called by the old one. I remember, several years after I had ceased to live at Tongala, falling in with a party of Bangerang young men. I had left them boys, but in the interim they had shot up into men, and grown quite out of my recollection. I had known them both by their native and white names. The former they had given up, and altered the latter, and I failed altogether, though I took some trouble in the matter, to induce them to enlighten me on either point. I may add that they received me with the most enthusiastic expressions of goodwill; laughed, talked, struggled to hold my horse, invited me to sit down, and so on; in fact, there was nothing they would not do for me, except tell me the names which I myself had given them, and by which they had been known to everyone for ten years.

As regards women, these customs did not obtain, for though perhaps generally addressed by a term of relationship, the name which they had received in childhood was often used. There were, however, several old grandpapas, and now and then a man of forty-five, to whom what I have said did not quite apply, as they were frequently spoken of, never to, by the name borne in childhood. How this variation of the general custom came about I never knew. When a man wished to address another, he used to call out Mirra! (look) or Mirramna! (look, I say) until he caught the person's eye. In speaking of absent individuals, a man would say—"I saw at Kaiooga your younger brother, and my elder brother, and two Kogomoolgas, the eldest son of Windyarning (a woman), and the second son of Miniga (a woman)," and so on. It was not long after our arrival at Tongala until the Bangerang began to find the want of names very inconvenient in their intercourse with us. They were, of course, aware that their Ngooraialum neighbours had all got white names, so they took the matter up, and several came to me daily to be named. The result of it was, that in the course of a week or two I christened the whole tribe, men, women, and children; and very amusing it was to hear them, as they left me, repeating the name constantly to themselves, so as to impress it on the memory, not unfrequently coming to me several times in the day to hear it repeated. One old fellow, of a particularly meditative and owlish countenance, I remember I called Plato, which he pronounced Pĭl-ĕ-tŏ, laying the stress on the first syllable, which my men, not understanding, converted into Billy Toole; so Billy Toole he remained ever after. One particularly jolly old fellow, with grey hairs and whitish beard, whose cheeks had an unusual tinge of red, I called Jolly-chops, and as he was alive in 1875, I think he must have reached his eightieth year. In 1841 he was a grandfather, and was always called "*thowmunga*" (old man) by the tribe. Another, a lad whom I used to take out kangarooing, afterwards rather a personage in the tribe, I called Tallyho.

Save as man and wife, but little conversation was allowed after childhood between the sexes; when such occurred, however, between individuals of discreet ages, they addressed each other by the terms of elder brother and elder sister, and spoke with their heads and eyes averted. This reticence on the subject of names, which I have noticed in more than one locality in Australia, like many other customs, has given way, more or less, in the general fusion of tribes which the advent of our civilization has brought about. Amongst the Bangerang it resulted from the superstitious belief that if the name of a person became known to an enemy, or any implement of his, or the leavings of his food, or any of his hair, or, in fact, anything which had been his came into the possession of an enemy, that by the performance of certain incantations over such objects the life of the owner might be spirited away. Hence, when eating, such leavings as the dogs could not consume were generally burnt. As wizards did not usually trouble themselves about the lives of women or children, they were called by name.

Another custom was to avoid mention of the dead under all circumstances, so that if a child, called, say, Punna (opossum), died, the name of the animal would infallibly have been changed. It was not common, however, to name children after animals. Nothing jarred on the feelings of the Blacks more than to hear a white man name the dead, even by his white name; indeed, a sort of horror came over them on such occasions, and they would endeavour to stop the speaker's mouth with their hands. I have reason to think, however, that after ten or fifteen years the names of the dead were again available for use. When, as sometimes happened, a girl attained the age of puberty before she was married, it was the custom on the occasion for the women in the camp to put an opossum-rug over her head, and insert smoking sticks beneath the covering, which were kept in that position until she was nearly smothered and almost unable to stand. The Bangerang arms, ornaments, and implements were pretty nearly the same as those described by Eyre in his "Discoveries in Central Australia." I may mention, however, that as there were no flints found in their country, they used often to cut the flesh of animals with a sharp bit of reed. Flints and tomahawks the Bangerang had, however, obtained from the Ngooraialum and Pimpandoor in exchange for beautiful light reed spears, which were easy to carry and most effective in hunting, which they made in large quantities from the reed-beds in their territory. These reed spears of the Bangerang found their way to distant tribes, and were in much repute.

Whether the Bangerang had the boomerang when I first came amongst them I am not quite sure; but, at all events, they never took kindly to that singular missile, nor evinced much skill in its use. Their great weapons were reed spears for hunting, and the war spear, sometimes edged with wooden teeth, and sometimes with quartz, the latter being obtained by barter. Circumcision, and other mutilations of the sort, were not in vogue; nor, as far as I am aware, the totems or crests

19

spoken of by Captain Grey and others as existing in some portions of the continent. The symmetrical scars on the arms, breasts, and shoulders, so general throughout Victoria, were the principal ornament of their persons. In their demeanour towards each other, as I have before remarked, they were habitually courteous and good-humoured, so that one seldom noticed any quarrelling amongst the men, nor heard anyone speak disrespectfully or disparagingly of any member of the tribe. Indeed, though their ways were different from ours, it always seemed to me that the bonds of friendship between blood relations were stronger, as a rule, with savages than amongst ourselves. The women not being related to each other, but members of several neighbouring tribes, quarrels amongst them, though not frequent, were more common than amongst the men. Their little disagreements were settled with their yam-sticks, without much injury being done, their husbands interfering with their clubs if matters went too far. Concerning the women, it may be also noticed that their sympathies lay rather with the tribe in which they had been born, than with that of their husbands. If asked of what tribe they were, they always gave the name of that in which they were born.

Religious worship the Bangerang had none. As the result of several conversations on such subjects, the conclusion to which I came was,

that they stood in considerable awe of a powerful
spiritual being, whose interference in their affairs
was usually of a malevolent character, but whose
principal attributes (such as power, knowledge,
&c.) we Christians attribute to God. This spirit
the whites have taught the Blacks to call *debble-
debble* (the devil), and hence people commonly say
the Blacks believe in the devil, but not in God.
As regards superstitions, however, the Bangerang
had a plentiful, if not a very interesting, crop.
In *Pekka*, or ghosts, they were firm believers,
and easily frightened with ghost stories, to which
they listened unwillingly. They had also a
superstitious dread of being caught in a whirl-
wind, and other fancies of the sort. As usual
with savages, there were certain individuals
amongst the Bangerang who enjoyed the character of being necromancers. These men used
to relate conversations of the most whimsical
character, which they averred they had held with
the dead, some of whose spirits were said to be
constantly lurking in the woods near the camp
in a disembodied state. The bodies of the dead
were said to remain in their graves—indeed, they
so secured the legs and arms of the corpse before
interment as to render its escape impossible;
but the spirits of the departed were often seen
and spoken to by the necromancers, and were
much given to fantastic tricks. What was
reported of their conversation was foolish and

trivial. These sage impostors of the Bangerang were also credited with the power of making rain, and of taking away the lives of their enemies by enchantment. One sovereign mode of effecting the latter result, as I have already mentioned, was through the instrumentality of a lock of an enemy's hair, or the remains of any food which he had eaten; by means of which, and certain mysterious ceremonies, his caul-fat was surreptitiously abstracted, when it was believed he either pined away and died, or some fatal accident befell him. As, however, the sage Bangerang conceded to others the same black arts as were claimed by their own necromancers, whatever deaths occurred, save in the case of extreme old age, were attributed one and all to enchantments of enemies, and revenged accordingly; not always by counter-charms, but occasionally *vi et armis*, or rather by midnight assassination. From this source proceeded those perpetual wars of which I propose to say more in the sequel. Another superstitious practice which prevailed amongst my sable friends when travelling, and afraid of being benighted, was to place a lump of clay on any conspicuous stump or log which they happened to pass near. This proceeding was believed to retard the setting of the sun. On quizzing them about little matters of the sort, as I often did, and pointing out to them how stupid they were, they used to laugh good-humouredly enough, but evidently set down my failing to see the effect of the lump of clay on the course of the sun as an instance of particular thick-headedness on my part. If I could deny that, I could deny anything! In their eyes I fancy I was what the Italians call *testa dura.* Though it has been narrated more than once— I believe correctly—that the Blacks, on seeing white men for the first time, had in their surprise taken up the idea that one of the party had risen from the grave, yet neither the Bangerang, nor any of the tribes which I have known in New South Wales or Queensland, had any general belief of the sort.

A respectable characteristic of the Bangerang was, that suicide was unknown amongst them. Whatever sickness, hardship, or misery fell to the lot of an unfortunate, he always found courage to bear it to the end.

The Bangerang built their huts of boughs in fine weather, and of bark in winter. Each family had its own hut. Unmarried men and boys of eight or ten years and upwards lived together, and separate from their parents and sisters, in what we used to call the bachelors' camp. The huts were nearly semi-circular in shape, and were set up in such positions, and at such distances from each other, as to secure a good deal of privacy to the inmates. Generally, they were about twenty feet apart, and all facing the same way, with their backs to the wind. I often noticed that, whilst the white man will go a little out of his way to camp where he camped before, the Black never does so, but, if practicable, occupies a fresh spot; on which subject a good deal in connection with the instincts of the two races might be said.

When the nights began to get cold in autumn, and after the first fall of rain made the forests remote from the river—in which opossums abounded—accessible, it was usual for the men of the Bangerang to set about making new opossum-rugs: their old ones, in due time, being given up to the women, children, or aged persons. Whilst engaged in this business, the men hunted opossums during the day, skinned them on their return to camp, and, after feasting on their flesh, pegged out the skins, each on a small sheet of bark, which were then placed in front of the fire, so as to dry gradually. This done, the skins were scored with a mussel-shell in various ornamental patterns, and were then fit for use. When enough had been collected they were sewn together, a sharp bone being used as an awl to pierce them with; the sinews of the animal itself, or of the kangaroo, serving very well for thread. This pegging out of opossum skins was a very favourite occupation, and the tap, tap, tap of the dusky workman, as he sat at his fire chanting his monotonous corroboree, might often be heard far into the night. The manufacture of weapons also used to occupy a considerable portion of the time not spent in eating, hunting, and sleeping. Their arms were wonderful productions, when it is remembered they were wrought with stone implements, pieces of shell, bone, &c.; and it is remarkable that, though their fabrication was enormously facilitated by the iron tools they got from us, they fell off in beauty, and got to have a sort of slop look about them. The making of nets and baskets was left to the women; as also the spinning of yarn out of the fur of the ring-tailed opossum, which was done with a sort of spindle. This yarn was worn in many folds round the neck as an ornament. The manufacture of implements, clothes, and weapons, as also cooking, were all carried on seated. The Blacks never stood whilst at work. The men sat with their legs crossed, a heel under each ham, the thigh being close to the ground—a position which the English thigh will not take. The women, when seated, had both heels close to one ham, so that only one thigh touched the ground.* Whilst engaged in their various industries the camp exhibited a very comfortable *ménagère* appearance, which was much increased by the introduction of smoking. Tobacco, iron tomahawks, and the tinder-box, which relieved the women from the

---

* See plate in Mitchell's "Expedition into Eastern Australia," vol. ii., p. 92, where the position of women sitting is well shown.

trouble of carrying fire-sticks on the march, were indeed the three boons which the Blacks received from the Whites in compensation for endless disadvantages.

Amongst the Bangerang there were also several pastimes and games in vogue. Occasionally, for instance, the men drew pictures of corroborees or hunting scenes, with charcoal, on the sheets of bark of which their mia-mias were composed. Then the boys had a game with a ball made of opossum skin, and mimic battles with toy spears and shields, to which in after life they owed entirely their dexterity in the use of their weapons. It was also common to practise their toy spears on round pieces of bark, the size of a dinner plate, which were bowled swiftly along the ground.* The girls and women used sometimes to amuse themselves with a game resembling our "cat's cradle," with the difference that it was played by one person, who used her lips as well as her fingers in the conduct of the string. Occasionally the children amused themselves very cruelly with half-fledged birds and young animals, which they invariably killed when tired of the game. In the summer season the women and

---

* The Blacks very seldom threw their spears except when actually hunting, for they were difficult to make, and their points easily broken, though less so in the case of reed spears than others. Certainly a Bangerang did not throw a spear once in a week on the average of a year.

little children, when not engaged in fishing, used to bathe a good deal for pleasure, swimming, diving, and romping in a hundred ways. Of course, neither boys above seven nor men were with them. On such occasions constant peals of laughter would be heard proceeding from the merry throng, accompanied by a singular noise reminding one of the beating of a drum, which they made by striking their hands on the water palms downwards, and forcing under it a quantity of air.

Like other tribes with which I have been acquainted, the Bangerang used to have messengers who went from one tribe to another to arrange the times and places of meetings and corroborees, and also to gather news. These men we used to call postmen. They were personages of no little importance amongst the tribes, and welcomed accordingly, for the Blacks were, perhaps, more fond of gossip than any other people I have met with; with this peculiarity, that if anything of interest had occurred, each black-fellow would make a point of hearing the news direct from the postman, never being satisfied with the relation at second hand. By means of these messengers the tribes kept themselves sufficiently well informed of what was occurring in their neighbourhoods; and, on this principle, I have no doubt that the first settlement of the whites at Sydney was known for two or three

hundred miles around before many months had
elapsed. Messengers occasionally brought with
them a small stick on which were several notches,
which they told us were *yiletta* (letters). I never
paid any attention to them, but I believe they
were a sort of evidence to their minds of the
truth of the message brought by the bearer.

As a rule the health of the Blacks in their
wild state was excellent; they decidedly ailed
less than Europeans. What they principally
seemed to suffer from was rheumatism, headache,
and an itchy eruption of the skin (shared with,
if not caught from, their dogs), which by the
Bangerang was called *bōra*. This complaint
prevailed most commonly in the winter, disap-
pearing in great measure in warm weather,
when bathing and diving for fish kept the skin
clean. During winter, when much tormented
with this complaint, opening with a sharp peg
the innumerable little pimples which it occasioned
was a great occupation in the camp, as also
scratching; and I have known a man walk forty
miles to procure mussel-shells, with which to
scratch himself comfortably. The treatment in
bad cases of headache, which seemed to me to
occur principally to the least intellectual, and
between the ages of twenty and thirty, was
slightly gashing the temples; whilst for rheumatism, friction and ligatures round the affected
limb were had recourse to. Treatment for snake-

bite I never witnessed, but a neighbour of mine informed me that one of a party of Blacks encamped at his hut, being bitten by a snake on the calf of his leg, he sat down by his fire whilst his friends covered the leg with ashes as hot as he could bear them. To this baking he submitted for some hours, when the evil effects of the bite were said to have passed away. I do not, however, recollect to have heard of any symptoms being noticed to show that the snake was a poisonous one ; whilst it is certain that the Blacks were in great dread of the bites of these reptiles, though they used to eat them occasionally *when killed by themselves*. On the whole, what I heard of the remedy gave me no great confidence in it.

For the purpose of holding or carrying water calabashes were used, which contained from one to two gallons. They were made out of the knots or excrescences which are common to both box and gum trees. Like other savages, the Blacks were skilful in producing fire from the friction of wood. This was done in two ways, in which, however, the principle was exactly the same. One of the methods employed was to rub a piece of wood about as long and twice as thick as a carving-knife (which was quickly shaped, either with the teeth or a tomahawk) with considerable pressure, and at the greatest speed attainable, transversely across a crack in a dry log. This crack would be about an inch wide, or a little more, and about an inch deep; or, if it were too deep, a little dry earth would be thrown in it, so as to bring it to the required depth. Both the log and the piece of wood selected were dry, but not rotten, nor, perhaps, entirely free from their natural oils. Whilst rubbing, the fingers of both hands were clasped over the stick, and the operator kneeling. From the powerful friction used there was a good deal of smoke, and a nick was soon worn by the knife-shaped piece of wood, in doing which a quantity of dust was produced; this accumulated in a small heap in the crack, and in the centre of this heap a spark was generated. The little heap of dust was carefully removed on a leaf or bit of bark, wrapped in dry grass (as is done with tinder), and blown into a flame. After many trials, I once made fire in this way myself, and the task is not by any means an easy one; even those accustomed to the operation sometimes failed once or twice before succeeding. The process occupied about sixty seconds, the last thirty or forty strokes being made with all one's might, as regards both speed and pressure. It began firmly and slowly, and went on *crescendo* till the *finale*. I never saw two persons assist in the operation, as I have read. The sorts of wood which I have seen used were pine, box, gum, and grass-tree. When a person failed in

an attempt, he always recommenced in a fresh
place on the log. Any blackfellow with the
proper materials would make a fire in this way
in a few minutes. In the other mode in which
I have seen fire made the operator began by
making a hole quite through the centre of his
wommera, which was generally (and when I
saw fire made) of pine. This hole, which at
the entrance was large enough to admit the
point of a poker, gradually diminished to a
fourth of that size. This completed, the
operator sat down on the ground, drew his
knees nearly up to his shoulders, placed the
wommera (stick with which spears are thrown)
under his feet, and with them held it tight on
the ground. He then inserted in the hole the
end of a grass-tree stick about thirty inches
long and of the thickness of a poker. This
stick he placed between the palms of his hands,
and rubbing them with great speed and a
strong downward pressure, backwards and forwards, caused the stick to move in like manner.
Smoke soon ensued, and a smell of burning wood;
the dust which the friction of the stick created fell
through the hole to the ground (through which
the stick could not pass), and collected in a small
heap, in the middle of which fire was found.
Descriptions which I have read of obtaining fire
by the friction of wood always left the impression
that it was the sticks themselves which ignited—

which, indeed, is generally supposed to be the case, but I doubt whether that is possible. Smoke in large quantities can be obtained by rubbing sticks together, but I never saw fire result from the process. The children often used to amuse themselves in trying to make fire in the crack of a log as described, but their efforts always ended in smoke.

The Bangerang mode of burial had nothing remarkable about it. The dead were rolled up in their opossum-rugs, the knees being drawn up to the neck with strings, when the corpse was interred in a sitting posture, or on its side, generally in a sand-hill, in which a grave about four feet deep had been excavated. A sheet of bark was then placed over the corpse, the sand filled in, and a pile of logs about seven feet long and two feet high was raised over all. Round about the tomb it was usual to make a path, and not unfrequently a spear, surmounted by a plume of emu feathers, stuck at the head of the mound, marked the spot where rested the remains of the departed. Women were interred with less ceremony.

To lay before the reader, however, anything like a full account of my Bangerang neighbours would require more time than I have at command, so I must content myself with a short summary of their principal characteristics as they seemed to me. Before doing so, I may premise that much of what I have to say concerning this particular people might without very great modification be applied to the whole of the tribes inhabiting the country between Port Phillip Heads and Brisbane.

The Bangerang, when washed clean, were of a dark copper colour—some, however, being darker and some lighter; the variations in this, as in all other particulars, physical or mental, being less than those found amongst Anglo-Saxons, French, Germans, Turks, or other races of which I have experience. Amongst the agricultural peasantry of Grenada I noticed many individuals who struck me as wanting little—at least as regards the parts of the body exposed to the sun, namely, face, hands, throat, and the lower portion of the leg—of being as dark as the Bangerang. When born, the children were almost white, but assumed the hue of their race in a few days. The men, as regards stature, may be described as nearer to the Englishman than the Frenchman, and less robust than either, whether in trunk or limb. The lower portions, both of the arms and legs, were slighter than amongst us. Individuals standing over six feet were not uncommon amongst them. As I have already said, the women were smaller in proportion to the men than is the case with European females, and weighed, as I ascertained by experiment, from 75 lbs. to 140 lbs. Under the conditions of civilized life, and plentifully supplied with food, it is noticeable that the

aboriginal increases vastly in bulk in one generation, and the female quite loses her comparative
diminutiveness. Many of both sexes have also
become corpulent whilst living with the whites, of
which I seldom saw an instance amongst them in
their wild state. Sometimes this happens even
early in life.

The head of the aboriginal, which he always
carries well, is generally oval in shape, the bone
of the skull being much thicker than that of a
white man. The hair is always black, with a
tinge of auburn in it; coarse and plentiful, and as a
rule straight, but occasionally wavy, and, amongst
the fishing tribes on the rivers, sometimes
shortish and curly. Besides the hair on his
head, the Bangerang wore his plentiful beard,
moustache, and whiskers pretty much as nature
made them, merely shortening them now and
then; an operation in which a small fire-stick
supplied the place of scissors. In quantity, his
hair was somewhat in excess of ours. Like
white men who wear beards, the Bangerang was
apt to become bald, but in a much less degree,
and later in life, than in our case; for I have
noticed that few white men wear a beard for
twenty years and retain a full head of hair. As
regards the women, I have seen them with very
thin hair in old age, without positive baldness.
Until middle age was past this defect did not
appear in either sex. As a rule the eyes of the

Blacks were smallish, dark-coloured, the white slightly tinged with yellow, set wide apart, and much overshadowed by the brow, but vivacious, expressive, and intelligent. Occasionally, however, they were large and liquid, and there were amongst the Bangerang one or two women whose eyes might be compared, in respect of beauty, with those of the Cypriote, Gaditana, or Maronite. As regards sight, that of the Blacks was marvellous, whether in the matter of seeing quickly or far. When a Black pointed out to another anything in the distance, instead of using his finger, he merely indicated the direction by obtruding his beard, which was always sufficient. The women pointed with a slight forward motion of the nose. Indeed, their gestures frequently differed from ours. For instance, they beckoned with the palm of the hand down instead of up, and they expectorated with the teeth closed, one of the incisors being removed in youth. When they sat cross-legged, the knee, ham, and calf of the leg touched the ground; and, as expressive of anger, they often thrust the end of the beard into the mouth. Occasionally aquiline, the nose was usually flat and wide-spread at its lower extremity; the lips, without exception, being full and ugly. The mouth was large, the teeth white, regular, and strong, and the breath sweet; the chin small and retreating, the jaw powerful and massive. The neck was shortish, and inclined

20

to be thick. As regards the chest, it was generally, but not always, round rather than flat, and well developed, as were the shoulders, the upper portion of the arm, and the thighs. The wrists and hands were invariably small, the men's being less than those of the European female. The fingers were of medium length, and the nails often filbert shaped. Below the elbow and the knee there was a decided want of substance. The heel also obtruded somewhat, and the women stood and walked with the toes a little turned in, and the heels out. The back was famously supplied with muscle, and being well curved and hollowed-out at the loin (so that a plummet-line dropped to the ground from midway between the shoulders would fall well free of the spine), gave that graceful carriage, firm and elastic tread, for which the Australian Black is remarkable. The skin was particularly velvet-like to the touch.

The Bangerang endured well hunger, thirst, fatigue, and climatic variations of temperature. Though individual white men surpassed our black friends as equestrians, especially in the particulars of a graceful seat, hands, and judgment, yet as scrub-riders and rough-riders the average Bangerang excelled the average stockman. He had better nerve, quicker sight, and stuck closer to his saddle. Indeed, it was wonderful to see with how little practice he would come to the front in scrub-riding; and how well he would enter and take his line through saplings, into which, at fifty yards distance, it was difficult to detect an opening. What made him, when mounted, a little deficient in grace was, I fancy, the somewhat short neck, which was characteristic of the race.

The Australian Black generally performs well at cricket and other games, survives terrible wounds, but succumbs readily to fever. I never saw or heard of an albino amongst the Blacks, though I have known several with imperfections which dated from early childhood, and even from birth.

On the whole, the Australian savage is lighter and less muscular than the Englishman, but more active, has a better carriage and figure, and in his wild state preserves his physical powers and elasticity to a later period of life. As regards the nude figures of the two races, I have remarked how many whites there are of forty years, who (presentable enough with the boot-maker and tailor's gloze around them) seem half-misshapen when stripped, a feature one does not notice when the Black drops his opossum-rug. As regards the inferior development of muscle in the Black, it is particularly noticeable up to his twelfth year or so, as up to that time he cannot sufficiently supply himself with food. At the same time, I never see a number of our

countrymen stripped at a public bath but I
notice how few there are not in some measure
misshapen, and how inferior in symmetry they
are to the Blacks.   Later on, when competent to
get his own opossum, the young savage develops
his muscle surprisingly.   When age has sapped
his food-procuring powers, the figure becomes
greatly debased.   In age, too, the face of the
savage deteriorates far more than that of his
civilized brother, a certain painful vacuity and
somnolency being frequently its prevailing expression.

The mental characteristics and development of
Australian aboriginals is a subject at which I
shall only glance.   When I first met them, the
impression they produced upon my mind was,
that, superficially so widely different from ourselves, they were in fact so like us; there
being, however, much about their conversation
which reminded one of children.   Yet, with a
mind confined to few ideas, and those of a low
class; with a language deficient in collective and
abstract terms, and which seldom supplies so
many as three numerals;* without history, almost

* The Bangerang Blacks have but two numerals, the
equivalents of *one* and *two*.   *Three* was expressed as *one two*,
four as *two two*, five as *two two one*, and so on; but I am
convinced that very few of them had a precise idea of any
number greater than five, or perhaps seven.   Frequently,
however, appointments to meet at certain places, at some

bereft of tradition, with but vague ideas of a Supreme Being, the Australian savage (though his mind seems to grow but little after twenty) appears to me, nevertheless, to have within him a latent capacity, moral and intellectual, equal to that of the white man. To cultivate this capacity to the highest standard would, no doubt, require time—perhaps a century or two—and favourable circumstances.

In mere intelligence and powers of observation, and powers of reason, the Black very frequently surpasses the British peasant, as at least one writer (I mean Major Mitchell) has noticed. His mind has a keener edge, if I may use the term. Nor, in making this statement, do I confine myself, for instance, to matters connected with the pursuits of bush life, which might be thought to be particularly in his line, as even in our schools he has given strong proof of his

period within the limits of seventeen days or so, were arranged in the following manner. The person who wished to fix the day of meeting used to take hold of his left ear, and say *jan-jan*, and that was the first day; he then put the fore finger of his right hand on his collar-bone, saying *krok-krok*, and that was the second day; and in this way he went on placing it on his left shoulder above the muscle of the fore arm; below that muscle; and then on two spots between the elbow and the wrist; and then on the wrist and on each finger of the left hand; after which he held up each finger of the right hand; each spot on which he placed his finger, and each finger held up, having its particular designation, representing a day.

capacity.* As an instance of his aptitude for primary instruction in our learning, I may notice that I have known black boys learn the principal portion of the alphabet in a very few lessons. The book from which the task was learnt was, no doubt, a novel one, being the backs and ribs of cattle on which the letters of the alphabet were branded. These we used to point out and name as we rode along; so that, after a few lessons, when your impromptu young stockman returned from a ride amongst the cattle on the run, to the question of whether he had seen any strangers (strange cattle), he would reply as glibly as possible—"Oh yes; mine bin see two pella white cow, brand rib AB (in) circle; 'nother pella bullock, CM, upside down, rump; 'nother pella ole cow, brand R (in) diamond, shoulder; one cleanskin (unbranded beast), too, mine bin see."

In respect of memory, that of the Black is unusually tenacious. What he has once learnt he seldom forgets and has at his finger ends. Looking at him as a linguist, it is to be remarked that he picks up very quickly any Australian tongue. In his English a good deal of the con-

* One of the inspectors of our National Schools reports, concerning the school for the aborigines at Ramayuk, that, under peculiar disadvantages, it is rather beyond the requirements of the Education Board: that at some of the examinations there were no failures, &c. Indeed, the efficiency of this school has been testified to by several inspectors.

struction of his own language is apt to prevail.
When speaking, there is a rather remarkable
absence of gesticulation. For personal courage
I consider our black friends decidedly above par,
especially in that constituent of courage which we
call nerve. In this particular our savage has the
advantage of civilized races, as may be noticed in
his fighting, climbing, and riding. This quality
was frequently displayed on his first meeting with
white men mounted on horse or camel. Though
man and horse seemed to the Black one terrible
animal, or a being from the other world, they
were generally encountered with tolerable firm-
ness; and one instance is recorded of a solitary
savage meeting an exploring party far in the
interior, and opposing its advance single-handed
with club and shield, a feat of resolution and
nerve, when his stand-point is remembered, which
seems to me to compare favourably with anything
recorded in the annals of the human race. It
reminds one of fabled heroes attacking monsters
and goblins. When placed in circumstances of
peril, as a rule, the blackfellow displays more
than average resolution, and can—and in this he
often differs from his civilized brother—prosecute
with unshaken nerve anything he has undertaken.
however perilous. Nor should his aversion to
the rifle—he being armed with spears—detract
from his character for courage. Reverse the case,
and how would the white man act? Indeed, we

may remember that, before Western Europe got used to the smell of powder, even the *Chevalier sans peur and sans reproche* himself thought fire-arms fitter for lansquenets and men-at-arms than for belted knights.

As regards courage, I should say that the white man has more resolution, and the black-fellow better nerve. Though the Blacks used to put up with a good deal of abuse from the station hands and take little notice of it, their very children would resent a blow or a push instantly; and when rough-and-tumble fights did occur, on most occasions of which I was a witness the Black worsted his white antagonist. It was curious to notice the tact of the Blacks in estimating the standing of persons they casually met, and that, after a few moments' conversation, they would say whether a stranger was a gentleman or one of the working class. Sometimes, however, they would say, in doubt, *imbat oberchia* (I believe overseer).

A remarkable faculty of the Blacks, which seemed nearer akin to instinct than to reason, is that by which he finds his way about the bush. It is born with him in embryo, and is strongly developed at an early age. It is rare to meet a white man, no matter what practice he may have had, who can compete in this particular with an average black boy of fifteen years of age. It is also noticeable that whilst a white man's steering

in the bush—directed by compass, or its substitute,
the sun—is generally attended with some mental
effort, that the Black finds his way without reference to anything of the sort, though he has
names for all the cardinal points, and almost
without reflection. He takes no notice of his
shadow, and not much of where the sun sets or
rises, or of how the wind blows; so that a cloudy
day is not so inconvenient to him as it is to us.
A friend of mine puts it, that he has a compass
in his head which always points to any place he
wishes to reach! And certainly his powers in
this respect are as like intuition as anything I
know. His recollection also, not only with
respect to the lay of a country, but of trifling
matters met with, is very remarkable, and he
will frequently recognize a tree, or a bush, once
seen, which have little that is noticeable about
them. With all this, however, he is not unerring. A blackfellow occasionally gets puzzled.
Neither is the faculty so strongly developed in
him as in cattle. Bush-bred cattle are, I believe,
unerring; so that a herd driven from its run, say
300 miles north, and then 300 miles west, will,
at pleasure, return step by step the way it went,
or make as straight a track home between the
two extreme points as a surveyor could with his
theodolite.

When not cut off prematurely, the Black lives
to a good old age, say sixty, seventy, or eighty,

and occasionally longer. To the end, of course,
he must hunt, fish, and follow the wanderings of
his tribe. Eminently good tempered and jocose,
the blackfellow is full of *bonhomie*. He is so
given to joking that he never thoroughly takes
to anyone who will not laugh with him. Fun is
a ready passport to his goodwill. His natural
way of life does not subject him to the labour or
anxiety which are the lot of his civilized brother,
to whom, it is needless to say, he is far inferior in
cultivation, morality, generosity, gratitude, truth-
fulness, steadfastness, perseverance, industry, and
the power of long-continued labour. He seems
hardly to feel that lying is wrong, and feels little
compunction at taking human life. I believe
that, on the whole, the blackfellow in his wild
state suffered less and enjoyed life more than the
majority of civilized men. Amongst themselves
the Bangerang were scrupulously honest: nor
had we anything to complain of in this particular
after we had come to understand each other.
Our huts were constantly left unprotected, and
yet it was very rarely, indeed, that anything was
missed. *Mauvaise honte* is unknown to the
Blacks, and they exhibit, as a rule, the most
perfect *aplomb* under all circumstances. They
are keenly alive to ridicule. Notwithstanding
much that was degrading in the position and
practices of what I may call the domesticated
tribes, the blackfellow had decidedly something

of the gentleman about him, when out of the
reach of drunkenness and town influences. Like
the gentleman reduced by circumstances to the
necessities of menial service, he was a good deal
bullied by the white labourer, who lost no opportunity of asserting his superiority over him;
whilst, on the other hand, he was generally
treated by the educated squatter with a familiarity
which argued something of equality, and in
which the white labourer never shared. Though
usually good tempered, the Australian savage is
subject to occasional outbursts of ungovernable
rage, and whilst the fit is on him he will stick at
no brutality. I should think he possesses an
equal aptitude with the whites for comprehending
religious teaching, if not for the practice of
religion. That tribes which have come in
contact with the whites have not been civilized,
is, in my opinion, owing to the fact that their
civilization has never been strongly desired by us,
nor perseveringly attempted. As regards the
aboriginal's inaptitude for steady labour, which on
his first coming in contact with civilization was
so very noticeable, it has already been pretty well
overcome. Even the old have been induced to
work pretty continuously, and to a great extent
have got reconciled to it; whilst, as regards the
schoolmaster, his labours have met with such
marked success that there appears to be but
little difference between the white boy and the

black under his hands. Indeed, as regards rudimentary education, I believe it has been found that the black child is more easily taught than the white. Altogether, the Blacks are a likeable people, and in consequence were generally welcomed at stations. The causes of their popularity were their kindliness, fondness for children, constant flow of spirits, love of fun, *bonhomie*, and the ease with which they accommodated themselves to the likes and dislikes of persons whom they wished to please. Of more important characteristics, unfortunately, one has to speak less favourably. Their stumbling-blocks are puerility and want of character, and the absence of morality and religion, which we have not taught them.

Passing on to other matters, there are in connection with the Bangerang some circumstances particularly noteworthy, as they seem to afford grounds for speculation on the subject of their past history, of a more reliable character than those vague traditions, which, in the majority of cases, are all that can be found to reward the perseverance of the inquirer. Concerning them I may premise by remarking that I shall proceed in what I have to say on the assumption (proof of which it would be out of place to give here, though it exists abundantly) that the progenitors of the Australian tribes landed on the north coast of the continent, and that their descendants, as they increased in numbers, spread along the sea-shore to the east and the west, occupying the land as they went, and peopling, as they met them, the rivers which they encountered flowing from the sea-coast ranges into the ocean or into the interior; disseminating themselves, in fact, in every direction until they had gradually occupied the whole of the continent from sea to sea. The reader then will remember that it has been related that there were nine tribes whose speech was either pure Bangerang or dialects of that tongue, and that they occupied the country between the Goulburn and the Murray rivers from their confluence, and a little below that point, as far east as may be defined by a line drawn from Yarrawonga, on the Murray, to Toolamba on the Goulburn, as well as the country on the north bank of that portion of the Murray, and on the south bank of that portion of the Goulburn. Of these tribes, which closely resembled each other in other particulars besides language, I shall speak collectively in what follows as the Bangerang race.

The reader should also be aware that, as far as is known (probably with some exceptions on the north coast), the several hundred languages found in Australia contain a number of words and grammatical peculiarities common to the whole series, and that, as a rule, the differences between them occur gradually—that one language melts

into the other as it were, so that it is frequently
difficult to decide where the dividing line between
two languages should be drawn ; and that
generally the amount of resemblance or difference
of speech between tribes can be estimated pretty
well by a knowledge of their geographical
situations and the distance and sort of country
which separates them. The ordinary exceptions
to this rule are found in cases in which two
portions of the race took their departure from
some point—say on the north coast, for instance
—by different rivers, the banks of which they
gradually peopled (leaving the arid and less
desirable country between them long unoccupied),
meeting finally again perhaps, after a *hiatus* of
centuries, as such wastes became peopled by an
expanding population ; in which case, as these
unwritten tongues are constantly varying, two
neighbouring tribes would find each other's languages unintelligible, and yet with resemblance
enough between them to prove a common origin.

Now, in the case of the Bangerang race (whose
tongue possesses a fair proportion of the words
generally prevalent throughout Australia), we
find them inhabiting a country on the banks of
two large rivers, and so situated topographically
as to entitle us to expect that their language and
dialects would, following the general rule, present
a mere modification of those in use by the neighbouring tribes ; whereas, on the contrary, we

find them in reality surrounded on all sides by tribes whose speech is lexically more distinct from theirs than English is from French, *the dialects of such surrounding tribes being all intimately connected the one with the other*, and being traceable, step by step, from the Castle-reagh, in New South Wales, by the Lachlan, Murrumbidgee, the Edwards, the Murray, and the Goulburn rivers to the banks of the Yarra Yarra in southern Victoria. It is also singular that the only language in which I can find any resemblance to Bangerang (less the words common throughout the continent above spoken of) is the Goughi tongue, spoken on the Mungalalla Creek, near the Balonne River, some five hundred miles distant.

Another peculiar circumstance bearing on the history of these tribes, to the accuracy of which I can testify, is connected with the native names of the river Goulburn. The Bangerang name for the Goulburn is Kaiela, and, as we have seen, that part of the Bangerang race which inhabited the lower portion of the stream called itself, and was called by the *Bangerang tribes*, Kailtheban, or people of the Kaiela. On the other hand, the Ngooraialum (a fraction of the Castlereagh-descended people which surrounded the Bange-rang race) who dwelt on the Goulburn imme-diately above Toolamba, where the Bangerang territory terminated, called the Goulburn throughout its course Waaring, but always spoke of the Kailtheban, *and not of themselves*, as the Waaringulum, or people of the Waaring.* The only way in which I can account for these facts is by supposing—what I have no doubt occurred—that when the Ngooraialum first saw the Goulburn they found the Bangerang already located on it, and named the river Waaring, and its people Waaringulum, some time before they established themselves on a portion of it.

That this conjecture may receive due weight it is necessary that the reader should know that *illum* (possibly from *yellom*, bark, their huts being made of bark) was the Ngooraialum equivalent for people or tribe; as instances of which it may be noticed that they frequently called the Wangatpan *Wangatpai-illum*, and a white man from Sydney they spoke of as Tidni-illum, and so on; but they never in their own language spoke of themselves as Waaringulum. or people of the Waaring, though they obtained the name of Goulburn Blacks from the whites, and came to use that term when speaking of themselves in English. My conjecture is that their name Ngooraialum sprung from their huts,

* It is noticeable that the Murray is called Kaiela by the Ngarrimowro, whose country is just above Wongat, and that below the country of the Bangerang it bears the name of Mille, and subsequently of Millewa. so far at least as its junction with the Darling.

when they first located themselves on the Goulburn, being at a spot a few miles above Murchison, on the north bank of the river, which they called Ngoorai, and that subsequently that spot came also to be named Ngoorai-illum, or, as the whites now call it, Noorillim.

From these circumstances I have come to the conclusion that, several centuries back, a portion of some tribe on the outskirts of what was then the occupied country—possibly the Mungalalla Creek—absconded, and marched away to the then uninhabited south, and when out of reach of pursuit located themselves somewhere in the vicinity of Yeilima (or Yiilima as I should spell it), from which point they spread as they increased, broke up into nine tribes, and occupied the country which I have already described. That subsequently, after their descendants had remained isolated for a long period, probably a century or two, they were come upon by the advanced portion of the race which had been gradually extending south from the Castlereagh river, and were found speaking several dialects of a language which the new-comers were unable to understand. That as time passed on the descendants of the Castlereagh tribes made their homes in the unoccupied country, gradually surrounding the Bangerang on every side; passed onwards, breaking, as usual, into many tribes, but retaining in their languages those evidences of

21

relationship which seem to the writer a record of the past.

No doubt cases parallel to that of the Bangerang have occurred more than once in the history of our tribes; nor will anyone learned in the ways of the race hesitate as to the cause which led to secessions of the sort. No doubt the common story was, that the elderly men of a tribe having, as usual, appropriated to themselves the young women as wives, some of the latter and a party of the young men eloped, made forced marches far into the unpeopled country, eluded pursuit, established themselves on the banks of some unknown stream, and became the progenitors probably of several tribes before the constantly-advancing stream of population came upon them.

I have given reasons for asserting that the Bangerang tribes were closely related, and formed a sub-section of the aboriginal race, and also that they were isolated for a long period from contact with other tribes. Of the last-mentioned fact another proof occurs to me. It is this. When I settled in their country the Bangerang tribes were all in close alliance, and in a chronic state of war with the Ngooraialum and the other Castlereagh-descended tribes which surrounded them. It must also be understood that one of the features of habitual friendship between tribes is that, though the dialects of such tribes may vary considerably, they have words in common for the terms *the Blacks, wild Blacks,* and frequently for the *negative adverb.* Now, in these terms the Bangerang tribes differed a good deal, which fact, with others which came to my knowledge whilst I lived amongst them, led me to the following conclusion, viz. :—That the Bangerang had not only lived long in seclusion, but that they had existed in a state of chronic warfare amongst themselves, and that the friendly terms on which I found them dated from the time at which the Castlereagh tribes occupied the country all round them and treated them as *wild Blacks*—in other words, as *enemies.*

CHAPTER XXII.

THE WARS OF THE BANGERANG.

In the world's history how little, comparatively, writers have had to say of the concerns of peace, and how much of war! Of this there are many instances, and some ludicrous ones. Lockhart tells a story of Sir Walter Scott, who, being in Paris during the occupation of the Allies after Waterloo, was invited to dinner by Earl Cathcart, who desired to present him to the Emperor

Alexander. On this occasion the Wizard of the North made his appearance (no doubt a good device) dressed in the red and blue uniform of the Selkirkshire Yeomanry Cavalry, in which corps he held a lieutenant's commission; and the Czar, overlooking, as of small importance, Sir Walter Scott's world-wide literary fame, questioned him, as was his wont, about the engagements in which he had taken part. In view of His Majesty's known prepossessions on the subject of soldiers, Scott found himself constrained to allude in reply to the actions of Cross-Causeway and Moredun-Mill, little known out of Selkirkshire, when the host came to his relief, and dexterously led the conversation into some happier channel, rejoiced, no doubt, that his illustrious countryman had been able slightly to mystify the imperial brain. But though, since the stirring times of the first Napoleon, neither rulers nor ruled have been quite so much engrossed with fighting matters as they used to be, still throat-cutting is natural to the species; and no doubt, in spite of peace parties, interest will always attach to the wars of peoples, civilized or savage, a circumstance which must be my excuse for saying something on the subject of Bangerang homicides.

When a tribe in our neighbourhood had a substantial grievance against another which admitted of adjustment, such as the violation of their territory or the abduction of some of their women, it was usually fought out in broad daylight with spears, boomerangs, and waddies ; and the scene of a score or two of active savages doing their best to kill each other with such weapons was not unpleasant to look on, when it was borne in mind that the *fracas* would probably result in nothing worse than a few ugly gashes and contused heads, and a general make-up when all was over. In my experience I never knew anyone killed in such engagements, though I have seen some narrow escapes, so dexterous were the combatants in the use of their shields and so quick of sight. The consequence was that the whites came to look on these encounters rather in the light of rough *assauts d'armes* than battles. When a real hatred and blood-thirst took possession of a tribe, matters proceeded very differently.

Amongst the Bangerang, as indeed amongst the whole of the tribes of Australia, so far as is known, the cause. not of fights, but of bloodshed, if we go to the root of the matter, was, nine times out of ten, the belief that the deaths of persons, no matter from what apparent cause other than old age, were attributable to the spells and incantations of some of their enemies—their enemies including all Blacks not their intimate friends and neighbours. This was an ever active and fundamental idea of the aboriginal mind, and

their hatred and fear of an enchanter were
infinitely greater than of a man who had slain
one of their tribe in fair fight with his spear.
With the deaths of women and young children
the Blacks did not generally much concern themselves, but to the savage machinations of wizards
were attributed, as I have said, all deaths,
whether from disease or accident; and for every
adult male who died from any cause save old age,
a corresponding victim was anxiously desired,
though fortunately not always sought by force of
arms, from the supposed offending tribe. Generally, indeed, revenge was gratified by counter-
incantations. When more active measures were
had recourse to, any adult member of the supposed
offending tribe would do as an expiatory victim,
though the death of a man was considered much
more satisfactory than that of even a young
woman. In connection with the history of our
aborigines there is, perhaps, no more important
circumstance than this; for this belief in the
taking of life by incantation, in its immediate and
collateral consequences, was the bane of the race.
It systematized murder throughout the continent,
rendered the friendship of the tribes at large
impossible, and was the great factor of savagery
and degradation.

Of these native wars and assassinations I will
proceed to relate an instance or two.

In the Kailtheban section of the Bangerang

people there was a fine, stalwart, jolly fellow, who, amongst the whites, rejoiced in the name of Pepper. Master Pepper, in 1845, the period to which I refer, was about twenty-six years of age, stood five feet eleven inches in height, and weighed thirteen stone or more. He was a bachelor, good-looking in his way, a first-class workman with spear and waddy, and one of the merriest and most genial souls alive, so that it was no wonder that he was a favourite in his tribe and beyond it.

It happened, however, one day, whilst Pepper was engaged with some others of the tribe in opossum-hunting, that the limb of the tree along which he was walking gave way and precipitated him to the ground. The height from which he fell was, I understood, about sixty feet, and the ground being rough and hard he was terribly injured, so that, after lingering for a few hours in a state of insensibility, the poor fellow died. The death of even one warrior being a calamity to a tribe, Pepper's death was of course the cause of much rage and grief in Bangerang, and many were the vows that the tribe of the enchanter who had caused the branch to break should pay the full penalty of the deed.

A few hours after Pepper's demise, the corpse was prepared for burial. Duly swathed in old opossum-rugs, the knees drawn up to the chin and the arms fastened to the side, the body assumed the shape of a large ball. It was then placed on a sheet of bark and borne by the men of the party, followed by the rest of the camp, to the nearest sand-hill, a distance of several miles. Sand-hills were selected as burial places on account of their easy digging, hollowing out a grave in the stiff clay with nothing but pointed sticks being a work of very great labour. Arrived at the place of interment, a hole large enough to receive the corpse was sunk about four feet in the sand. Whilst this was being done by a few of the party, the rest, to the number of about five-and-twenty, sat quietly round, smoking their pipes and talking of their ordinary affairs. The grave completed, the body was quickly consigned to its last resting place, one blackfellow descending into the tomb to arrange the corpse on its side. At this juncture the onlookers arose to their feet, and, with that facility for passing from laughter to sorrow so characteristic of the race, gave vent to lamentations and yells which might be heard a mile off. The men beat their heads with the butts of their iron tomahawks until the blood streamed over their faces and backs, whilst the women (especially the old ladies, who were always prominent actors in such scenes) proceeded to burn their thighs, sides, and stomachs with fire-sticks, amidst general cries of lamentation. After a time, when these paroxysms of grief had subsided, a sheet of bark, rather larger than the grave, was stripped from a neighbouring tree and placed over the remains in a somewhat arched form. On this were laid logs which had been cut into suitable lengths; and finally the sand was filled in, and heaped into a mound, some two feet in height and seven in length. An oblong space of about fifteen feet in length was then cleared around the tomb, swept smooth, and the war spear of the deceased, decorated at the point with a plume of emu feathers, reddened with ochre, was driven firmly into the sand at the head of the grave; a simple ornament which always struck me as particularly picturesque and appropriate. Finally, a slight fence of green boughs was erected round the spot, and the mourners returned in silence to a camp which they had made not far off; those more nearly related to the deceased to plaster their heads with mud and daub their faces with pipeclay.

The following morning, just before daylight (and at the same hour for months after), arose from the camp that long-drawn-out wail of some female relative of the deceased, which persons familiar with our Blacks forty years ago will no doubt remember. Here and there also, had any-one stood in the camp, might have been noticed a woman sitting at her fire, silently weeping as she listened to the song of sorrow. Shortly after sunrise the men, spear in hand (for no one ever left the camp without at least one spear), went

over to the new grave. Entering its enclosure,
they scanned with eager eyes the tracks which
worms and other insects had left on the recently-
disturbed surface. Concerning these tracks, I
was told by my brother, who was present, that
there was a good deal of discussion, as in the eyes
of the Blacks, as we all know, they were believed
to be marks left by the wizard whose incantations had killed the man, and who was supposed
to have flown through the air during the night
to visit the grave of his victim. The only difficulty was to assign any particular direction to
the tracks, as in fact they wandered to and from
every point of the compass. At length one
young man, pointing with his spear to some
marks which took a north-westerly direction,
exclaimed, in an excited manner, " Look here!
Who are they who live in that direction ? Who
are they but our enemies, who so often have
waylaid, murdered, and bewitched Bangerang
men ? Let us go and kill them." As Pepper's
death was held to be an act particularly atrocious,
this outburst jumped with the popular idea of
the tribe, and was welcomed with a simultaneous
yell of approval which was heard at the camp,
whence the shrill voices of the women re-echoed
the cry.

The principal point being settled, and all doubt
as to who caused Pepper's death being thus
removed from the Bangerang mind, grave

deliberations followed for many days around the camp-fires. The main body of the tribe was collected, and messengers sent to the neighbours to learn whether they had any objections to an onslaught on the devoted people, as, owing to the intermarriages of tribes, difficulties sometimes arose in such cases. Spies, too, went quickly into the hostile country to gain information as to the whereabouts of its inhabitants. These preliminaries having been gone through, those men of the Bangerang who chose to be of the party, and one or two volunteers from neighbouring tribes, started on the war-path. As they had a long forced march before them, and they had agreed to go entirely without fire and to leave their tomahawks behind, lest the smoke and the noise of chopping out opossums should discover their presence to their intended victims, they applied at the last moment to my brother, who was on the station at the time, for a small quantity of flour, with which, of course, he declined to supply them. All being ready, and the dogs secured in the camp to prevent their following, the war party, consisting of some fifteen men, one by one, clubs and spears in hand, without a syllable of adieu to wife or child, took their departure, the sable forms of the dusky warriors, who gradually fell into Indian file, being quickly lost to sight amidst the shades of the forest. What occurred on the occasion of this expedition

was related to me some time after by more than
one of the actors in it, and may be taken as a
fair specimen of Australian warfare. It was as
follows :—

On leaving their own country the party proceeded stealthily, and chiefly by night marches,
to the neighbourhood of Thule station, visiting
on their way those spots (known to one of the
volunteers) at which parties of the doomed tribe
were likely to be found. After several days'
wandering from place to place, subsisting on a
few roots hurriedly dug up, and suffering considerably from hunger and fatigue, they caught
sight, as they were skulking about towards sundown, of a small encampment, without being
themselves seen, upon which they retired and
hid in a clump of reeds. About two o'clock in
the morning the war-party left their hiding place
and returned to the neighbourhood of the camp,
and having divested themselves of every shred
of clothing, and painted their faces with pipe-
clay, they clutched their spears and clubs, and,
walking slowly and noiselessly on, soon found
themselves standing over their sleeping victims.

I can well realize the scene, for I have often
heard such described. Had there been an on-
looker at that moment near the camp, he would
have observed in front of the mia-mias several
small fires, some smouldering, some burning up
brightly, and, to windward of them, the recum-

bent figures of perhaps a dozen sleepers, little
and big, wrapped in their opossum-rugs. Close
by some of them he would have seen a number
of spears stuck upright in the ground, showing
where the men lay, and almost in the ashes
of the fires a pack of half-starved dogs.
Directing his eyes to the distance, he might
then have become vaguely sensible of some dark
objects in motion. If they had attracted his
attention, it would have been, however, only for
a moment, as their speedy fading from sight
would probably have led him to imagine them to
be only the result of changing clouds, and moonlight in the forest. Suddenly he would once more
have caught sight of the dusky shapes, but this
time unmistakably, and nearer at hand. Then
he would have watched their approach, now lost
amidst the shadows of the trees, now re-appear-
ing and flitting lightly over spaces shone on by
the moon. Had he been a novice in such matters,
even then he might have failed to realize the
import of what was passing before his eyes, so
shadow-like and silent would have been the apparition. By degrees, however, the objects he
was observing would become more distinct: he
would recognize them to be men, naked, armed
with spear and club, bent nearly double, and approaching with quick noiseless steps. Soon they
would be at hand; within the halo of the camp-
fires, standing erect; when circles of white clay

around the eyes, and streaks of the same material along the ribs and legs, giving them the ghastly look of skeletons, would become visible. He would now see the expanded chest, the inflated nostrils, the flashing eyes of the sinister visitors.

According to native custom no one was on watch at the camp, and I have often heard the Blacks say that their half-starved dogs seldom gave the alarm in cases of strange Blacks, though they would bark if the intruders were white men. Arrived at the fires, the attacking party paused a moment, held the points of their spears in the flames and allowed them to burn a little, so that another pang might be added to the wound they were about to inflict; then with their fingers they gently raised the rugs a little from the chests of the doomed wretches, and at a given signal, with a simultaneous yell, plunged their long barbed spears into the bosoms or backs of the sleepers. Then from the mia-mias, which were quickly overturned, came the shrieks of the dying, the screams of the women and children, blows of clubs, the vociferation of the prostrate, who were trying to defend themselves; the barking of the dogs and the yells of the assailants, who numbered fully three to one. Altogether it was a ghastly, horrible scene that the pale moon looked down on that night at Thule; and with its enactment it might be thought that the death of Pepper had been avenged to the full. Such,

however, was not the case. Whilst the massacre
was in progress, the men in the camp being
troublesome to despatch, as each struggled des-
perately as long as he was able, and with an
energy which few white men are masters of when
grievously wounded, a number of women and
children had made good their escape. These, it
was rightly judged, would return to the camp
after some hours, and to wait their coming and
murder them was at once determined on. With
this view the assailants betook themselves, whilst
it was yet dark, to a patch of scrub close at hand,
having first mutilated the slain in the most horrible manner, torn out the kidney-fat from the
wreaking corpses, burnt the camp utensils, and
possessed themselves of such food as was to be
found.

From their lurking-place the half-starved
savages watched the camp until shortly after
sunrise, when the defenceless mourners made
their appearance and were at once seized. What
followed cannot be described. At last all were
killed, except one young woman, whom a blackfellow rescued from the slaughter and took away
as his wife. Her fate, however, was not long
delayed, for, on the march home, which was
begun at once, a brute, whose thirst for blood
was unusually deep, walked up behind her and
knocked her brains out with his club. After the
slaughter of the women and children, daylight

disclosed the fact that one of the attacking party, a volunteer from a neighbouring tribe—the murderer of the young woman—had slain his own brother in the *melée* without recognizing him.

One evening, late, a few days after these occurrences, I was at home when the war-party reached their camp at Tongala, to which they had returned by forced marches. Plump and greasy when they started, they were now wasted in frame and haggard in feature. Their habitual kindliness of manner and *bonhomie* were gone, and in place of them there was nothing but boasting and braggadocio, and a sort of look difficult to analyze, but, as it seemed to me, expressive of guilty fear. The night of their return, though a reprisal was apprehended, I noticed they adhered to their custom of not keeping watch, and we felt relieved, the next morning, when the whole horde commenced its retreat of a hundred miles up the Goulburn. During the absence of the war-party, those left behind used to say that the ghost of Pepper appeared constantly at night to the chief conjurer, to whom he had given a clay pipe of a different pattern from any previously known in the camp, and also to his sister-in-law, to whom he had taught a new corroboree, which she sang, and which was afterwards in vogue. Except statements of this sort, showing a good deal of childishness and deceit, and the peep-of-day wailings of the women which were still to be heard even when the tribe returned to our neighbourhood some months later, nothing further was said about Pepper.

As another instance of the bloodthirsty proceedings of the Blacks, which, happily, were not of frequent occurrence, may be related the fate of a youth in my employment. Jimmy-Jack, as he was called, was a Bangerang boy of about fifteen years of age. Of a particularly mild disposition, he seemed to take to civilized ways more easily than his fellows; and for that reason, though he was somewhat less robust than others of his age, he was installed in the post of "general useful" about the place, in which capacity his obliging disposition made him quite a favourite. The boy took his meals in the kitchen, his duties being to get up the saddle horses and working bullocks in the morning, accompany the wool dray to town occasionally, and ride with my brother and myself when we went out kangarooing or duck shooting, with other light services of the sort. After Jimmy had been a year or so in our service, and, as the effects of his residence in the kitchen, had got to shine all over like a well-polished boot, it happened that I was setting out on one of my periodical hunting trips (of which I shall have something to say in a subsequent chapter), and that I asked the boy if he would like to accompany me. As, however, he preferred

22

remaining at Colbinabbin, I left him to the care of the four worthies then resident at that out-station. These individuals, I remember, were, like most of my servants, rather a nondescript lot, and consisted of the hut-keeper, Antonio Fiore, a native of Calabria, and originally a sailor, who (though, as far as I had experience of him, a good servant and an honest old fellow enough) I always used to fancy might possibly, in his youth, have had some slight experience of the gentle craft of pirating in the West Indies. Besides Antony, there were three shepherds—one of whom, in days gone by, had been huntsman to a crack pack of fox-hounds in the Green Isle; the second had found his way from the same country to Australia, as the result of his connection with some secret society and an unlucky blow with his shillalah; the third being an active young Scot, who, if he had not seen the view about which that playful old lion, Sam Johnson, twitted Bozzy as the one which possessed the greatest charms for the dwellers in the land of cakes—i.e., *the road to England*—had, at all events, availed himself of the, perhaps, not less agreeable track to Australia. In charge of these four worthies I thought the boy quite safe, no danger, indeed, being apprehended. On my return to Colbinabbin, however, a month later, from the trip to which I have referred, I received from old Antony the following account of his fate.

Some few days after I left the place, it appears that four strange Blacks from the neighbourhood of Hamilton's Sugar-loaf came to the hut. They were unaccompanied by women or children, and as soon as Jimmy saw them he said in a somewhat excited manner that they had come to kill him. The strangers camped at a little distance from the hut, to which, however, they constantly came during the day, as Blacks will, pretending to be friendly, the poor boy making them presents of tobacco and other trifles. When the shepherds brought their flocks to the folds that night, they heard of the arrival of the Blacks and of Jimmy's forebodings, and the young Scot, with native good sense, endeavoured to get the poor fellow to make a start for Tongala during the night, and so give his enemies the slip, offering very kindly to accompany him with his gun for several miles on his road, so as to see him past all danger. This, however, the boy declined to do, alleging that he could not walk the intervening five-and-thirty miles, as there was no water on the road; the true reason, I fancy, from the inquiries I made, being, that he was paralyzed with fear—fascinated by his enemies. Be this as it may, the Scot next day loaded the only gun at the hut, and insisted on Jimmy accompanying him out shepherding, giving the Blacks to understand that he would shoot any of them who attempted to follow him. They, however, disclaimed any intentions of mischief, and remained some days at the place, Jimmy always going out with the shepherd.

On the fourth morning they came to the hut at breakfast time to say good-bye, and then started, as they said, for their own country. The unwelcome visitors having left, it was thought unnecessary for Jimmy to go out with the shepherd, so he remained with old Antony at the hut, and shortly after breakfast was bending over a sheep which the hut-keeper was skinning, when they heard the exclamation "Waugh!" and were raising their heads when Jimmy's back was pierced by a heavy jagged spear, which went clean through and pinned him to the ground. The weapon was hurled by one of the four Blacks thought to have left, who had approached unobserved, and now stood close to Antony and the boy, naked and painted for murder. Two of these wretches then seized old Antony, half-dead with fright, and hurried him to the hut, threatening his life in case of resistance; whilst a few blows of a club completed the murder of the boy. The corpse was then carried off by the murderers, and was found floating in the creek a few days afterwards, the kidney-fat having been abstracted through an incision in the side. I need hardly speak of the sorrow and indignation which this catastrophe caused me, especially as I well knew there were no hopes of bringing the murderers to justice.

Besides these disgusting assassinations, without a description of which the life of an Australian savage would be but ill understood, fights between tribes and individuals also occurred occasionally in the locality about which I am speaking. These were usually the result of acts which, according to their code, were injurious in a minor degree only, and were atoned for by fighting, and, of course, the risk of death or wounds, as used to be the case in duels. Of encounters of this description I saw several at one time or another. One of them was on a fine autumn morning as I was about to take a plunge in the river.

As I passed by the camp on my way to the water, I could see the Blacks rolled up in their opossum-rugs, taking their morning nap. The air was somewhat chilly, and here and there an old man sat before the fire, which he had drawn together, smoking the heel of his pipe and warming his fingers in the blaze. As I stood for a moment looking about me, the sun appeared through the trees red and round, when a young Towroonban Black, called Monoorumbe, got on his legs, gazed on the sleepers, stretched himself, took up some reed spears, his throwing stick, two shields, a boomerang, and a club, and walked about fifty yards on to the plain. "There!" said he in his own language as, drawing himself up, he turned round and faced the camp. "There!" repeated the savage; and his exclamation, and the rattle of his shields and club as he threw them on the ground beside him, seemed to awake some of the sleepers, who sat up, rubbed their eyes and looked about, but did not speak. As these were the premonitory symptoms of a fight, of course I halted, towel in hand, to witness it. At first, matters went on a little slowly. Monoorumbe was still alone, standing at his ease in the sunshine, covered with his opossum-rug. He leant lightly on two or three reed spears, which he held in his right hand; the sole of his left foot resting on the opposite thigh. As yet no one moved in the camp, so he again broke silence. "Ngooraialum men," said the Tow-roonban, "talk at night in the camp and say they'll fight when the sun comes. When the sun comes they forget to fight—they sleep. I spit on them." And so he spat demonstratively on the ground. At this juncture the shrill voice of a middle-aged woman gave vent to one or two rather uncomplimentary phrases; then came a reply from a younger female, when most of the persons at the camp sat up. Then followed a rejoinder, when the young woman dropped the rug from her shoulders, and, dragging it along the ground in her left hand, walked threateningly towards the elder woman, abusing her at the top of her voice.

This dragging the rug along the ground was always the culminating sign of anger in the

female; the men occasionally dropped theirs
entirely when moved to much anger, but the
women never let theirs go altogether. At this
juncture two or three female relations seized the
young woman, and forced her to cover herself
and be seated. Next followed a little delicate
abuse from our early-rising friend, Monoorumbe,
when a young man at the Ngooraialum fire called
out in contradiction, "Thago" (No!) "I spit on
you!" said the Towroonban. "Yes; and did you
ever spit blood?" was the reply; and with these
words the Ngooraialum rose, deliberately conveyed
his weapons one by one from the ground to his
hands, by the medium of his toes, shoved a
boomerang through a belt of opossum skin which
he wore round his waist, and stalked majestically
on to the plain. The combatants now stood
facing each other about thirty yards apart, the
manly attitudes of the savage erect and on foot
offering a marked contrast to the figure presented
when squatting at his fire. "Pir" (proceed),
said Monoorumbe, and simultaneously they let
fall their opossum-rugs on the ground. "Take
that!" said the Towroonban, who had shipped
on his *yoolwa*, or throwing stick, one of the reed
spears, which he now launched at his foe.

All that listlessness of manner common to
persons who have just awoke, and so noticeable a
few moments back, had now left the combatants,
and every nerve was braced to the utmost, for a

spear well planted is death. The right arm of
Monoorumbe was no sooner thrown back than
the Ngooraialum was in position, his shield
before him, his knees and back well bent, and his
left shoulder in advance. As the spear came on,
he sprung forward a pace, quivering his shield in
his left hand, and with it touched the light
weapon which flew swiftly towards him breast
high from the ground, deflecting it from its
well-aimed course. Then followed another spear,
which the Ngooraialum, stepping aside, avoided.
A third nearly fell short, and he only raised his
right foot, the weapon sticking quivering in the
spot vacated. The next was better thrown, and
the defendant only just escaped its entering his
loins by bending his back till I thought it would
have broken. He had miscalculated its flight a
few inches, and a half-shy smile, such as one may
see on a schoolboy's face when caught tripping at
cricket, came over his countenance at this want of
dexterity, which had well-nigh cost him his life.
"There!" said Monoorumbe, as he paused, his
spears all thrown. It was now the Ngooraialum's
turn, within a few yards of whom I was standing.
A savage shadow passed over the smile which had
been on his face. He now meant to do his best
to kill his adversary, so, clutching his boomerang
by its extremity, he drew it deliberately from his
belt. This weapon, as the reader probably knows,
is in shape very like a scimitar without the

handle, but broader and thicker. The Ngoo-raialum drew it out, held it opposite his cheek, turned it once or twice from side to side by a movement of his wrist, as if to calculate its weight, threw back his right arm and leg, and then, with a step forward, hurled it at his adversary. Straight flew the she-oak blade, with a hurtling sound, such as the hawk makes when, almost grazing your horse, he swoops on a quail which your kangaroo dogs have flushed from the grass. Just in time to save his head, Monoo-rumbe stepped to one side, raised his shield, and let the missile pass by. Then followed three or four spears, thrown with great force and accuracy, which the Towroonban deftly turned aside with his shield.

At this stage of proceedings the old men in the camp interfered, to prohibit the throwing of more spears, suggesting that enough had been done in that line to satisfy the *pundonor* upon which the misunderstanding had arisen, inviting the combatants to conclude the business with shield and waddy, from which——so thick is the aboriginal skull—little danger used to be apprehended. To this the combatants consented. In a moment they laid aside the weapons they had been using, and stood foot to foot, a heavy shield in the left hand and a club in the right. Their left shoulders were in advance, the weight of the body being supported by the right leg, the shield and club forming an arch over the head. Then followed blow after blow in quick succession, yielding a jarring sound when warded off by the shield, and a soft thud when the club fell on the flesh. The bronze-coloured combatants were well matched, lithe, and strong. Resolute, and savage of aspect, their keen eyes glistened from under their heavy over-hanging brows. They fought hard, but, as it seemed to me, without *acharnement*. The exertion, however, was so great that it could not be long upheld. As an exhibition of the primitive fighting of savage men, the passage of arms might have found favour as an interlude in the Flavian amphitheatre. On this occasion, however, the *habet* would not have been heard, for, after a time, the friends on both sides again interfered and stopped the fight, the combatants being much gashed about the head, and blood flowing freely ; a dazed, drunken sort of look being the expression of their faces as they walked back to the camp.

CHAPTER XXIII.

COLBINABBIN TAKEN UP.

I HAVE already related that I took up Coragorag in August, 1843. In the January following I squatted on Colbinábbin Creek, occupying subsequently Cócoma, Dírra, Wóllenjo, Gargárro, Námerong, and Ullumbúbbil, which gave the station (inclusive of two large gaps) a length of between fifty and sixty miles from end to end, with an area of more than three hundred square miles, as will be seen by reference to the map of the station. But though most of our occupations of country had some little history connected with them, I think, out of regard to my readers' patience, and in fear of the *Ohe! jam satis,* I must restrict myself to that of Colbinabbin, which came about in this way. During the months of November and December, 1843, a fire had run over the Púrnewong, Corágorag, Gargárro, Colbinábbin, Wongúlta (now pronounced *one halter*), Gobérip, Redcastle, and Rushworth country, and how much beside I cannot say. Where, or in what manner, such fire originated, nobody in those days troubled themselves to inquire, or thought much about. Probably this one was set a-going by someone burning a patch of country near the Campaspe to lamb his sheep on ; or by a black-fellow dropping a fire-stick whilst travelling from one water to another. At all events, constant clouds of smoke visible at Tongala made it evident that an extensive conflagration was going on in that part of the country. Some time, however, in December it was extinguished by a heavy downpour of rain, which occurred just as I was on the point of making a trip to town. As the reader is aware, I had several times crossed the Colbinabbin Plains in 1841 and 1842, when the creek was almost destitute of water ; and it will, no doubt, seem natural that, as my father's flocks were increasing, and that for country, like other things, *l'appétit vient en mangeant*, I should wish to become possessed of so fine a sheep-run. Indeed, almost the first time I saw Colbinabbin, I made up my mind to take it up as soon as heaven sent it a supply of water.

Such being my intention, it occurred to me, on my road to town, that no time should be lost in applying for a license, as the late heavy fall of rain on the burnt ground must certainly have flooded the creek. Accordingly, on reaching Melbourne a day or two later, happening to meet the Commissioner of Crown Lands in the street, I made a verbal application for the country. Whether, however, the Commissioner, whom I had always found very ready to grant the applications which I considered myself entitled to make, had begun to think them of too frequent recurrence, or what, I cannot say; but, at all events, he hesitated on this occasion, and only consented to grant my application on the condition that I should be the first to put stock on the country. This decision I remember rather annoyed me at the time, as it seemed unreasonable in itself, and I had made up my mind to remain a few weeks in town, which I now felt myself unable to do with any satisfaction, as it struck me that the Commissioner, who was likely to be informed on such points, might know someone beside myself who was enamoured of Colbinabbin, and that delay in the matter might be fatal. The consequence was, that, the morning after our interview, I started hurriedly for Tongala—not, however, by the Goulburn road, by which I had come to town, but by the Campaspe, as I was afraid that my unexpectedly early return might lead to suspicions about Colbinabbin, if any one of my neighbours was really thinking of taking it up. Pushing on, I got over the hundred and fifty miles between Melbourne and Tongala early on the third day, having learned from a blackfellow on the road that the Colbinabbin plains were, as I expected, covered with magnificent feed, and the creek full to the brim. As it happened, the further I rode, the more I thought of the subject, and the more uneasy I became lest someone should be beforehand with me; so, when I arrived at my hut, I set to work to get ready to cross from

the north to the south bank of the Goulburn the
flock of scabby sheep with which I intended to
occupy the new run. Next day, by making a
great effort, this was managed, and the flock
started on the road; my brother, who conducted
the expedition, taking two men with him, and
on the bullock-dray, which was about to start
for town with lambs' wool, such provisions and
tools as would be immediately wanted. As, however, boilers, materials for dressing sheep, and
other bulky articles, for which there was no room
on top of the wool, required to be sent out, I
determined to ride over to Kotoopna, a station
some fifteen miles off, and borrow a horse-dray
in which to convey them.

Starting early next morning I found my neighbour at home, who very kindly placed his dray
and harness at my disposal, so that so far I was
fortunate. There were, however, two difficulties
in the way of my making use of it which had to
be overcome, for the dray was on the wrong side
of the Goulburn—a deep and awkward stream to
cross, as the reader is aware—and my chestnut
mare which I was riding had never been in
harness, and might object to be utilized in that
way. However, as I was not possessed of a
draught horse, there was no choice but to try
what could be done with the chestnut, or wait a
month inactive for the return of the bullock-dray.
So, as no harm could come of trying, I set to

work at once to get the dray across the river.
As there was neither boat nor log-punt at the
station, this had to be done by floating it, the
first step being to lower it down an almost
perpendicular bank of twenty feet to the water's
edge by means of a bullock-hide rope passed
round a tree. Having accomplished this with
the assistance of my neighbour and his cook
(the only two persons at the head station), we
lashed a cask on the centre of the dray, leaving
about ten feet of the rope as a painter with which
to tow it across the stream. That job fell, of
course, to my lot, and I remember it cost me as
severe a struggle as anything of the sort I ever
undertook, though at that time I was a good
swimmer. Everything being ready, we pushed
off the dray, and, taking the painter between my
teeth, I struck out for the opposite bank, or
rather for a sandspit on the other side about a
hundred yards below the point of departure.
To overcome whilst swimming the *vis inertiæ* of
so heavy and clumsy a body as a dray, and
keep it progressing athwart stream, was, as I
have said, a difficult task, and I only accomplished it after a hard struggle and any amount
of " buffeting with lusty sinews."

Arrived at the sandspit, I was met by the
cook, who had crossed over in a miserable bark
canoe which seemed as likely to sink as to swim,
and with him unlashed the cask, and, having

improvised a sort of rough Spanish windlass, with much trouble we got the dray up an inclining bank on to the level ground.

So far, all had gone well, and it only remained to be seen whether I should be able to get the chestnut, who had never had a collar on in her life, to perform her part of the business. At that time, I may remark, I had never seen a horse put into harness for the first time, and was quite ignorant of the process, or possibly I should not have undertaken what I did; but with the blissful inexperience of a young bear whose troubles are all to come, and with a helpmate more ignorant than myself, I set to work at once to grapple with the remaining difficulty. On this occasion a facility which my friends used to say I had with horses possibly stood me in good stead and supplied the place of experience. At all events, having put on the harness, I mounted the mare and rode her about a bit, and then put on the winkers, allowing her to feed for a while on the grass, whilst I held the rein and had a smoke and yarn with the cook, who was a sailor by trade, about windlasses and purchases generally.

When " old Mary," as we called her, had got a little accustomed to the harness, with the assistance of the cook I put her quietly into the shafts—for she was so used to my ways that she would allow me to do almost anything with her—and with very little trouble, though a very old lady, got her started, and carried off my dray in triumph. The next day, loading it with about twelve hundredweight of necessary articles, I set out, with one of my men, to follow the sheep to Colbinabbin. The distance we had to go was about thirty-five miles, which took three days to accomplish, for the ground was rough, and I did not care to distress the mare with the unaccustomed work. Altogether, though I was anxious about the occupation of Colbinabbin, the trip was enjoyable enough; the plains, at the time fresh and verdant, abounding in turkeys, ducks, emu, quail, and ibis, some of which I knocked over, and out of which I learned my brother had made a fine bag as he went along. Indeed, in our part of the country there was no better shot or keener hunter than my brother Richard, who had also an intuitive knowledge of the ways of animals, wild and tame, which I have seldom seen equalled, and never surpassed.

Arrived at Colbinabbin, I was delighted to find my party in undisturbed occupation, and that the little serpentine creek, embosomed in trees, now full to overflowing, and the green rolling plains and picturesque ranges were indeed possessions of my father. Of course, only squatting possessions, which, however, before the discovery of gold it was generally thought would last our time at least. As for the value of the country thus secured, it could easily have been sold for a thousand pounds even in those times, so that we had every reason to be pleased.

The day after my arrival we set to work to make a hut for the men, the sheep camping without any trouble in the bend of the creek, which is now Mr. Winter's garden. We had also to cut down a number of trees, and put up some bough-yards, in which to erect a bullock-hide dip for the sheep, as I had determined to clean our last scabby flock.

The arrangement of the new station, putting up an extra hut or two, &c., and dipping the sheep occupied about a month; and I remember I was sitting one evening, shortly after my arrival, on a water-keg before the fire, covered with dust, and very dirty, smoking a quiet pipe, when one of a party of Blacks who had found us out, and camped close by, informed me that three horse-men were coming over the plain. Of course we wondered who they were, and what their business. Half-an-hour solved the question, as the trio proved to be my neighbour from the Toolamba station, with his storekeeper and a blackfellow; the two white men being armed with guns. As was the custom, I invited them to dismount, and ordered tea to be made. My neighbour, whom I installed on the keg, appeared to be in the worst of humours, and it soon came out that he had taken up Wongulta creek, which lay some five miles to the eastward, and had come over to Colbinabbin (which he had also decided to occupy, not knowing that I had been beforehand with him) for the purpose of determining the site of the hut which he meant to erect there for his men. It rather amused me that my neighbour, having no one else to make a confidant of, in a very complaining sort of way sought my sympathy in his disappointment; especially when he informed me that he had never seen the country before that day, but only heard of it from the Blacks, and that he now regretted exceedingly my having forestalled him. "I cannot tell you," said he, "how much annoyed I am at finding you here. I had no idea what fine country this is. I thought you held a large country on the Murray, and did not expect to find sheep of yours out here."

Whether puerility or pure selfishness predominated in these remarks of my neighbour, the reader can judge for himself. I merely laughed and said, "I might say the same of your occupation of Wongulta;" but that I had injured him was, I could see, a fixed idea in his mind. Having finished his pot of tea and met with no sympathy, my neighbour very shortly got up to go. As he was mounting his horse an expression escaped him that led me to infer that he intended to dispute my right to the country, and send a flock of his sheep on to the creek for that purpose. Not appearing to notice his words, I said carelessly, "How I regret I cannot, like you, leave this rough work behind me and ride home. However, in another fortnight the sheep-dressing will be over and I shall be at liberty." "What," said he, with something almost fierce in his tone, "are your sheep scabby?" "Oh yes," I replied, "this flock is a little so, and I have brought it here to be out of the way." This answer rendered his bringing his sheep near mine, for the purpose of disputing my possession, out of the question, and was, I think, the last drop of bitterness in his cup that day: at all events he turned his horse's head and rode away without a word in reply. But peace to his ashes! Though he was only a young man at that time, it is now nearly thirty years since, as the result of losing in the old country the money he had realized on the Goulburn, he laid violent hands on himself.

My sheep had not, I think, been more than six months at Colbinabbin, to which I had also brought a second flock, when the owner of the Ardpatrick, or Cooma station, on the Goulburn, sent a couple of flocks to the plains, locating them about five miles from my hut on a water-hole called Tongalum, which lies at the southern extremity of Paboinboolok, or Lake Cooper, as it is now called. Their owner was the person of whom the reader has heard before as entertaining inimical feelings towards the unfortunate " Prince

Chairlie;" the same who good-naturedly lent me
his mare on an occasion when I was hard up for
a mount. Though at the time the country
absolutely abounded with grass, and, save where
my Toolamba neighbour and myself had located
ourselves, was unoccupied and unclaimed in every
direction, my Cooma friend persisted in feeding
his sheep on what I considered to be my country.
This no doubt was natural enough in a purely
selfish point of view, as he was merely endea-
vouring to provide for the future by establishing
through occupation a claim to as much of the
country as lay between our two huts as he was
able, leaving to the future his boundary battles in
other directions with new arrivals when they
should come.

Though I took this proceeding in high dudgeon,
we met, nevertheless, to talk the matter over in an
amicable way; but as we failed to agree, I made
an application to the Commissioner of Crown
Lands to define the boundary line between us.
Of that official, and his multifarious duties in his
district, I have already spoken; but I may repeat
that not the least important of them were to
grant licenses to squat, to decide the amount of
run to which the stock in possession of each one
entitled him, and to determine the boundaries of
runs. To the discharge of these functions, on
which depended results most important to every
sheepowner, the Commissioner of our district

brought, it was pretty generally agreed, I believe, a thorough impartiality, unaccompanied, unfortunately, by much common sense or business habits. In accepting my applications for country, for instance, I never saw him mark a tree, take a compass-bearing, or make a memorandum—a neglect which, if a common practice with him, as I believe it was, accounts for much of the subsequent disagreement and litigation between run-holders; and yet I think I am correct in saying that even his autocratic and lax mode of doing business was held generally to be more satisfactory than the cost and delay which would inevitably have accompanied any elaborate system. But though the official acts of public men are fair subjects for comment, I should have abstained from relating what follows, had it not been that the gentleman to whom I refer is no longer alive, whilst the failure of duty which occurs in my story will, I hope, be found of a nature not calculated to trouble any of the friends he has left behind. Indeed, but few will recognize the gentleman to whom I refer, who, with many good qualities, had, like the rest of us, no doubt, his weak points.

The Commissioner's reply to my application about the boundaries reached me at Tongala, I think, two or three months after it had been made; a letter appointing a day of meeting at Colbinabbin for the purpose of settling

the question being delivered to me by one of
his troopers, a few days in advance. On the
morning before the day specified, I remember
I left Tongala on a well-bred, showy young
horse, of which I was not a little proud, and
which it gave me pleasure to think would attract
the admiration of the party I was about to meet
at Colbinabbin. This little vanity, however, met
its appropriate punishment, for when I got up
next morning I found that my quadruped had
absconded during the night in his hobbles, and
left me in the lurch, which a less flighty animal
would most probably not have done ; the consequence being that when the Commissioner, my
two neighbours, and a *posse* of police troopers
arrived at Colbinabbin, I was obliged to join the
party without him. At any time it is unpleasant
to accompany on foot a lot of mounted men ;
doubly so when one has business on hand, and
the dismounted unit is unaccustomed to walking.
On this occasion, too, it was an additional
nuisance to find, from words which reached my
ears now and then, that my two neighbours
were quietly talking over the unsuspecting
Commissioner in a manner which could not
have occurred had I been able to join in the
conversation. In fact, I found that my prior
and authorized occupation of the country was
being lost sight of, and that the Commissioner
was being induced to treat our several claims as

equal, and to fix the boundary midway between our huts, a proceeding which to his mind, I have no doubt, appeared the perfection of equity.

However, nothing could be done at the moment, so I comforted myself with the reflection that the Commissioner would certainly dismount before he settled the matter, when I should have an opportunity of drawing his attention to what I thought my rights in the case.

Whilst affairs were in this state, and I was striding along in anything but a pleasant mood, the Commissioner's orderly cantered up from behind, and reported two emu on the plain. "Where are they?" asked the Commissioner. "About half-way between us and the ranges, sir," replied the man. "Well," said the Commissioner, as he leant down to shake hands with me, "I am going to the Campaspe to-night, and the galop will be all in my road—Good-bye;" and so saying, and before I had time to reply, he put spurs to his horse, and, hallooing to his dogs, set off, followed by the rest of the party. Of course all this was particularly pleasant to me, so I cooeyed to the Commissioner, and when he had pulled up, shouted to him in a rather indignant tone, "I think you have forgotten the business we came on." His reply, after looking about for a moment, was, "You see that single tree on the plain: an east and west line through it will be the boundary on this side of the creek, and, on the other side, the blackfellow's oven; and so saying, the whole party turned and rode *ventre à terre* at the emu, which were still feeding unsuspicious of mischief.

Of course I was left standing alone on the plain. I have seldom felt more indignant or more galled than on that occasion. The circumstance that the boundary line was thus fixed within two miles or so of my hut, whereas I claimed five—was even more unfavourable to me, or rather to my father, than the half-way arrangement the Commissioner had intended to make, and against which I had determined to protest—formed but a portion of my vexation, which rested a good deal on the autocratic manner of a public servant, who seemed to forget that I was there to claim a right and not to ask a favour, and who evidently considered the performance of duty a condescension on his part, and liable to be set aside at any moment by the merest whim or trifle; a train of thought which I fancy the reader will consider eminently natural under the circumstances. So I stood for a while on the plain chewing the cud of bitterness and mechanically watching the chase. No doubt it would have been easy in so flagrant a case to have brought the Commissioner to a serious reckoning, a course which, in the first instance, I felt very much inclined to take, and had subsequently some trouble to prevent my father from adopting.

A few weeks after the emu-hunt I went to Melbourne to wait on the Commissioner and get what compensation was possible. At his office I recalled very curtly to his recollection the circumstances under which his boundary settlement had been made ; and, indeed, to judge from his manner, I should say that he had thought a good deal more about the matter since it occurred than he did at the time. He was evidently nonplussed. I then pointed out in a few words the loss which his decision had entailed on my father, and handed in an application to extend the Colbinabbin boundary, on the unoccupied side, to the end of the plain, some six or seven miles south, which would give me a frontage of nine miles to the creek, by five miles in depth on its western, and two or three miles on its eastern side. This extension of country, which I did not consider more than the equivalent of what I had lost, being granted, the matter ended.

CHAPTER XXIV.

A MAIL ON THE LOWER GOULBURN—NEWS-PAPERS AT TONGALA—OUTCRY AGAINST THE SQUATTERS.

I THINK we had been about five or six years at Tongala, when the enterprising owner of a punt and public-house, at the place which afterwards was called Moama, proposed to run a mail between that rising township and Bailieston. Previous to this, the letters in our neighbourhood used to come only by chance opportunities. The first I heard of the proposed mail was from a horseman who rode up to my hut one evening and handed me a prospectus of the undertaking, which set out the disadvantages we settlers on the Goulburn laboured under for want of a regular mail, suggested that one should be started, and that my contribution to the undertaking should be to allow the mailman to stop at my men's hut two nights in the week, and put his horse in my paddock as he went backwards and forwards. Though I was not conscious of having suffered from the inconvenience spoken of in the prospectus, I acquiesced at once in the proposal; and, as the thing was generally popular on the river, the establishment of our post became an accomplished fact very shortly after. Preliminaries being settled, in due time a horseman..

with a new leather bag hanging rather con-
spicuously from his saddle, announced himself
at Tongala as the postman. He was well
mounted on what he called a Theôrem mare
(putting the accent on the second syllable), and
was evidently inclined to be obliging. He went
by the name of Charley the Barman, though
probably he had a surname. Naturally, Charley
became shortly quite an institution on the river,
and reminded one of what we read of the pedlers
of eighty years ago—I mean as newsmongers and
retailers of gossip. Few who met him let him off
without a yarn of some sort, and shepherds would
feed their sheep so as to intercept him as he
passed along the road, in order to make inquiries
about what was stirring in their line, and take
their chance of getting a little news to talk over
at night with their mates in the hut. I was once
present at a conversation of the sort, on the road
side, which ran something in this way :—

SHEPHERD.—Good day, Charley! I've been
waiting this hour to see you. What's the news
up the river ?

MAILMAN.—Good day! Good day! Well,
not much. All I've heard of was a Devil's
River lot, six or eight of them, knocking down
their cheques at Young's. I don't know their
names.

SHEPHERD.—How long had they been there ?

MAILMAN.—Oh! three days or so. All top

ropes, of course; but were, as I heard, close up fly-blown (*i.e.*, nearly penniless) the day before yesterday. Long Bill Warrigal told me of them, and that they had pretty well polished off Young's rum-keg. But I must be jogging.

SHEPHERD.—Well! well! to think the keg's given in. What will the next poor fellow do as wants a drain? Won't you have a light?

MAILMAN.—No time. Good-bye. I must push on.

And so Charley started the Theōrem, the shepherd shouting after him, "Tell Billy I'll send the bacca next week."

Our post, so much in favour with the gossips, did not last many months. The reason of its discontinuance I never heard, nor did it interest me much, as I could always go or send to the punt, twelve miles off, without much inconvenience when I had letters or papers to receive or send.

One of the things I recollect in connection with our mail is, that I began newspaper reading at this time. Though about twenty-five years of age, I doubt whether up to that time I had read a newspaper more than a dozen times in my life, a circumstance easily accounted for by the fact that I had always happened to be somewhere where newspapers were not obtainable—in the forests of Tasmania for instance, on the sea during several very long voyages, at college in the old country, at Tongala and Wolfscrag for some four years, and so on. On the other hand, having been studious of books, I was a good deal struck with the contrast presented by this class literature, with its medley of advertisements, editorial articles, collections of news, letters, scraps, &c. At first it seemed to me curious in the extreme. But what most attracted our attention at Tongala in the newspaper line were the leading articles on bush matters, as their writers displayed on the whole but a very superficial knowledge of the subject.

At first, in our inexperience, we were inclined to set down some of these articles as merry hoaxes, something in *Punch's* vein. Time, however, showed that their writers were earnest enough, so that "Who on earth writes these things?" was not an uncommon expression at Tongala. It was also about this time, or perhaps a little later, that we learnt from the papers that a Melbourne resident, who delighted to style himself the first settler on the banks of the Yarra Yarra, was exerting himself to set by the ears the class which had originally invested their capital in town allotments and such as had taken to pastoral pursuits ; the former having grown poor, and the latter being prosperous, as was made apparent by quite an eruption of dog-carts and tandems which broke out amongst the squatters at this time, they being the outward symbols of a good lambing and a rise in the wool market.

Of course, the grievance, as it stood, was a very pretty one; so a cry was got up that the squatters had monopolized the public lands. Representations that half of the Port Phillip District (not to speak of New South Wales proper) was as yet untenanted, and open to persons who thought squatting desirable, had, of course, no weight, any more than the fact that the squatters were the only producers in the colony, and that the Crown lands could be utilized in no other way. Neither did it seem to matter that the public-spirited individual to whom I have referred had so shady a reputation that he was constantly jeered by the mob at public meetings; and that few decent people would like to have been seen speaking to him in the street. He was listened to all the same.

So the busy old sinner posed to the last as the founder of the colony and a great public benefactor, to neither of which he had any title; became one of our *patres conscripti*, and in due time passed away and received apotheosis.

I must not forget to notice, in connection with the newspapers, that we saw in them constant mention of my father. Indeed, his position in connection with the Victorian question of the day—separation of the colony from New South Wales—was so well known that people with

whom I was not acquainted used often to stop
me, when off the station, to inquire when the
colony was likely to obtain the desired boon—a
question to which my general residence in the
bush, and consequent ignorance of political
matters, often left me unprovided with an
answer.

CHAPTER XXV.

PROGRESS IN SHEEP-FARMING AND DAILY LIFE ON THE STATION.

HERETOFORE I have endeavoured to describe the
more prominent features and occurrences of my
squatting experiences, and said little about the
financial concerns of the station or of my every-
day life in the bush. Naturally, the financial
position of the station, its successful or unsuccessful management, and the quantity of stock on
it had much to do with my daily life, so that
it is convenient to speak of the two subjects
together.

The reader is aware that, at the outset, my
squatting had been a losing business. On
getting settled at Tongala, my brother and
myself made great efforts to bring this unfor-

tunate state of things to a close, and the property into a paying condition. As it was impossible for the time to increase the yield of wool, the change had to be brought about by lessening the expenditure. To effect this the most important steps in our power were, after lambing and weaning, to run the whole of our sheep in two flocks instead of four, and discharge two of the shepherds, a hut-keeper, and the two bushmen. But, though wages fell shortly from £45 to £18 a year, servants were as scarce as ever, so that we had a great deal of trouble in getting our shepherds to agree to have their flocks increased. For notwithstanding that there was no difficulty in shepherding larger flocks, as the event proved, the convict instincts of my men led them to make a point of their labour not being too profitable to their master, so that I thought it best to compromise the matter by offering them a small increase of wages, which would bring them up to about £20 a year, making the advance contingent on a successful lambing, which depended in great measure on their exertions. These changes, however, were only brought about gradually, as existing agreements terminated. Subsequently I further raised the minimum of my flocks—weaners to two thousand, and grown sheep to between three and four thousand, and on one occasion had as many as ten thousand ewes and lambs in one flock.

Carrying on the station with this reduction of hands brought about two results, for it both made the undertaking a success financially, and gave my brother and myself a great deal to do; for partly that our large flocks consumed quickly the grass which they could reach from any particular hut, and partly that our country was subject in one portion to floods in winter, and in another to the absence of water in summer; and that it was necessary besides, in order not to lose possession of our straggling, and, for those days, large run, to use every portion of it occasionally, removals of flocks were always going on, and, as a consequence, my brother and I constantly repairing shepherds' huts and helping in the removals of sheep.

Thus our system was necessarily a migratory one, and, so far, both exceptional and troublesome. During the winter months our sheep were fed principally on the undulating plains at and near Coragorag; when the water had dried up in that country—which, in average years, would be in September—they were driven to Tongala, shorn, swam over the Goulburn, and placed at Madowla, Wolola, Pama, and other places. In November or December they were again moved to the Moira country, where they remained until the first frost withered the couch-grass, which was generally in April, after which they returned to Wolola, Tongala, Bunderi, &c., in expectation of the rain which was to make the Coragorag, Namerong, and Ullumbubil country fit for their winter's run.   In this way a constant change was going on.   As regards Colbinabbin, we generally kept the weaners there the year round, as they were more easily shepherded, and did best on the plains.

Another job which cost us some trouble every year was burning off portions of the run on which we had had no sheep for some time, or had only partially fed off; it being well known that the feed which springs up after a fire is particularly wholesome and fattening.   Though February was the month in which burning off was most easily and commonly done, we generally delayed it until March or April, when rain was expected, as we found that a fire not shortly followed by rain lost much of its efficacy, probably from the ashes, which act as a manure, being blown away by the wind.   Indeed, our experience was that country which remained three months without rain, after being burnt, only recovered itself slowly and partially, as many of the tussocks perished, apparently for want of moisture.   But when the fire was a strong one, and was quickly followed by heavy rain, the result was excellent.   In burning off country, our practice was to set to work on the windward position of it on some hot windy day at about eleven o'clock.   If possible, we got a blackfellow to go with us to lead our horses, whilst we set

fire to dry branches, which we dragged along the
ground across the wind ; if boughs were not
to be had, we made torches of bark, with which
we lit a few tussocks here and there as we passed
quickly on. In this way a fire was set a-going in
a line of from one to five miles, and then left to
chance. Sometimes burning off was a very troublesome job, on other occasions the flames went
merrily ahead in every direction, now rushing up
the tall stems of a thousand eucalypts, the leaves
of which it shrivelled like old parchment, shed-
ding around a pleasant odour ; now passing
slowly over scantily-grassed patches, again to
seize on the bushes or dry herbage which stood
in its way.

In addition to a reduction of wages, we also
practised a number of minor economies of one
sort or another at Tongala, which, in the aggre-
gate, were of considerable importance at a very
critical time, when the want of small sums of
money wrecked many promising undertakings.
One of these was killing for station use a number
of ewes, too old to breed and too poor for sale—a
practice which enabled us to keep our wethers for
market. To carry out this system, as we did for
over a year, was disagreeable, no doubt, as I had
to put up with the complaints of my men, in
addition to those of my stomach. But economy
is always a nuisance, and one looks for nothing
else ; so we persevered, and swallowed the last of

discover a little grievance of my Granadine friends, which cropped up on my making inquiries about the "bright-eyed Dolores" of the "New Sketch-Book." "Oh!" said José, "she married a doctor, and lives down there on the Vega." But on my suggesting that I ought to endeavour to see her, as one of Irving's celebrities, he at once threw cold water on the proposal, being strong on the point that she was no longer pretty. It also leaked out that the Ximenes, both father and son, who looked on Irving's work as the last of any note which had appeared in Europe, were not a little jealous of the inquiries made by travellers generally respecting the Señora Dolores, so that the old man took occasion, when speaking of her, to inform me that Irving "*la ponía en el libro porque guisaba por el;*" or that he had given her a place in his book because she used to cook for him. On the whole, therefore, as insisting on seeing her might have disturbed the harmony of existing relations, and besides—as

"'Time will come with all his blights"—

have led to what the Spaniards call *un desengaño*, or, *una ilusion perdida*, I thought it prudent to forbear further mention of the subject, and turn the conversation to the worthies of the declining days of *Morisma*, whose histories are so mixed up with that of the Alhambra. So, as we wandered about the apartments of the old palace, or sat in the sunshine of its courts and gardens, we talked of Boabdil el Chico and the gate by which he last left the city ; of Aija la Horra, La Lindaraja, El Zagal, Hamet el Zegri, Hernando Perez del Pulgar (*el de las hazañas*, or he of the exploits), of Ponce de Leon, and the great Alonzo de Aguilar, Marquis-Duke of Cadiz, to whose countrymen are still familiar the old story and the old rhyme—

> " Decid conde de Ureña
> Don Alonzo, donde queda?"

besides many other matters connected with the history of Granada and the Alhambra which it is needless to enlarge on. Altogether there was something very pleasant in going over in Andalusia the histories which had occupied our little circle on the Goulburn, as well as in looking back on past discussion and conjecture concerning localities from the vantage-ground of personal experience. Indeed, in re-reading history—if I may use the term—on the ground where its scenes were enacted lies one of the great charms of travel. To me there was also something congenial in the every-day life of a community into which the disquietude, bustle, and hurry of the Anglo-Saxon world had not yet succeeded in forcing themselves.

Another episode in history which interested us a good deal at Tongala, and gave us something to

couple of bushmen, with some assistance from the Blacks, could very well do the extra work of the station.

Having endeavoured to give the reader an idea of the struggling times of my bush life when I had plenty to do, and the profits of the station were small, we come to its second phase, when the concern had grown, leisure become plentiful, and time often difficult to dispose of. At that period reading became our chief resource at Tongala. In the matter of books I believe we were better off than most of our neighbours, though those in our possession had been got together in a haphazard sort of way, at various times and without any idea of making a collection for the bush. However, from a pair of stout wooden pegs in the wall-plate of the sitting-room. of our rough, but not uncomfortable, slab hut at Tongala, surrounded by a miscellaneous collection of fire-arms, foils, masks, wooden sabres, fencing gloves, stockwhips, spurs, and other articles which embellished the walls, hung, in the place of honour, some shelves made of bark, on which were ranged our literary treasures. These volumes, our great resource for years against *ennui*, for want of something new, were read, re-read, and discussed, I cannot say how often. In fact, several of them became studies in our small circle. Amongst them were a number of histories, ancient and modern, Bourrienne's

" Napoleon," Segur's " Histoire de Napoleon et de la Grande Armée," O'Meara's " Voice from St. Helena," " The Court and Camp of Bonaparte," " The Alhambra, or New Sketch Book ; " the plays of Racine, Corneille, and Molière ; the poetical works of Milton, Shakespeare, Byron, Tommy Moore, Scott, and Burns.

There were also several of the Waverley Novels, some of them in French translations; " Travels in the East," by Lamartine, Stephens, and Chateaubriand ; " Silvio Pellico's Le Mie Prigioni," " Horace's Odes," Pope's " Iliad," Junius's " Letters," some of Florian's works, Sterne's " Sentimental Journey," " Blackstone's Commentaries," Adam Smith's " Wealth of Nations ; " two or three elementary works on natural science ; " Youatt on the Sheep and Horse ; " and a pile of old magazines, chiefly Blackwood's, and amongst them those in which the " Noctes Ambrosianæ " had appeared. We had, besides, a few colonial works, such as " Major Mitchell's Explorations," and the " Memoirs of Jorgen Jorgenson, ex-king of Iceland," whom I remember to have seen when a clerk in my father's office.

Altogether our collection amounted to about a hundred and fifty volumes, of which those mentioned are fair samples. None of them, perhaps, were left entirely unread; diversity of taste, however, leading to one of us interesting himself in one subject, and another in another. A subject we all enjoyed was Eastern travel; and, indeed, two of our little circle visited later on many of the scenes we so often read and talked about in our solitude at this time. As the reader may imagine, the confinement of our reading within such narrow limits was not a matter of choice. It arose from the circumstance that books were hardly obtainable in Melbourne in those days. As an instance of this, I may mention that, having taken a fancy to learn something of the discovery and conquest of America, I tried to obtain " Herrera," " Bernal Diaz," and some other works, but without success. Of the volumes in our collection, very favourite ones with me were those of Washington Irving, which treat of Moorish times in Spain; and as that writer's studies on the subject at his villa on the Hudson were the cause, as he tells us, of his visiting Granada, so my acquaintance with the pages of the American resulted subsequently in my paying a visit to Andalusia.

When I reached Granada, in 1851, I had already been the best part of a year in the Peninsula, and spoke Spanish pretty well. As a matter of course, full of my Goulburn recollections, my first inquiry, after getting settled in my hotel, was for Matteo Ximenes, Washington Irving's guide in 1829, and famous in the pages of his " Alhambra, or New Sketch Book," and very pleased I was to find that he was still alive and hearty, though he had ceded his more active duties to his son José, then a young man of some twenty-three years. José, who had had more care bestowed on his education than the original *hijo de la Alhambra*, spoke French in addition to his native tongue; had read the lives of Christopher Columbus, and several other worthies; heard of Australia, and entertained a hazy idea that it formed a portion of North America; was looked on as quite a man of learning by the dwellers in the purlieus of the old palace, and was a very good cicerone. Besides showing me whatever was noteworthy in the Alhambra and Jeneralife, bringing to my recollection episodes of history connected with them, and pointing out from the palace towers the sites of many a bloody battle between his countrymen and the Moors, José used to bring his father to talk to me about Washington Irving, and of his stay amongst them. Indeed, conversation on this topic was the old man's hobby, and he quite took me into favour when he discovered that I had some acquaintance with Granadine lore, and that I knew something about *la cuesta de lagrimas*; *el ultimo suspiro del Moro*, or, *el suspiro Moro*, as it is called on the spot; the Vivarambla, the Zacatin, and other features of the city and neighbourhood. Whilst living in this old-world atmosphere, it amused me to

our old ewes as best we could. The preservation of flour bags, which had a marvellous tendency to go astray, also claimed our attention. As for sheepskins, the sale of which in town covered the wages of a man or two, I cannot tell the reader the trouble they were to collect on a run like ours, though I was very painstaking and systematic about it. In fact, rather than allow any laxity to grow up in the matter, I have occasionally walked five miles to secure a single skin, and carried it home in my hand. As regards dress, the same economy prevailed as in food, and I cannot help smiling at the remembrance of the straits to which I was once reduced in the matter of boots. I had limited myself to a certain number of pairs for the year, and though they held together for that period, the last of them became so hard from constant wet and frequent greasing that for the last fortnight I could only get them off and on after soaking them in water ; so that, when I came home from riding, I had to sit exposed to a little gentle chaff with my feet in a bucket of water until the leather got soft. Besides practising economies of all sorts, we also so managed (contrary to common custom) by drafting out our dry ewes for a summer lambing at the Moira, where the grass was always green at that season, and by lambing our ewe flocks twice every alternate year, to raise our increase from ninety to one hundred and thirty per cent.

per annum, which rate was maintained for several years without any very striking bad consequences as regards the quality of the offspring. The result of these measures was, as I have said, that we quickly paid off the liabilities of the station, and, with wethers at five shillings a head and wool at a shilling a pound, succeeded in bringing it into a very prosperous condition. However, the hard sort of life we led at first did not last more than two or three years, as about this time two of my brothers returning from college in England came to lessen our labours. A little later on, also, as our sheep increased, we found it advantageous to give up work, in great measure, for supervision, and, indeed, to divide amongst us the management of the flocks now spread over a large area of country. To effect this a second head-station was formed at Colbinabbin, where my brother Richard went to reside, and another at Kokoma, near the Moira, for one of my younger brothers: besides a little *sans-souci* at Gargarro, at which we could put up comfortably when busy about Coragorag. From this time our chief occupation was riding about the run looking after shepherds and hunting wild dogs; and having got rid of scab and foot-rot, and taken to camp our sheep in place of hurdling or yarding them (a great improvement, which I believe I was the first to adopt), we found that a

think and talk about, was that of Bonaparte. Many were the discussions and comparison of authorities we used to have on matters touching that hero—concerning Brienne, Toulon, the passage of the Alps; Mont Tabor; Marengo, Austerlitz, the raft on the Niemen, the glories of Tilsit, the Kremlin, the terrible passage of the Beresina, Leipsic, Elba, Waterloo, and lastly, " *le rocher de Sainte Hélène*"—the refrain, by the way, of a plaintive song which, in youth, I had heard the peasant girls, forgetful of the blood he shed, sing in the harvest fields of France.

At other times we discussed the actions of the Corsican's historic companions,—Massena, Desaix, Soult, Ney, Murat, or Talleyrand; or the singular fortunes of Mademoiselle Tascher de la Pagerie—in early life the Viscomtesse de Beauharnais, and known at the court of Marie Antoinette as the Creole beauty—shortly after, in the darkest days of the Revolution, a widow in Paris with the future Viceroy of Italy and Queen of Holland to provide for; subsequently the wife of General Bonaparte; Madame la Consulesse; the Empress Josephine; and at last the dethroned sovereign and discarded wife of Malmaison.

To this subject of Bonaparte—if a digression may be pardoned—I had been led by a number of those impressions of boyhood days which seem to cling to one through life. In fact, I attribute my first bias towards a subject which, as I have said, was a favourite one in my solitude (much as Sir Walter Scott did his predilection for border minstrelsy, so pleasantly described in "Marmion"), to stories related to me, when quite a child, by two servants in my father's house who had served under Nelson in one or other of his great battles, and had, of course, plenty to say about Bonaparte. Both of these worthies had been wounded, and were "assigned servants" to my father in Tasmania; and one of the pair, an old African negro, used, to my astonishment, to be allowed to drink the health of the departed sea-king in Jamaica rum on the anniversary of each of his great battles, the dates of which he very accurately bore in mind, always accompanying the ceremony with the words, "Here's to the memory of that glorious clipper, Lord Wiscount Nelson, wice-admiral of the blue." Adding, if I were present, as he smacked his lips with true African unction, "Master Edward, Nelson's old sea-dogs never drank his health in nothing but rum ashore or afloat!" This old African used also to relate to me, in a highly dramatic manner, what he knew of the great sea-fights; his information, of course, being confined to what he had been able to see through the smoke of his own particular port-hole.

Later on, also, besides perhaps fifty volumes

which I had read about Napoleon, it happened
when a stripling in France, that, being a good
deal addicted to fencing and exercises of the sort,
I was accustomed to "*espadroner*" with men of
Auerstadt and Jena, and knew a number of *vieux
moustaches* who had fought under the Emperor's
eagles at Leipsic, Monterau, Quatre Bras,
Waterloo, and other places, from whom I heard
a thousand incidents of battle and bivouac,
of which, subsequently, Erckmann-Chatrian's
delightful " Conscrit de 1813" vividly reminded
me. In my childhood, too, I fancy Bonaparte
was a good deal more talked about than any
historical personage has been since his time, and
I often listened to my father and his friends
discussing his doings.

Talking of the state of the English postal
system at the time of the war, I remember
hearing my father relate an anecdote which will
perhaps bear repeating. It is this. When quite
a lad he was walking in Sheffield (a city between
which and London now-a-days there are probably
a dozen railway trains daily), when he noticed a
number of people congregated about the post-
office, so he crossed the street and joined the
crowd. The moment was a critical one in the
affairs of Europe, and as the anticipated news
was likely to affect the price of bread, the funds,
and property generally, the crowd which was
waiting to hear it was both animated and

impatient. So a few of the people who had watches looked at them and informed those about them that the post was late ; others wondered what the news would be, and what Pitt would have thought of the times had he been alive. Others talked of " Boney's" last battle ; but still the mail arrived not. Then someone remarked that the clock might be fast. " Clock fast ? clock be hanged !" said another in a long green and white waistcoat, " Tommy has got Herod to-day, and he ought to be as fast as any clock in Yorkshire, 'cos he's as thoroughbred as Eclipse, and in rare fettle. Clock indeed ! it's not the horse's fault, I know ; like enough he's cast a shoe."

" If Tommy had the Black Prince under him," rejoined another stableman, " I'd a-warrant he'd a bin here afore now."

" No," remarked the first, " Herod for my money ; as good a horse as a man ever threw leg over."

After some further horsey talk there was a cry that the postman was coming up the street. so the crowd opened, and a light muscular horseman in livery, booted and spurred, with a postillion's cap on his head, mounted on a magnificent bay horse, reeking with sweat, dashed through the lane of human beings up to the window of the post-office, into which, having detached them without dismounting, he flung a pair of saddlebags containing the mail. In the meantime the crowd closed quickly round him, the ostler admirer of Herod having secured a position near his favourite, whom he patted kindly on the neck. Many an anxious face was turned on the postman and many a look of eager curiosity, whilst some half-dozen of the crowd blurted out simultaneously, "Well, Tommy, what's the news of Bonaparte?" As his reply was given in a low tone, those who could not catch his words yelled out, "Speak up, man, Tommy—we cannot hear thee." So Tommy stood up in his stirrups, and shouted out, "There's but bad news, I reckon; they say as Bonaparte has won a great battle. They call it—Wag—Wag—well, it's a foreign name as I can't get round. Folks seems to say there's no knowing where it will all end;" which said, Tommy sat back into his saddle, gave Herod the rein, and trotted off to the stable, followed by the ostlers.

But to return. For the first few years at Tongala we hardly ever saw a newspaper, and seldom made an addition to our library. Neither, when a new book did find its way to us, was it altogether an unmixed blessing, as it was not pleasant to be aware of the fact and not take advantage of it; nor, on the other hand, could one read in comfort with one's brother sitting opposite smoking, and apparently going through "Hamlet" for the hundredth time, whilst conscious that he was in

25

reality only waiting for the new volume to be laid down, that he might take a hurried glance through its pages. And, talking of books, I am reminded of how seldom now-a-days one sees some which were met everywhere forty years ago. A few of this sort, such as Addison's "Spectator" and Johnson's "Rasselas" and "Rambler," we had at Tongala, but they were not much in favour. Unfortunately, Boswell's "Life of Johnson," which all of us had read before, was not in our collection; so that the conversations of the brawny lexicographer at the Mitre Tavern with Burke, Garrick, Beauclerk, Goldsmith, and his other intimates—not forgetting those with the *belle* Thrale, at Streatham—were only amongst the recollections of our readings. We used, however, to laugh over some of the funny episodes scattered through the work, such as Johnson's calling at the lodgings of George Psalmanazar, "the *good* Psalmanazar," and carrying him, as they used to say, to a neighbouring alehouse, to talk over matters of importance, and then setting to work in the public room to discuss such lively subjects as *the natural tendency of the human mind to improvement!* or something of the sort. But though books in those days were scarce in the colony, the squatters' shelves, as far as I saw them, were better provided than at present, and typical of a more educated class; for if, now-a-days, from many a house elaborately furnished from attic to basement, Chambers's Cyclopædia and a score of novels were removed, the remnant would not be great.

As, however, one cannot always be reading, especially the same books, we used sometimes, in the evening, by the light of our tallow candle, to pass an hour at cards, chess, or draughts. We had also a number of out-of-door amusements, which stood us in good stead, and enabled us to while away many a morning which otherwise would have been dull enough. Amongst them were swimming, shooting, throwing spears, and so forth. To such exercises, indeed, we were much more given than any of our neighbours; and as for horses and hunting, many of my happiest hours were passed in the saddle, for which, in my youth, I had a perfect passion.

But though in those days I doated on horses, and especially on a horse at a gallop through a pleasant sapling scrub, where the chances of getting a broken neck or a knee knocked out of joint seemed about equal, still in wet weather, when the then untrodden soil was too soft for galloping, I made shift to amuse myself with hunting on foot. In this pursuit the charm of the thing was the scope it gave for the exercise of ingenuity in tracking and reading from the tracks the history of the chase. On the whole, I do not know but that one got as much amusement and excitement out hunting on foot as on horseback. Of course,

the nature of the amusements was quite different.
At that time tracking was comparatively easy,
where it is now impossible. Starting from the
spot where the dogs, first feathering about, made
a sudden rush, and, taking up the scent, quickly
vanished from sight amongst the trees, the tracks
of kangaroo or emu were quickly come on by the
hunter, and the number and sizes of the animals
learnt. If the scent was that of a wild dog, the
matter was more difficult; if kangaroo or emu, a
short examination also made clear whether the
game had noticed our approach, and started at
score, or whether the trail had been made whilst
feeding. Such matters decided, the tracks of the
dogs were energetically followed up, possibly for
two or three miles without any fresh indications,
when suddenly matters altered. Now the foot-
prints of the mob were all in one line—and, if
kangaroo, a very narrow line—more deeply in-
dented in the soil, and the stride longer. Here,
then, the kangaroo had first seen the dogs and
taken to their heels. A few hundred yards further on, the dogs had got so close to the rear-
guard as to disturb the order of the flight, and
had so pressed the *old man* (who usually brings-
up the rear) as to make him leave his mob and
take off to one side. Probably the dogs had kept
together, and closed in on the patriarch of the
lot, who had shown fight at the foot of a tree.
Around are the marks of the scuffle; there they

have had the brute down, and a rough-and-tumble
fight. There is a drop of blood, probably from a
dog, for the tracks show that the kangaroo got on
his legs again and made off. In another fifty
yards the dogs are again up with him. But what
has mudded yon crab-hole? There the dogs
fought and threw him a second time. The imprint of his hand in the mud is as big as my own.
I stop, look round, and sound my horn, for I
know that he must have been killed not far off,
or have finally beaten off the dogs and made his
bow. And sure enough there is the pup coming
back on the tracks; when I get up to him I find
him covered with blood, and a large patch of
loose skin hanging from his neck. Another hundred yards ahead there is a second dog lying
down resting himself; he wags his tail as I pass
him by, for not fifty yards off I see a dark-
coloured object under a cherry tree, which I
know can be nothing else but the old man, though
I cannot yet make out the parts.

And so the chase is done. There is a wound
or two to tie up, and the dogs to be fed; so I
take my little brass tinder-box off my belt, light
a fire, skin the beast, and take his hide and tail
as my share of the spoil, cut off as much flesh as
I think the dogs will eat, and throw it on the
coals to cook, with, perhaps, a kidney for myself,
and so sit down and rest a while whilst I smoke a
pipe.

Another out-of-door amusement to which I was
much given was duck-shooting, especially in
winter and spring, when trees and shrubs and the
banks of lagoons are in their best attire. To me
the stillness and freshness into which this sort of
shooting led were always a great attraction. Another of our pastimes was breaking young horses,
though, as we had only a dozen brood mares,
our pleasures in that direction were necessarily
limited. We also domesticated some emu and
wild pups, the observance of whose habits used
to amuse us. Corroborees, which were very
frequent at one or other of our stations, were
another resource, though eventually we became
rather *blasé* as regards that amusement, and only
sat out the choice *morceaux*. After all, however,
yarning with the Bangerang, swimming, climbing
trees in the native fashion, throwing spears, and
hunting principally occupied our leisure hours;
and, as the poet says—

" Thus the days of Thalaba went by ! "

As the reader may imagine, these were dull
enough at times ; but there were others worse
—lengthy intervals of mixed *ennui* and low
spirits, literally of times *à fumer pipette et à ne
rien faire*. When overtaken by this complaint,
which, of course, was when we were out of work,
horses, dogs, guns, spears, and books became alike
insufferable. We came to loathe everything

about us, and for the time it seemed to me
there was little to choose between our position
and that of Pellico in the Spielberg; conversation dried up, and gloom gradually overshadowed
us.

When things came to this pass, it generally
resulted in several of the party—perhaps all but
one—leaving the station for a time, one for
town, a second, perhaps, on a visit to a neighbour, and so on; or, if more than one remained,
they separated and went to different stations for
a few days, perhaps one to the Moira, and the
other to Colbinabbin. This seemed the only
remedy. The step decided on, a few preparations ensued; favourite horses were got up, their
manes and tails pulled, and hoofs trimmed with
a chisel. Then coats, neckties, and cabbage-
tree hats were extracted from boxes in which
they had lain for months, and spurs and Hessian
boots got an extra polish. The next morning a
start was made, the unfortunate who remained
behind, mindful perchance of Stoneyhurst and
old college days, addressing those who were
going in the words of the poet,

> " Si quis, ut in populo nostri non immemor illic
>   Si quis, qui, quid agam, forte requirat erit,
>   Vivere me dices, salvum tamen esse negabis."

Intervals of solitude, too, each of us had
occasionally to go through. Once, for instance,

it was my luck to pass three weeks at Tongala,
during which I did not see a face, white or black.
We were short-handed, so one of us had to
remain at the head station, and by chance it fell
to my lot. The weather was frightfully hot at
the time, and, being a prisoner with nothing to
occupy me, I fell into very irregular ways. Of
the days of the month I soon lost count. Sometimes I went to bed late and sometimes early.
When I rose late in the morning, I fancy the
crows thought the silence of the place, the un-
opened doors and smokeless chimneys, portended
something suspicious. At all events, they used
to annoy me a good deal with their cawing, as
they stealthily approached the hut along the top
rails of the paddock fence. Probably the muzzle
of my gun thrust through the window, and the
discharge of one or both barrels, conveyed to them
the first intimation of my being still in the flesh,
and of my objection to being disturbed. Quiet
restored, I used to sally out with my kangaroo-
dog into the intense glare of the sun, despatch
the wounded, have a look round, and saunter to
the bathing-place, some fifty yards away. The
weather was so hot that even at an early hour
the *choondoonga*, as the Bangerang called the
little birds, had taken shelter in the trees, out of
which occasionally one dropped dead. Days of
this sort were, of course, very hard to get
through. Except to cook for myself and chop

my firewood, I had no employment. Reading I found it difficult to settle down to in the absence of bodily labour, of which I got but little, as it was probable if I left my hut to hunt or shoot (the only things I could do) that it might be robbed in my absence. Still this idleness, compulsory though it was, always brought with it feelings of self-reproach.

Sometimes, however, impatience got the better of me, and I sallied out in desperation with my gun to have a walk, and get a duck for dinner. On one of these occasions I met with a little adventure which might have cost me my life. With my gun on my shoulder, I was sauntering along the banks of one of the lagoons, around the edges of which grew a bright green plant which resembled floating moss. I had not proceeded far when I caught sight of a flock of ducks, which I stalked up to with some little trouble and fired at, knocking over one, which fell into the middle of the lagoon. Having no retriever, there was nothing for it but to swim in for the bird, so I undressed, leaned my gun against a tree, and plunged into the water with an impetus which carried me through the border of water-plants, of which, indeed, I took no notice just then. A few strokes took me to the duck, which I picked up and swam back with, until I got near the margin of green stuff, when I threw it on shore, as it occurred to me that my passage back through the weeds would not be so easy as the first had been. This done, I struck out for the bank (the water being deep to the very edge), and only got part of the way through when I found my arms entangled and the mass of floating green stuff, which I had disturbed. closing in on me. Any swimmer will realize the danger of such a situation. How I managed I can't say ; all I remember is that, after a violent struggle, I found myself again floating in the deep water, the green stuff still between me and the shore. So there I was, free once more, a little skeared and a good deal blown.

Being an excellent swimmer in those days, I soon cooled down and began to consider quietly what was to be done ; but though I turned the matter over in every way during many minutes. as I quietly floated on the water, I could see no escape from the facts that the whole margin of the lagoon was equally covered with the water plants, and that there was not the faintest probability of anyone passing that way from whom to expect assistance. Things being so, I made up my mind to charge the weeds at the original spot, using the hand-over-hand stroke of the Bangerang, in which I was well practised, as most likely to pull me through. So, as chances seemed about even, or perhaps somewhat against me, I reflected for a few moments on death : had a look at the green trees around, gave a thought to those I might possibly never see again, and went at the weeds full speed, hand-over-hand, and feet almost on top of the water, as I had determined. Fortunately I got through, and with less difficulty than I had anticipated, but with an antipathy to swimming amongst weeds which I never got over.

Periods of loneliness, such as I have described, were our bad times, and were not very common, though we had a good deal of less complete solitude which became habitual, so as ever after, in my instance at least, to render a reasonable amount of loneliness quite acceptable. As a rule, when thus shut out from conversation, we employed ourselves very actively with our books, and, on one occasion of the sort, I took up vigorously the study of Italian for some weeks, a step which proved very useful to me some years afterwards. The drawback to the bush, however, seemed to me the want of mental occupation. This I could not find in sheep-farming. Its advantages were that it was a lucrative occupation, and secured much personal independence.

In thus recalling the memory of our everyday lives at Tongala, I have perhaps dwelt more on the *désagréments* of the situation than on its bright features. On the whole, however, it was passable enough; we had no anxiety; money-making went on swimmingly; we were our own masters, had generally plenty of out-of-door work ; good dogs and excellent horses, in which we much delighted ; our spirits, as a rule, were prime, and our digestions excellent—altogether, as it seems to me, a reasonable share of the good things of life.

CHAPTER XXVI.

HUNTING WITH FOX-HOUNDS.

THE first urban settlement near Tongala was "Maiden's Punt," so called after its energetic founder. The little hamlet was on the north bank of the Murray, not far from the junction of that river and the Campaspe, and began in the time-honoured way with an inn and blacksmith's shop. Its most prominent feature, however, was Mr. Maiden's capacious, flat-bottomed punt, by means of which bullock teams, wool-drays, and flocks of sheep were quickly and securely passed over the river. Of course the punt was a great convenience to the travelling public, and resulted in due time in the little settlement developing into the not unimportant border town of Moama.

I mention these circumstances because it was at this place that the squatters in our vicinity were in the habit of meeting a pack of fox-hounds, which our neighbour of Turumberry had got together for his own amusement, and that of his friends. The pack, which our horse-riding little *coterie* came to look on with special pride and satisfaction, had sprung originally from a few couples of fox-hounds obtained from Mr. Pike's pack, near Melbourne. They were fed on the boiled flesh of the worn-out sheep of the master's station, supplemented by forties and fifties of similar animals which neighbouring stock-owners contributed from time to time for their support. In comparison with English fields, our meets were very small, for I do not remember to have ever seen more than a dozen horsemen turn out at once.

If the hunt was not very numerous, however, it was certainly a very merry one. Of our symposiums on such occasions (a not unimportant part of the business) I regret I am unable to give more than a faint idea, for, indeed, the memories of merry-makings, even when of rare occurrence, are not the sort of things which dwell most vividly in the mind; and yet characteristic incidents were always occurring at ours, which, if I could remember them, would give the reader a picture of our ways at the time. This, how-ever, I am unable to do, so he must make the best of a meagre description. As regards the main object of our meetings—the actual hunting —still less is to be said, for the country being unenclosed, there was but little jumping and no falls, so that, omitting the working of the hounds, the find, the first burst, and the kill, sights which have been depicted somewhat too often, all that remains is the jovial scamper through the bush of ten or a dozen practised horsemen—a matter hardly worthy of description. No doubt, however, the predominant features of our gatherings were the evenings after the hunts. Indeed, from the solitary life we all led, the very fact of three or four of us meeting together, were it only over tea and tobacco, brought on such an attack of high spirits as was almost painful to bear.

The first time we met was on a beautiful evening in the month of June, 1849, if I recollect right. The winter in our neighbourhood had been a dry one, so that the ground was in fine condition, and the mornings and evenings clear, frosty, and exhilarating. The company came dropping in at "Maiden's" in ones and twos about an hour before sundown. Several were without coats, arrayed in red silk shirts. Hessian boots, and cabbage-tree hats, and everyone on his best horse. As we were all well acquainted, each new arrival was received with many greetings. Then came a visit to stables, and, of course, complimentary remarks on the nags. Such matters satisfactorily gone through, an adjournment followed to the dining-room of mine host, for the purpose of commencing to allay that peculiar thirst which gets hold of one on gala days; so the landlord was summoned to give an account of his tipple. As it happened, there was brandy and beer in the house, and a little gin; but what Boniface chiefly recommended, I remember, was his rum, the strong point of which seemed to be, that it was, as he termed it, "bootiful cool." "Possibly"—chimed in some one aside—"in comparison with his own coppers." "Bring in your 'bootiful cool,'" said another; "it must be some new drink, for I never heard of it before, and should like to taste it." This order seemed to jump with the general humour, as it was decided that it should be "bootiful cool" all round.

The first libation poured, the company strolled out to see the twenty-five couples of hounds whose acquaintance we were to make on the morrow. Whether any of the field were judges of hounds I can't say. For myself, I had never seen a pack of fox-hounds before, and so knew nothing of the matter. At all events, a good deal of favourable comment ensued, and the pack was taken to our hearts right off, when another arrival, on a bay cob, attracted our attention. Anticipating an increase to our numbers, several hurried to the door of the "public" to greet our fellow-sportsman.

The new-comer, however, who proved to be a

resident some twenty miles up the Campaspe, was not one of hunting kidney, but a "canny body" from the "land o' cakes," who could by no means be got to join us, or even to dismount, though invitations were many and pressing. So, after he had lit his pipe and tossed off a glass of "bootiful cool" with which one of his friends presented him as a new drink, he exclaimed, in that douce tone and strong brogue which were his wont—"Hunt! Hunt, man! No, no! It wudna do for an auld fellow like me to gang scouring through the bush wi' a lot o' demented young folk. Syne, though Barney, the puir wee bit horsie, is gleg aneuch wi' his legs, he's aye ill to please an he's not let gang his ain gait; so I must just canter him hame, where I shall be glad to see ye all, if ye'll tak' a turn up that way to-morrow." After which, amidst some pleasant banter, the douce man took a second nip, and, with a kind word to each of us, and a few caresses lavished on the "horsie," made tracks. And, after all, the ways of the good man, though "awfu'" thrifty, were not without a strong savour of good sense about them, as, three years later, he sold out and returned to the "land of brown heath" with forty thousand pounds in his sporran, no doubt to spend his remaining years in something more to his fancy than hunting.

At six o'clock came dinner, for which all practicable preparations had been made by mine host, as, besides mutton and damper, we were treated to potatoes, dough-boys, and cabbage. Then succeeded pipes, and, later on, grog, and conversation fast and somewhat uproarious. I should not care for such doings now, but thirty years ago it was different, and our gatherings at the punt were *Noctes Ambrosianæ*, hours of fun and yarning, and rum our nectar. As for Byron's saying,

> "There's nought, no doubt, so much the spirit calms
> As rum and true religion,"

I only know that the beverage had not that effect upon us, as the more we swallowed the less calm we got. By eleven, however, a good deal of steam had been let off; some were getting sleepy, and the company had broken into groups and were talking of all sorts of things, and more about horses than anything else. "Oh, yes," said one, whose horse had been under discussion, "O. B.'s a grand horse, but a rather fractious-tempered devil if anything goes wrong. I wish you had seen him some nights back. I was riding him home late through the bush, when it came on to rain so heavily, and got so dark, that I began to be hazy about the direction, and was obliged, however unwillingly, to camp; so I hung up Master O. B. to a sapling whilst I made a fire. In the meantime the thunder roared and the lightning flashed in great style. After I had

26

got a fire, with the assistance of my tinder-box, which fortunately was on my belt, and a good piece of my shirt, I unsaddled the nag and hobbled him with a stirrup leather, and was taking off the bridle when he began shaking his head, which, of course, he held as high as he could, so that my Pelham caught on his tushes, and I was unable to get it off. The wretch then reared, wheeled, and snatched the reins out of my hand. I heard a grunt or two, and if it had not been for the lightning I should not have known what he was doing. However, there he was, not two yards off, standing on his hind legs pawing the air, his head as high as he could get it. I never saw a brute stand so straight or so long. To go near him with nothing but the uncertain flare of the lightning to guide one, especially in the muddy state of the ground, was to risk one's life; so I retired a few steps and waited. At last he got his fore feet entangled in the reins, fell on his side, and I was able to get the bit out of his mouth, when he got up and stood beside the fire for some time, a good deal done."

Besides sundry relations of bush incidents of this sort, there was a good deal of racing talk and discussions on Whisker and Satellite blood and buck-jumping yarns, to which your young bushman is right much addicted. "Did you hear," said one, "that B.'s cob has been lame these six months—no one can say why—and no signs of mending ?"

"Of course, he could never have lived with hounds; no pace."

"Just so," said a third; "not for him the sweet music of hounds, but still a rare slave; slow, you know, but sure. So he's gone lame, and only rising seven! Why, when I saw him last, I thought him good for another ten years. A fine nag, was he not ?"

"Well, to tell you the truth, I don't like cobs."

"What! not like cobs ?"

"Not a bit. No doubt your cob, with his short back, short pasterns, great ribs, and straightish shoulder, is a fine feeder, has lots of constitution, and often lots of muscle, and so, for a time, will get through any quantity of work; and when you've said that I think you've given the favourable side of his character. On the other hand, no one, I think, who cares to be pleasantly carried would select a cob for his hack. He is the sort one keeps about the place for *anyone to ride but one's self*. Then, as a rule, he is subject to go lame suddenly and without any cause, as people say; but I have always attributed the catastrophe to the concussion which the short back and pasterns, straight shoulders, and general want of elasticity entail on the legs. Depend upon it, when a rider feels a horse rough, the horse's legs are getting it."

At another corner of the long deal table a knot of young worthies were talking shop—the value of sheep-dogs and the ways of shepherds. "The other day," said one, "I came on one of my shepherds, who seemed just then to be what people call eccentric, for to my surprise I caught him running round his flock like a madman, giving vent to terrific screams. I rode up to him, and asked what was the matter. What do you think was his answer? Pointing to his dog, which was sitting under a tree, and had evidently struck work, he said, 'Talk to him, sir; he's the shepherd, I'm the (adjective) dog.'"

A roar of laughter followed this yarn, which seemed to us just then immensely humorous.

"That was your new-chum shepherd, was it not?"

"Yes, he of the laughing jackass."

"What was that?" said another.

"Oh! a very good yarn, I think. This shepherd of mine—a Paddy, by the way—when he arrived in Melbourne, some months back, was going about the streets with his mate seeing the lions, when they came to a poulterer's shop, in which, besides fowls, there were some birds in cages of sorts new to Paddy. Naturally enough he thought they were native poultry, and, being of an experimental turn of mind, asked the shopman, *pointing to a laughing jackass,* 'What might be the price of yon quare-faced turkey, or whatsomever you call him?' 'Why,' said the shopman, 'he's not a turkey, man, he's a owl!' 'Oh, thin,' said Paddy, in that peculiar whining tone of voice in which an Irishman sometimes gives vent to his fun, 'devil a care I whether he's ould or young, so long as he's fat.'"

Another lot before the fire were talking of the Blacks and their doings. "Stalking!" said one, "I heard a blackfellow boast that he had stalked so close up to an emu, with a bundle of boughs in his hand, that the bird put his head round the bush to see if there was anyone behind it, and he caught him with his hand."

"Well, they are witty enough in their way," said another. "I was bathing with old Jacky-Jacky in the Campaspe last summer, and the mosquitos were so bad that I wished I had a tail to switch myself with. I could not bear them, so I said to Jacky, 'I don't mind them on my hands and face, but I can't bear them on my body. How do you manage without clothes?' 'Oh, you see,' said Jacky, *'Blackfellow all face,* so nebber mind!'"

"But their idea of cleanliness amuses me," said another. "Would you believe it? I explained to a darkey out camping, not long since, that he should wash his hands before putting on the chops, and not lift them with his fingers; so, sure enough, before the next meal he went to the creek and washed his hands, and then took his seat before the fire to commence operations, but as I had told him not to touch the chops with his fingers, and said nothing about forks, how do you think he placed them in the pan?—with his toes!"

"Well done, Jacky! he took his instructions *au pied de la lettre!*"

"And yet, after all," said another, "with a good deal of the grotesque, and even of the nasty, one is constantly stumbling on something picturesque in connection with the Blacks; for instance: on one of the hottest days of last summer I went to the camp of a blackfellow, whose lubra was sick. He was seated naked before his mia-mia straightening some reeds, of which he was about to make spears, on a little mound of hot ashes, in the usual way. Inside the mia-mia was a young woman, his wife, covered with her opossum-rug, her head resting on her bag, and suffering from fever. I had been talking to the man for a few moments when the invalid raised herself a little, supporting herself on her hand, her back towards us. Her rug partly fell off, her head drooped, and her hair hung down in close heavy masses, reminding me of the appearance of hair in statuary. Indeed, the *pose* was not unlike that of the 'dying gladiator.' 'The flies!' said she, in her own language, and in the tone of one impatient and suffering; and her husband took up a small bunch of twigs and drove away the tormentors. She did not move, however, but in a moment exclaimed 'I am hot;' so the Black filled his mouth with water from his calabash, and, turning towards the sick woman, gently drew down the rug a little and ejected the fluid from his mouth upwards, in such a way that it fell on her skin in the form of spray. After this had been repeated once or twice, she pulled her rug over her and lay down apparently relieved. Altogether, I thought the mode of nursing and the little scene picturesque enough."

"Talking of Blacks," said another, " let me tell you of what happened to me. Last winter I was suffering from rheumatism, and about eight o'clock one night was lying before the fire, very weak and done for want of sleep, when two or three lubras came to the door and asked me to let them have the head of a bullock which was to be killed next morning. Not wishing to be troubled, I consented to the request at once; but instead of withdrawing they remained consulting together in an undertone, and at last I asked them what they were waiting for? 'We want you to tell the cook to give us the head,' said they; to which I replied that I would tell him in the morning. But still they did not go, and after some time it came out that they were anxious I should tell him at once, as *they thought I should be dead before morning.* The idea amused me a good deal, as I did not feel a bit like dying, though no doubt I looked very ill; so I insisted that they should seat themselves on the hob and give me their death-song on the spot, which they did. But the best of it was that my cook, hearing the cry, rushed in and removed the rug with which I had covered my face, exclaiming, when he saw my eyes open, ' Praise be to God, sir ! I made sure you were dead when I heard the lubras " *waking*" *you !'* "

By degrees, as the evening went on, there were a few songs, and the tobacco smoke got crowded, and conversation involved and difficult to follow; but I remember there was a good deal said about new chums, who had been accustomed to hounds at home, getting on poorly in the timber. About midnight we went to bed, and the last thing I recollect was a loud scream, which roused me for an instant. The next moment I was asleep.

As the master of the pack was under the impression that the scent of the wild dog did not lie long after sunrise, we had to dress and breakfast by candle light, so as to be in the saddle as soon as we could see the hounds. On this occasion talk at breakfast was about the scream to which I have just referred. It had proceeded from one of the company, a bold rider and a heavy weight, who had some practice with hounds in England, and his account of it was the only incident of a rather dull breakfast. " I was very sleepy last night," said the narrator in a somewhat strong provincial accent which few retain out here, " and must have dropped off almost as soon as my head touched the pillow. Probably but a short time had elapsed when I dreamt I was with the hounds, sailing along, scent breast-high, when suddenly I got into a crab-hole and came to grief. I thought the shadows of death were fast settling over me "—and here our worthy friend, who seemed inclined to get into the realms of poetry, cast a solemn glance round the table, and stirred his tea with his spoon—" I felt I had come to the last gasp ; I didn't think I should ever draw another breath, as the Badger was lying on top of me, the pommel of the saddle in the pit of my stomach." With every desire to appear sympathetic, the anti-climax was too much for the company, and we all burst into a roar of laughter. It might have passed in the evening with the " bootiful cool," but would not do at six o'clock in the morning.

Breakfast over, there was a cry of " to horse," and the steeds were led forth, looking but in-differently after their night in the stable, to which they were unaccustomed. As a heavy frost was on the ground, and the stable cold, none of them appeared very pleasant. However, we were soon in the saddle and the hounds turned out, and we had not gone three hundred yards when there was a whimper or two, and the moment after a crash, and I heard for the first time a pack of hounds in full cry. Then followed a scamper through sand-hills and scrubs on the scent of a wild dog; but, unfortunately, there was no kill, so we were fain to slacken our girths, light our pipes, and ride back quietly, trying the qualities of our horses over some rasping logs as we went along. After lunch some played quoits and some indulged in a nap. I remember I was very sleepy. Next morning there was another forenoon with the pack, and better sport, after which the company lunched; had a stirrup-cup; congratulated the master about the sport; made appointments for a future meet; shook hands; admired everybody's horse; lit their pipes; had a few more last words, and rode home.

CHAPTER XXVII.

LAW IN THE BUSH—AN INTRUDER ON THE RUN.

THE reader has seen that an official of the Supreme Court did break in on us at Tongala on one occasion, but I dare say he will have understood

that otherwise we had not much to do with law.
Indeed, for the first several years, as far as I
remember, no court of any sort was held nearer
to Tongala than Melbourne, which, for any use it
was to us, might as well have sat in Timbuctoo.
The consequence was, that, as the " Masters and
Servants Act" could not be appealed to, men and
masters took the law into their own hands, the
former leaving their places when dissatisfied, the
latter dismissing and sometimes fining their men
for misconduct—a mode of procedure which, with
all its imperfections, seemed to give as much
satisfaction as any other with which I am
acquainted; for the result was that an ill-
behaved man soon ceased to find masters in the
neighbourhood, whilst a master who had not been
tolerably honourable in his dealings with his men
would before long have found himself without
servants. In fact, that a proprietor should be
well served in our neighbourhood, a character for
straightforward dealing with his men was indispensable. However, as our first bright days of
Arcadian simplicity passed by, and our lands
came to be more fully stocked, conflicting views
of *meum* and *tuum* sprung up between stock-
owners on the question of runs, which could only
be set at rest by the intervention of law, and led,
in 1848 or '49, to the appointment of officials
styled Caveat Commissioners, whose duty was to
hear evidence and determine disputes concerning

boundaries. On my father's run we had to do with two of these functionaries. In both instances my father was the defendant, and in both the plaintiffs withdrew their cases on hearing a portion of the evidence adduceable on our side, so that in our regard the Commissioners had only to register the boundaries agreed upon by the parties in their courts. Prior to the appointment of Commissioners, however, we had a little unpleasantness at Tongala on the subject of one of our boundaries which occurred in this way.

At the junction, or, as the Yankees term it, the fork, of the Goulburn and Murray there were two or three square miles of country not included in my father's run which were periodically flooded to the depth of several feet. About this scrap of country I never troubled myself, as it was of no use to me, or anyone else. It so happened, however, that a misguided Frenchman, the possessor of a hundred and twenty head of crawling cattle, three mares, and a dray, on the outlook for some place in which he might squat in an inexpensive way, heard of the spot, and, thinking it would suit him, transported thither his stock, household effects, and his wife Jinny. With the exception of these belongings, which, without attempting to value the lady, represented a capital too small to attempt squatting with, I think the Frenchman was not

blessed with a five pound note in the world; so
that, being unable to employ labour, he used to
look after his cattle himself, the Blacks at that
time being thoroughly quiet, whilst *Gini*, as he
called his helpmate, attended to the *ménage*.
Being a horse-farrier by trade, he certainly earned
a few pounds now and then by docking colts in
the neighbourhood, and jobs of the sort, otherwise I have no idea how he managed to live during
the year or two he was at the junction. However that may be, I used to notice that wherever
I went, whether to Mount Hope, the Punt,
Kilmore, or elsewhere, I always heard of my
mercurial neighbour, and not unfrequently of some
little act of violence he had committed, or scrape
he had got into. In fact he was a wandering,
unquiet sort of person, and as fond of being on
the move as a *coureur de bois* in the wilds of
Canada. Personally, for a long time I had
nothing to complain of in connection with him,
and indeed rarely saw him except perhaps when
he paid a visit to my cook, or called at Tongala
to inquire about " ma bool " (my bull), an animal
which seemed to share the gad-about propensities
of his owner.

In this way matters went on very quietly
till one day a shepherd of ours, who had
been down the river with his flock, brought
in word that our volatile neighbour had left
his unpleasant place near the junction, and

transported himself and his belongings, Gini
inclusive, to one of our out-stations on the
Goulburn, just then unoccupied. It also appeared
that he had been there some time, as he had
thoroughly repaired the hut, and erected a yard
in which to muster his few head of cattle. So
unusual a proceeding, which seemed to us as
much an act of invasion as the landing of a
French *corps d'armée* at Deal would have done
to an Englishman, rather startled our little circle
at Tongala, and at once put a stop to the *entente
cordiale* which had hitherto existed between the
Frenchman and ourselves. Personally, I am
obliged to acknowledge (being then in the hot
days of my youth) that I should at once have
carried fire and sword into the enemy's camp, had
it not been for a servant who for several years
had discharged the functions of cook and storekeeper on the place, to whom I committed my
intentions. This worthy, who rejoiced in the
sobriquet of " The Peeler," a complete Caleb
Balderstone in his way, after having been informed of what was uppermost in my mind, and
directed to look me up some pistol bullets, proceeded, as he always did when he was in a hurry,
to take several pinches of snuff, when he burst
out into the exclamation, " I am very glad to
hear it, sir; if you'll allow me, I'll just rinse out
the double barrel and go with you. Yaw-hugh!
it will remind me of the evictions in the county

Wicklow years ago, and I shall be there to give a hand."

Everyone knows how a word will occasionally turn the current of one's thoughts, and in this case the word *eviction* brought to my mind circumstances I had read of, which led me to doubt whether turning out the Frenchman in the summary manner contemplated might not in effect be to let myself in for some disagreeable intervention of the law, of which I had a great horror. In fact, when I reflected on the hubbub which had occurred in the old country on the subject of ousting persons from houses and farms which did not belong to them, with the whole force of the law and its guardians within easy beck and call, I began to think that my plan might not be the right one. At all events I thought it better to begin by making "The Peeler" the bearer of a note to the Frenchman, in which I expressed my surprise at the step which he had taken, and called upon him to remove from my father's run, authorizing my ambassador to assure him verbally that in the event of his sending a written acknowledgment of the wrong he had done, he would be allowed to remain where he was for a few weeks until he could make his arrangements to leave. This parleying with the foe I felt, it is true, to be a miserable concession to expediency, especially as I was convinced that an intruder who had gone the length of putting up a stockyard was most unlikely quietly to walk out on a mere summons on the part of the owner. Nevertheless, acting, as I was, on behalf of my father, I thought it my duty to be circumspect and prudent.

In the course of the evening "The Peeler" returned, and on asking what had been the result of his mission, he said, "The Frenchman didn't write, sir, though I asked him to do so, but swore horrid ; partly in what you may call English and partly in his own language, and said he would stick to the country up to the Towro sand-hill ; " and at this point "The Peeler" relieved his feelings with a long pinch of snuff.

"Well, what else did he say ?"

"Well, sir, he swore horrid at first. I never heard anything worse, and then went down on his knees and took Jinny and myself to witness that if you or any of the masters touched the hut or interfered with the cattle, saving your presence, he'd shoot you like one —— duck."

"Yes! and what did you say ?"

"Well, yaw-hugh! Mr. de S——, says I, it's not my business to say anything about the master's affairs, but for-in-as-much as you were talking about shooting, I may just as well recommend your wife to send out her invitations to a wake before you begin, for it's well known there's no one on the river that seems so natural with a gun or a pistol as the family, and that it is safe to turn out a Waterloo if you begin." After which my servant gave utterance to several cackles peculiar to himself, which it is quite impossible to give an idea of in writing, and set to work to lay the cloth for dinner.

Having thus ascertained beyond a doubt my neighbour's intention to appropriate a slice of the run, I sent my father an account of the circumstances, and in due time received a letter in reply, in which he informed me that he had consulted his lawyer, and been advised that there was nothing for it but to have the stockyard and hut pulled down, and things in general made disagreeable for the intruder. My course thus marked out, the next step was to indite a quiet letter to my Gallic neighbour, which I sent by "The Peeler," informing him that, on a certain day, I should chop down the stockyard and hut. In the course of the evening I received his verbal reply that, if I attempted to do anything of the sort, he would shoot me. On the day appointed my brother and I, accompanied by one of the men, who carried a couple of axes, paid a visit to the foreigner's establishment, and to our disgust found him absent, and his wife only at home. Under these circumstances we chopped down the stockyard, but did not touch the hut, as "Gini" informed us that her husband would certainly be at home in a day or two, and begged us not to leave her alone and houseless. We left her, therefore, with the understanding that we should return that day

27

week and pull down the hut, Frenchman or no Frenchman. This leniency was, however, quite thrown away on our neighbour, who, thus twice invited to be present at the demolition of the premises, failed to come to the front; so that, at last, we had to pull down the hut in his absence, merely leaving the bark table and bedstead standing. The job was a disagreeable one, and "Gini," of course, shed "some natural tears;" but there was no help for it. A few days later, finding a score of my neighbour's cattle on the run, I drove them across the Murray, whence it would be difficult to recover them, and sent him notice of the circumstance, and an assurance of my determination to persevere in that course. This step brought our friend to his senses; and on receipt of a letter from him, which satisfied me in every particular, I allowed him to remain where he was for a few weeks, when he departed with his stock and travelled on, as I heard, to some distant part of New South Wales. At all events I never saw him again; and to make the recurrence of such troubles impossible, my father got the useless scrap of country which had led to the unpleasantness added to his run.

At a later period I think a feeling grew up in some neighbourhoods that courts of petty sessions in the bush had become desirable. At all events, the Governor, Sir George Gipps, gazetted a number of stockowners to the commission of the peace, and had clerks of petty sessions stationed here and there. Our neighbourhood, it is true, was not favoured in this way, but I had more than one opportunity of observing how the measure worked in the Western District. In that locality court days were a sort of holiday, and there used to be considerable musters of justices on such occasions, and, when the business was over, not a little brandy-and-water, and discussions respecting the decisions arrived at. To tell the truth, however, though the squatters in those parts were very jolly fellows, they got on but indifferently in the magisterial capacity. One of their great difficulties, I remember, was *making out committals*, which, on one point or another, almost always turned out bad. This, however, was fairly enough set down to the incapacity of the clerks.

On one occasion, one of the justices determined in despair to try his hand at drawing a committal, which he did with much deliberation. However, his experiment was not a success, and it was said that the document fell into the hands of some limb of the law in Melbourne, who, after (speaking metaphorically) ruthlessly tearing it to pieces in court, said he would have it framed and hung up in his chambers, as a sample of what a bush justice could produce.

Occasionally, however, the doings of the little court did hold good, which tended very much to encourage the plucky young J.P.'s to persevere in their duties.

Being present on one occasion at the Chepstowe court, I heard a decision which struck me as very whimsical, and which may be adduced as characteristic. There were on the bench at the time four or five gentlemen (stockowners of course) who, I am sure, urgently desired to administer the law with the utmost impartiality, but who were in a position which, unknown to themselves, rendered them utterly incapable of taking a dispassionate view of the facts brought before them. The parties concerned were two rather rough sheepowners, who were neighbours, and the complaint was that the defendant had trespassed on the plaintiff's run with a flock of scabby sheep—a crime of the blackest dye, of course, in a pastoral country. For the defence, it was urged that the land on which the alleged trespass had been committed was the property of the defendant and not of the plaintiff, and that a *caveat* had been lodged respecting it. The decision of the bench in the case, which was delivered by the chairman with not a little of the manner of a chief justice, was, that commissioners having been specially appointed to decide cases of disputed boundaries, it was beyond the province of the bench to offer any opinion as to whom the land on which the scabby flock was found belonged; and that, without prejudice in that matter, *the bench fined the defendant five pounds for travelling with scabby sheep!* and so the matter ended. The justices, on joining their friends outside the court, seemed, I noticed, much pleased with this their decision, which to their minds met both the law and the equity of the case admirably, and at the same time showed a lawyer-like discrimination on the subject of their jurisdiction. When all was over, the bench adjourned to the house of a brother justice to lunch, to which they did ample justice. The little court at Chepstowe, I used to notice, supplied the justices with endless topics of conversation, and in this respect was a success. Many of the justices were gentlemanly young fellows, and excellent sheep-farmers; kept good liquor, rode good horses, and were usually well placed with a pack of fox-hounds which hunted the neighbourhood.

CHAPTER XXVIII.

OLD DAVIE.

On one or two occasions there came to Wolfscrag, with others of the Nerboolok tribe, a lubra, for whom a freak of nature had earned the name of

Six-fingered Polly. The last time I saw Polly, which was just before I left Wolfscrag, she had a little urchin of a daughter who peeped with bright eyes over her shoulder from her nest between her mother's back and her opossum-rug. The baby seemed just a second edition of its mother—save the six fingers, an ordinary well-made young woman—except that, in addition to her superfluity of fingers, she had also six toes on each of her tiny feet. Amongst the Blacks such things were not common, but there was a Wongatpan or Moira family which was a little remarkable in this way. The father of the family, who was known for a hundred miles round, bore amongst the whites the name of Old Davie. When I first came to Tongala he had only one lubra, one of whose eyes had been put out—I forget now by what accident. By her he had no family; but being, like the rest of his race, addicted to a plurality of wives when obtainable, Old Davie one day brought to the station a second spouse, who, strange to say, like the first, had also but one serviceable eye—with this difference, that her's was a natural and not an artificial defect. This gravitation of single-eyed charmers to one camp, odd in itself, was, however, rendered more remarkable when in due time Davie's youngest wife presented her husband with a little daughter, charming in every particular except in the matter of the family failing, one of its eyes, like its mother's, being—as he who sung "of man's first disobedience and the fruit" expresses it—" by dim suffusion veiled."

Later on, however, a son was born to Old Davie, who—probably from being an only one, unexceptionable in the matter of eyes, and a reasonably fine child in other particulars—became, as soon as he could walk and talk a little, the very idol and delight of the paternal heart. This offshoot of the tribe of Wongat, and the house of Davie, received at a very early age from his father the name of "Jack Jumbuk-man"—*Anglicé*, "Jack the Shepherd;" as it was to the employment of tending sheep at Tongala that his father destined him from the first, as he often told me in high glee. Possibly the old man had done a little castle-building in the matter, thinking it not a bad thing for a hungry savage to have a son in charge of two thousand fat sheep; at all events, there is no reason to doubt that he thought the employment in question thoroughly desirable for his son. To watch the gradual expansion of the Jumbuk-man's faculties; to see him balance himself with his feet astride, and throw his spear at his sister's back; to observe him tomahawk the sleeping dogs, maltreat any birds or insects he could lay hands on, bite his mother; to hear him lisp foul words, and give himself up to the charming ways of savage infancy, became henceforth the chief delight of his father. Though I had known Davie for several years, it was only about this time that he attracted my attention, and that I began to make some inquiries about him. When the Jumbuk-man was born he was verging on that period when a man is said to be "somewhat stricken in years," or, as I have heard an Irishman put it, "a thrifle ould." The wrinkles in his face were beginning to show somewhat strongly; the hair, which grew with remarkable profusion on his back and chest, was waxing grey; whilst the locks on the top of his head were getting scant, though this last peculiarity (undoubtedly not a sign of youth) was probably the consequence of his having a very long beard; as it seems to be a fact that such an appendage and an abundant head of hair rarely manage to exist together for a lengthened period.

I may remark of the mental capacities of this savage that they were below the average of his tribe; that he was the reverse of demonstrative; slow and unemphatic in speech; that he spoke habitually in a low tone and with a lisp; that he was kind to children, and never known to tomahawk his lubras; so that he bore the character amongst us of being a particularly humane and inoffensive specimen of his race. In person he was rather stout, bull-necked, capacious of chest, muscular and unencumbered with fat, and an adept in the use of his spear and waddy. In-

deed, than him none of the Bangerang did more
"excel in fact of arms." Of his passions or pre-
judices, likes or dislikes, but little was known to us
at that time, though constantly at the station,
as he seldom asked for anything or brought himself into notice. In fact, to escape notice was
one of his characteristics, his seeming small
amount of individuality leading one to overlook
him as a vegetable sort of being. At a later
period, however, we came to know that beneath
Davie's commonplace exterior there dwelt a
strong will, great courage, and a passion which,
probably from frequent indulgence, had become
overruling. His special craving was for murder;
particularly for quiet, unostentatious murders,
which he used to perpetrate alone, and at considerable distance from the haunts of his tribe.
Indeed, until he became the father of the Jumbuk-man, it appeared afterwards that he had
never had any strong liking for anything else,
but stuck to his solitary pleasure on every
available opportunity, just as an angler will to
fishing his favourite stream. Had De Quincey
known him, he would have been charmed with
him. He was unique in his way, and on this
score I will just glance at some of his doings
which came to my knowledge. I remember
hearing related how once, for instance, he happened to descry two strange Blacks making their
camp at sundown as they were passing from one

part of the country to another, and of how he stole upon them during the small hours of the morning, and speared them as they lay asleep. That, on another occasion, prowling alone in the country of another tribe, he had discovered a large camp, a hundred yards or so from the banks of the Murray; approached the spot, swimming noiselessly, after nightfall, and then waited patiently amongst the long grass until chance sent a lubra to replenish her kooliman, when he slew her with a single blow of his waddy, and got away before the deed was discovered. But the last exploit of this fiend which came to my ears, possibly from hearing the circumstances related more in detail, I thought a piece of exceptional barbarity. It was as follows :—

In the commencement of 1849 there was a large gathering of tribes on the Edwards river. Amongst others the Wongatpan were there, and with the rest one known to the whites as Colonel Henry; as also Old Davie, his wives, and the all-important Jumbuk-man. This Colonel Henry, a good-looking bachelor of five-and-twenty, fell violently in love with a young lubra who had come to the meeting with her parents. They had never met before, and the object of the Colonel's attachment had long since been promised in marriage to some fellow old enough to be her father, who probably had one or two wives already. At the time, however, she was single, and, as my informant said, had barely reached womanhood. During the time the tribes remained together, it seems Henry lost no opportunity of paying his court to the young lady, as far as circumstances permitted, sending her secretly, through the medium of his female relatives, frequent assurances of undying affection, together with presents of fat opossums, manna, and other delicacies. It was also said that he used large quantities of red ochre and grease in getting himself up for the nightly corroborees, in which he took a distinguished part, being in this particular, as I understood, rather in the extreme of the fashion. In fact, it was over again the old story which the world never gets tired of enacting; so Colonel Henry gained the maiden's heart, and before the tribes separated she eloped with him. This event caused considerable noise in the camp, so that the tribe to which she belonged—one from about Cobram, and of Bangerang tongue—returned to its own country somewhat in anger.

Whilst affairs were in this position, and shortly after the Wongatpan had reached their own country, it happened, unfortunately, that the Jumbuk-man was taken seriously ill. Whether that promising child had surfeited himself with fat fish, or what, I cannot say positively, though it is not unlikely. At all events he became dangerously indisposed. To avert the threatened calamity the conjurers exerted themselves to the utmost. Every incantation believed by the sages of Wongat to be efficacious on such occasions was had recourse to. Nothing, however, was of any avail, and after a few days the boy died. Though the death of a child was not in reality much felt by the tribe, they made—as my brother Richard, who was present, informed me—in deference to the father, who was a great warrior, a certain display of sorrow on this occasion, which took the shape of working themselves up into a state of excitement, in which they accused the old man of want of vigilance as regards the wizards, and beat his head with sticks in a friendly way as he sat unresistingly on the ground, streams of tears welling from his eyes. But if the tribal sorrow was rather assumed than real, the death of the boy was a terrible blow to Old Davie. He had been his special delight, and it was remarked at the time that though the old ruffian had made more widows and orphans than anyone within a hundred miles—had, in fact. rioted in ruthless deeds—when death came to his own mia-mia he took it very hard, and bore his loss in a very unstoical way. They said he more than once asked, "What had the boy done that he should die ? If the doctors of another tribe were angry, could they not have charmed away the life of someone else ?"

The first paroxysms of grief over, the considerations which occurred to Davie, of course,

were—" Whose witchcraft killed the child ? and
on whom could his death be most readily
avenged ?" for, with the Australian Blacks, the
death of a kinsman in such cases is nearly as
satisfactory as that of the offender himself.
These questions were, unfortunately, too easily
answered in this case.   " Colonel Henry," argued
Davie, " stole a young woman ; in revenge, the
conjurer of the tribe has charmed away the life
of the Jumbuk-man.   I will clear the score by
killing the woman."   Having made up his mind
on the subject silently and irrevocably, as was his
wont, the bereaved parent became more calm,
and, keeping his resolves to himself, set out with
his family and two or three others of the tribe in
the direction in which he was likely to meet
Henry and his wife, and quickly came upon the
young couple, with a few others, midway between
Wyuna and Kotoopna.   With them his party
encamped, and of what occurred on the occasion
I gleaned from the Blacks as follows.

Shortly after the meeting of the two bands
Old Davie's party made known to the others the
death of the Jumbuk-man, when the usual
expressions of sorrow were indulged in.   Next
morning, when the women had gone out yamming,
Old Davie addressed the men, and told them how
Colonel Henry had eloped with a young woman
of another tribe, and how, in consequence, the
conjurers had taken the life of his child.   Then

getting on his feet, and warming with his subject
as he proceeded, he said to Colonel Henry, with
considerable emotion, " The people of that woman
have killed my boy. Give her to me and I will
kill her. There is clay on my head and my
beard, and on the heads of my wives, and
it cannot be washed off until I have revenge.
Let her tribe wear clay. Let me kill her."
Colonel Henry replied—"You have come to
kill my wife. She is a Wongatpan now. She
is your niece now. You have no right to kill
her. Am I to lose a wife because you have lost
a son ? Besides, it was not her tribe who killed
the boy. I saw the conjurer of another tribe
looking at him. It was he who killed the
boy. Let us go and kill some of the tribe.
I wont give up the woman. You always
kill someone. I have long desired to have
a wife. Now I have a young wife, and
you want to kill her !" " It is our custom,"
replied Davie. "I cannot find the man who
killed the boy. His sister is here : I will kill
her. It is my right. You cannot always stand
before her. I may not spear her whilst you are
there, but when you take your eyes off
I will kill her." " I will take her over the
Murray," said Henry, "and let her go. She
will find her way back to her tribe. I will not
let her be speared." " And," said Davie, " what
will that profit you ? Will you have a wife

then?   Better, like a true Wongatpan, let me
kill her and revenge your nephew, who is gone.
Take care her tribe do not bewitch you next.
But why do I talk? Do as you like, say what
you choose, I will never change till I have killed
her.   I thirst for her blood.   I hunger for her
blood.   I will have it!"

After this style, as I heard, the matter was
discussed for a considerable time, and eventually
the old tiger worked himself up to the last pitch
of frenzy.   The more he talked, the more furious
he became.   Meanwhile Henry had little to say
in reply.   He was wavering.   He was oppressed
by superstition, and the doubtful right to kill his
wife, which Davie claimed.   Then, too, the
immense animosity of his opponent, his concen-
trated energy, his mad craving for revenge, to
which Henry had nothing violent to oppose, were
weighing him down.   In the matter of understanding Henry was vastly his superior, but in
energy, resolution, tenacity, and constitution he
was weak in comparison to Davie.   In fact—and
to this persons of our race will find it difficult to
allow full weight—I have no doubt Henry was
growing weary ; the discussion had exhausted his
endurance, and he was going to give way to get
rid of it.   As usual in such cases, as Colonel
Henry's replies waxed faint, the savage energy of
the old murderer increased.   As some of my
informants said, he was hardly recognizable in his

excited state. The veins stood out on his forehead, his chest heaved, he foamed at the mouth.

"Talk as you like," shouted he; "complain if
you choose, I will never relent : I will kill her !"

To this there was no reply. Several hours had
been spent in the discussion. Henry was worn
out, so he held his tongue. No one felt called
upon to interfere. The wife had no relative in
the camp to take her part; so Davie stooped
down, and took a small parcel from his bag,
which he threw to Henry.

"There," said he, is money : take it; leave the
camp; let me revenge my son. Let her be got rid
of, otherwise we shall soon stand by your grave,
for the conjurers will take your life. Go! make
haste! I am ready! shut your mouth! Go!"

Though it is more than thirty years since these
brutalities happened, it pains me still to remember them, and costs an effort to conclude.
Henry took up the silver. It was only a trifling
compensation for the loss he was to sustain, but
he gave in because he was weary. Probably his
own loss of a wife pained him more than the
thought of the girl's murder. So he took up the
silver, as there was nothing which appeared to
him wrong, much less horrible, in the act ; indeed,
I doubt whether he was capable of being made
to understand its turpitude. He had yielded to
superstition, to fear of the conjurer, to the
tyranny of custom—above all, to the force of a

will stronger than his own ; and he did not feel that there was anything to prevent him accepting compensation, much or little, for the loss which was being forced upon him. So he stood up, the silver in his hand, collected his weapons, and, with an exclamation not so much of sorrow for the fate of the girl as of petulant anger at his loss, left the camp in company with another of his tribe. Davie watched him, and then sat anxiously expecting his victim. Not long after, the women and children were seen returning. They were, of course, ignorant of what had occurred, and each went to her own camp, and amongst others the young wife. Hardly had they seated themselves, when the old murderer quietly took up a club and a huge war-spear, the point of which bristled with fragments of glass, and walked leisurely towards Colonel Henry's camp, and as though he was going to pass behind it. There was nothing remarkable in his doing so, and hence it attracted no attention on the part of the women. When close to the young woman, however, he stopped. With a sudden jerk he flung from him his only garment and stood naked within a few yards of the mia-mia, the spear quivering in his hand. At this instant the young wife turned her head and saw him. A plaintive cry escaped her, for, no doubt, she realized in an instant the full meaning of the Satanic apparition. Before she could rise to her feet, however, the fatal weapon was plunged into her back with a force which would have slain an elephant; then a blow with the club, and her sufferings on earth were at an end.

This murder—the last, I believe, which Davie committed—did not find favour with the tribe. "He always kills," said they, with an expression of pain; "she was a poor thing, an unfortunate!" and so the matter ended. As for me, I was so disgusted at what I heard, that I sent word to the two men that if ever they crossed my path again I would seize and deliver them to the police, and I never saw either of their faces again. Otherwise it was an idle threat, for I knew nothing would be done.

CHAPTER XXIX.

RAMBLES IN UNOCCUPIED COUNTRY

I AM afraid I must plead guilty to a somewhat vagabond turn of mind, and a constitutional love of rambling, especially into solitary and out-of-the-way places. Perhaps it is the consequence of many voyages and journeys made early in life. At all events, so decided are my propensities in this way that I have seldom passed a lonely mountain, unknown stream, or ruin of any sort without feeling strongly moved to make myself acquainted with its secrets; and, I suppose, this is how it happened that I had no sooner got things in order at Tongala, than, instead of quietly giving myself up to the enjoyment of my hut and the comforts of station life, I took to making excursions into the unoccupied country around me. These outings, which began with a day's ride in one direction or another, gradually extended to Mount Hope, Lake Meering, Swan Hill, the lower Edwards, the Wawkool, Niemur, and so on; so that for several years, until the country got occupied with sheep, it became a practice with me to pass two or three weeks in the bush shortly before lambing, which began in the middle of May. One, or sometimes two, of my brothers were usually of the party, and not unfrequently a couple of Blacks.

What we proposed to ourselves in our outings was a little change of life, plenty of shooting and hunting, and a sight of the unexplored country. This custom of ours, I may say, was an exceptional one, as bushmen generally took their holidays in town; "the pleasure in the pathless woods," of which we have all read, being indulged in no oftener than was absolutely unavoidable. With me the reverse was the case, as I preferred hunting excursions into unoccupied country to visits to the city; hence gradually I came to look

on the country of our rambles, which in extent
might be a hundred and fifty miles by fifty, as a
sort of *plaisaunce*, or grand park, on which I was
free to wander, shoot, hunt, fish, and do as I
chose, my only care being to escape getting a
spear through me.

Besides hunting, and a little exploring, I was
also very fond of scenery in those days, and loved
the Murray and the grand trees on its banks, its
reed-beds, its plains big and little, edged with
mallee, box, gum and other evergreen trees, its
pine-shaded sand-hills and long winding lagoons
crowded with waterfowl. Indeed, for the pleasure
it gave me to observe nature at that time—to
look on the trees of the forest; the quiet lakes;
the *mirage* mocking the sight with expanses of
unreal water; the ways of bird and beast; the
lowan with her peculiar nest; the wild dog,
seemingly impervious to heat and thirst; and a
hundred other objects of the sort—I might have
been a painter and a naturalist, though I knew
but little of their pursuits. Then, when the camp
was made, what a relish we had for roast duck,
grilled fish, or a kangaroo's tail done in the ashes,
followed by a *bonne bouche* of manna got from the
Blacks! And how pleasant it was, when the
cravings of hunger had been appeased, to lie in
one's blanket before the fire in the full enjoyment
of quart-pot tea and negro-head tobacco, whilst
our little party discussed the crack shots and

other hunting incidents of the day, or the relative merits of shot-guns and rifles, or the geography of the country about which we were wandering. That our forests were not stocked with lions and koodoos, buffalo, and elephants, like those of more favoured lands, was no doubt a drawback, and one which we often regretted.

With one exception, these excursions were made with only a horse a-piece, which at the outset were rather heavily laden, as, besides their riders, they had each to carry several pounds of flour, a blanket, ammunition, some tea and sugar, and other odds and ends. Our appetites, however, soon lightened the loads, our food afterwards depending on what we could get with our guns, dogs, and fishing lines—a mode of existence rather savage in its tendency, no doubt, but to us, at the time, very enjoyable, as a relief from the sameness of station life.

On our return from these trips our black friends at Tongala, who took a good deal of interest in them, had a host of questions to ask, which let one somewhat into their ways of thinking. Of course, as they themselves seldom left their country except on the war-path and for the purpose of knocking some one's brains out, they naturally thought we had been taking our pleasure in the same way, and that there could possibly be no other inducement for our excursions; so the first inquiry always was, " Well, massa, how many wild blackfellows you bin shootum?" our reply in the negative seeming rather strange to them, and leading, I fancy, to the conclusion either that we were not much given to telling the truth, or that we must have fearfully neglected our opportunities. Another question was, whether we had seen all the worn-out old moons, which they described as about the size of a dray-wheel, and as laying about Lake Boga, which they considered to be the outside of the world; or whether we had seen the sun, after its reaching those parts, take its course to the southward, behind the trees, so as to be ready to rise next morning in the east, evidently being of opinion that the world was a plane, of which the Bangerang occupied the centre and Lake Boga was the western edge. That I had seen these things I stoutly averred, as a matter of course, and on pain of being set down as an impostor, and I was not a little amused to notice that one of the black boys who had been out with us not only supported me with the weight of his testimony, but applied himself out of hand to the embellishment of my yarns, in accordance, no doubt, with the time-honoured custom of travellers all the world over.

The first of our more prolonged excursions, I remember, was to Mount Hope, the Kanbowro Creek, and the Murray River thereabouts; my brother Richard, a blackfellow, and myself making the party. As we crossed the Mount

Hope plains we had some capital runs after red kangaroo (by far the fleetest of the species), which I then saw for the first time. Eastward of the Campaspe this variety of the kangaroo was not met with, neither was it found at any great distance from the saltbush plains. On this trip it was exceedingly hot during the day, though not at night, and the pigs'-faces were covered with ripe fruit, so, naturally, as we had been living on mutton and damper for months, we indulged in them rather more than we should have done, and suffered in consequence a smart indisposition of a few hours. The plain, for the thirty miles we followed it, from the Campaspe to Mount Hope, was one bed of ripe fruit, some juicy and some dried like raisins. As often, however, as I crossed the same country afterwards, I never again saw the pigs'-faces ripe, so that I fancy they only came to maturity in exceptional years. The plant is now nearly, if not quite, extinct in that locality.

In our hunting rambles we liked to have with us a black boy or two, if we had horses enough, which was not always the case; not, new-chum like, to find our horses for us in the morning, and eventually the road home, for in such matters we were well versed ourselves, but as adding to the strength of the party in case of a fight, and taking trouble off our hands in camp. Besides, whatever he may be about towns and

public-houses, there is no one more pleasant and
genial, when really in the bush, than a blackfellow; besides that, he is always ready with
information on a hundred points connected with
bush-craft.

In addition to the explorer's pleasure of
traversing unknown country, and being the first
white man to see streams, lakes, and pasture
lands, I took, as I have said, great delight in the
landscape and enjoyed the pine-topped sand-hill,
the mallee-bounded plain, the towering row of
river gums, and the virgin sward unprofaned by
flock or herd, as I fancy the English landscape
painter does the green field, the snug cottage,
and flowery hedgerow which for centuries have
supplied the subjects of his art.

This reminds me—though, from the desultory
manner in which these pages have been written, I
am not sure that I have not already referred to
the subject—that whilst Monsieur Buvelôt, Monsieur Von Guerard, and other painters of high
merit, have of late years given us excellent
renderings of the scenes which characterize the
sea-board of our continent, its ranges and water-
holes, gnarled gum-trees, and so on, no one has
yet attempted to utilize for art purposes the vast
plains and desolate hills which constitute the
leading features of the continent in its interior.
Whether they are capable of being made sub-
servient to the painter's aims, or whether canvas

can be made to convey the feelings they engender,
I know not; that they have, however, a charm of
their own, bathed as they are in the fierce glare
of the sun and wrapped in eternal stillness, I
should think many must have felt. Another
kindred subject, which seems to me to abound in
picturesque and characteristic detail, is the camp
life of the Blacks, and I have often been surprised
that no artist has taken it up. Possibly their
ungainly appearance about towns, where alone
the artist is likely to see them, may have had
something to do with it. There, certainly, they
are neither picturesque nor prepossessing; but
it is different when one sees the half-nude,
statuesque figure in the native cloak, and the
stately carriage of the untamed man amidst the
surroundings of camp life, beneath the appropriate
gum-trees of the lagoon, or the deep shadows of
some luxuriant pine-ridge. Indeed, if Australia
possesses a subject out of which a new and
characteristic school might come, I should say it
was the aborigines. No doubt, to learn their
ways, and depict them, would entail a good deal
of time and application, but how novel such
paintings would be, and what admirable records
of the ways of the race!

But to return. Our happy hunting-ground was
inhabited by several tribes whose languages were
unknown to our Bangerang companions. Many
of the men, however, we made out, had seen Sir

Thomas Mitchell's party when it passed from
Swan Hill to the Loddon in 1836, and this was
all, or nearly all, they had seen of white men.
Though to all appearance friendly, and very
ready to supply us with fish, manna, and things
of the sort, which we were very glad to accept,
we were quite aware that in accordance with
their customs they would very probably knock
our brains out if they got a chance ; an amiable
penchant which not only entailed on us the
necessity of keeping our arms ready and our
powder dry, but—what was very tiresome—of
watching at night, and spending many a weary
hour, gun in hand, painfully alive to every sound
and every shadow, when the blanket would have
been more acceptable. However, we never were
attacked, nor did we ever detect anyone approaching our camp. On one occasion, indeed,
I remember a false alarm startled us somewhat.
It occurred at Mŏŏrerbat (*Anglicé*. Mŭrrābŭt
Creek), whither I had taken one of my neighbours, whose run on the Goulburn was overstocked, and who was on the outlook for new
country. Besides my friend and myself, an Irish
station hand and two Bangerang Blacks were of
the party. It was about nine o'clock at night
that the scare occurred, and we were thinking of
getting into our blankets, when Paddy gave
utterance to a yell which I should think savoured
strongly of Donnybrook, and hurriedly discharged

both barrels of his fowling-piece. Making sure that the Blacks were upon us, I sprang to my feet, and, seizing my rifle, rushed to the nearest tree for cover. Still I could see nothing but Paddy standing, gun in hand, as if rooted to the spot. At last he broke silence, " Tare and ages ! a thundering big snake anyhow ; fifty feet long if he's an inch. Dead enough now, by jabers ; sorra move he'll ever move again !" This exclamation of Paddy's took our fingers off the triggers, and I really began to hope that we had bagged the mythical snake of which the Blacks have stories in all parts of the country. On examination, however, our snake turned out to be a new tether-rope, which one of us had left on the green grass, and which by moonlight did not look altogether unlike a snake—of course barring the length. Occasionally, when there seemed to be no Blacks about, the whole party used to turn in and trust to chance ; but as a rule we preferred watching, for otherwise our sleep was so disturbed, and we woke so often, that we thought half a night's sleep in peace preferable to a whole one spent in a sort of intermittent nightmare. In those days Major Mitchell's dray tracks were quite visible on the plains, especially near what he called Moonlight Creek, which was in fact the same stream which he again came upon higher up and called the Loddon. The native name for the Loddon I learnt was Woppoon, and that of the Murray just there Mille, lower down Millewa, and higher up, as the reader has seen, Tongala, and still higher up Kaiela.

Speaking of Mitchell reminds me how few of our explorers were either good bushmen, or good men in the bush. By the term *good bushman* is usually meant one who possesses in a high degree the faculty of finding his way about a country without a compass; one whose knowledge of the positions of places is but little affected by the course he may take, however winding it may be ; in fine, one who finds his way by the exercise of a special faculty rather than by extraneous help. By the term *a good man in the bush*, on the other hand, is meant a man well versed in bush craft ; one who can find his way fairly ; track, shoot, and swim well ; who can bear hunger, thirst, and fatigue ; is able to look after his horses under circumstances of every sort ; understands the Blacks and their ways ; has a good idea of where to look for water, and so on. It is also a fact that a man may succeed very well as an explorer, even though he is not a good bushman, and may by aid of compass and sextant find his way very well from a given point to a river or mountain range a thousand miles off, and back again, who might be much puzzled to get back to his camp, after riding hither and thither in a cattle-trampled paddock of only a hundred thousand acres. Upon this statement the reader will probably ask how

it has happened that our explorers, whom I
have characterized as generally indifferent bushmen, succeeded in finding their camps under all
sorts of circumstances. My reply is that in a
country unoccupied by stock the fresh track of
even one horse can generally be followed pretty
easily, and that the track of a party is almost as
plain as a road, and remains so in many cases for
weeks, months, or even longer periods, so that
an indifferent bushman is generally able to follow
back his own horse tracks to his camp; and if he
cannot do this, his custom of travelling by
compass will enable him to intersect the main
track of his party and get to the camp by
following it, though he might never be able to
return to a camp in a stock-trampled country.
In fine, when an explorer leaves his camp in an
unoccupied country, he can return to it either by
retracing his steps or by intersecting the track
which leads to it; whilst, in a country which is
stocked, the tracks left by his party may not be
such as can be followed, and in many cases he
may only be able to get back by the exercise of
the faculty, the possession of which constitutes a
good bushman.

Another feature of interest in our excursions
was the ways of the Blacks, their stone tomahawks, weapons, and belongings in general. Being
a small party, they never fled from us, nor seemed
disturbed at our horses, though the discharge of a

gun made them a little nervous. It was on these occasions I noticed that in the presence of a person who might be an enemy, a Black, who has risen from the camp to go, never takes up his weapons or effects from the ground with his hands, as he might be easily killed when stooping, but lifts article by article with his toes, and so conveys them to his hands without exposing himself. This feat, as I know from experience, is not a difficult one, and certainly does not necessitate a big toe like a thumb, as I have read. Any young person accustomed to go bare-footed, who had seen such things done, could do the same with a little practice.

One of the articles of food which we found most in use amongst the Blacks of the Lake Boga neighbourhood and the mallee scrubs was manna. There were bags full of it in almost every camp, and I understood the Blacks to say that they used to set fire to a portion of the mallee every year and gather the manna the next season from the young growth. As we rambled about we came upon Blacks under all sorts of circumstances, and we used to remark how little our appearance—mounted on animals of which few of them could have any idea even from description—used to disturb their self-possession. On one occasion I remember I had wandered from the party near one of the lakes, when I heard a tomahawk in the distance. Riding in the direction of the sound, I was not long in coming on a solitary young Black, who was busy chopping a slab of wood out of the lower part of a pine-tree, probably to be made into a wommera, or throwing stick. As the ground was sandy my approach was not heard; so, without dismounting, I pulled up at some little distance to watch the young savage at his work. He was naked, and in the fillet which encompassed his head was stuck a white feather, which became him well, and contrasted admirably with his black hair and bronze-coloured skin. He rested on his toes, his posteriors nearly touching his heels; the posture and occupation displaying to advantage the muscles of his back, thighs, and arms, and the remarkable elasticity of his frame. A white man at his work would have knelt, and taken off much of the strain; but the Black, I have noticed, seldom kneels. Indeed, in many little matters the action of his race and ours is a little different.

After waiting unobserved for a few moments I called out to him in English. At the unusual sound he turned his head, and, catching sight of me, with an exclamation of surprise sprung to his feet, and, catching up his spear, stood confronting me. I also brought my rifle to my shoulder, but otherwise did not move; but I could see the savage's inflated nostril and heaving breast as he stood for a moment in his attitude of defence.

His first surprise over, he lowered his spear, as I did my rifle; then a few words and signs ensued, not very well understood on either side, when he shouldered his bag and left me.

The Lake Boga tribe was the one we saw most of in our rambles. Its members were a stalwart race, many of the men being six feet high, and few under five feet eight inches. Opossum-rugs seemed scarce amongst them, and our black boys said that they covered themselves at night with their fishing nets; but possibly this was a mere calumny, for strange Blacks are very fond of criticising each other's ways.

On one occasion we came across a party of about twenty of the Lake Boga people, men, women, and children. They were seated on the sandy beach of the lake, just out of reach of the wavelets which came rippling in before the wind. A little blue smoke, from a fire made of a substance composed of dead reeds and other decayed vegetation mixed with clay, then very plentiful round the lake, went upwards in the sunlight. As we approached they got up and seemed a little uneasy, so, not to alarm them, I halted the party a short distance off, and two of us dismounting, walked up to the camp, and, chucking one of the picaninnies under the chin, and pulling the nose of another, by way of introduction, seated ourselves by the fire. Seeing that we were peaceably inclined, the group followed our example, and my friend and I began to discuss the attainability of some delicious-looking perch which was roasting on the embers and emitting an odour just then far from disagreeable in our nostrils. Of course they would have given us some at once if we had asked for it; but it was voted that this would not do just then, as we felt ourselves to some extent representatives of the imperial race, and so on our dignity. Whilst the matter was under discussion, however, one of our new friends brought our difficulties to an end by putting a large quantity of the coveted food on two wisps of fresh green grass and laying it before us. This being so, we thought the proper thing was to accept the fish as a proof of good feeling on our part, and that to act otherwise would be decidedly churlish, so we set to work accordingly with great gusto, and without the help of forks, our hosts being apparently much gratified to notice ways so entirely in accordance with their own.

The repast over, the rest of the party having been supplied like ourselves, I thought it well to make some little present to our entertainers, but the question was, which of our belongings would they appreciate, and what could we spare? Of tobacco and tea they knew not the virtues; and, besides these articles and our ammunition, there was little in our packs. Fortunately, in this emergency I recollected a new cotton handkerchief of the Union Jack pattern,

29

of pre-eminently gaudy colours, which it struck
me would be emblematical of our country, and
quite an appropriate present in every way, so,
getting it out of the kit, I looked at the group
for some one with whom I might have a little
fun in the presentation. As the fittest, I fixed
on a young girl at the shy period of life, who
was stealthily peeping at us with wild eyes from
behind the little crowd ; so I beckoned one of the
Blacks to tell her to come to me. This he did,
but she apparently refused point-blank to advance
an inch, and at once became the object of the
outcry of the whole camp. So the old women
bullied, and the old men coaxed, whilst the girl
peered at me from behind a beldame who sat
between us. At length, after some little delay,
partly pushed forward by the women, the young
one got up and slowly approached me with a half-
bold, half-frightened air. She was as erect as a
reed, and, as far as I could judge, the nearer she
came the more terrible I appeared in her eyes, as
I stood with the handkerchief dangling from my
hand. There was a look of unutterable wildness
about the creature, mixed with curiosity and
apprehension, which was extremely amusing and
characteristic. When within a couple of yards
of me she stopped, disengaged her right arm from
her opossum-rug, and, reaching as far as she
could, was in the act of taking the handkerchief
when I sprang forward with a yell as if about to

seize her, a measure which resulted in her hasty retreat, and screams of laughter from our new acquaintances. Your blackfellow always loves a joke, and the camp understood the matter at once ; but the girl, I have no doubt, set down the proceeding as our manner of wooing wives, and congratulated herself on her escape.

On our return to Tongala after our trips, civilized ways were quite welcome again : damper, so despised a fortnight ago, now seemed savoury as plum-cake ; and horsehair mattrasses, on sheets of bark, beds for Sybarites. And then the pleasure of sleep, unbroken by watching and unvisited by visions of spears and waddies, can hardly be reckoned up. Besides, there were the greetings and congratulations of our Bangerang neighbours, who were constantly telling us we should sooner or later get our brains knocked out in our wanderings, and were glad to see us back, and so forth. But my pages are coming to an end, and I must have done with my sooty friends and their ways, of which I have, perhaps, said more than enough. So adieu, my Enbena, for I cannot even now, amidst the din of the city, forget thee, friend of my lone days. In truth, many a time when weary of books, with nothing to fill the vacant hour, right glad was I to see thee coming over the little plain at Thathumnera, with lubra, picaninni, and all thy belongings ; to count with thee thy hunting spoil and listen to thy budget of small news, even though thou heldest an empty pipe somewhat prominently before me, or pressed on me thy longing for a share of the contents of my flour-bags. Many a time, too, was I glad to have thee as a companion in hunting and shooting, for a merry fellow thou wert, and a genial scamp! But our civilization has rolled over thee, my Enbena, somewhat rudely since those times; ending alike, for the most part, thy merry ways and thy rascalities. Of thy tribe scarce one is left. Forest and swamp know thee no more. Adieu! Let the cry of the *jaaring** hurrying to the Murray to drink at sundown, and the loud laugh of the *wigilōpka*† from the towering river-gum, be thy memento; thy monument the lone *mulōga*‡ grave, or the grass-grown oven which smokes no more; and the west wind, whistling through the streaming boughs of the oak, the dirge of a people which have passed away!

CHAPTER XXX.

MY SERVANTS.

In the bush, as elsewhere, a good deal of one's success and comfort depend on servants, and when I began squatting, servants seemed little

---

* Cockatoo.   † Laughing Jackass.   ‡ Sandhill.

calculated to make their masters either successful or comfortable. Convictism at that time had not gone out, but was on the wane; and my men, when I got them, were an average lot of ruffians, who had all shortly before been convicts, some in New South Wales and some in Tasmania, and hated anything like work, and everybody who was not a convict—their employer for the time being especially. From first to last they were a motley crew, composed of housebreakers, thieves, drunken soldiers, and a Paddy or two, who in their jovial way had hit one of the boys at Donnybrook a trifle too hard with the shillalah. Now-a-days one never meets with men of this type, probably because the last of them died of drink not long after the gold discovery, when all things, nobblers in particular, went a little fast in the colony. Nor was the loss a great one, being, as it seems to me, a very proper exemplification of Darwin's principle of the survival of the fittest. Should, however, scientists in the future desire to know more of this extinct class of men, they will meet a good deal about them in the colonial literature of the period; or, in the event of that failing, in the bones of the departed, which will be met with amidst the *debris* of salt-bush and pigs'-face, which disappeared from Victoria about the same era. From this source, no doubt, as in the case of pre-historic races, any facts required may be elicited. Be this as it may, there is no doubt that, for some time after Batman's settlement, the craving labour market, high wages, and numerous grog shops of Melbourne had placed the ex-convict working class who flocked to it in a very independent position, and the employers of labour were not slow to learn that the workman had set his heart on a future of pretty constant excess and debauchery, and that for the time, at all events, he was in a position to give a very practical effect to his ideas on the subject.

Hence, at first, engagements in the bush were short, and but little steady labour could be had. Luckily for all parties, the giddy days of the colony did not last long, and expiree convicts (as well as others) soon got a good deal sobered down in more senses than one. In the case of the working class, the first step towards better things was a great fall in wages, which practically had the effect of transforming them from drunkards and idlers into shepherds and hut-keepers, and, so far as my experience went, eventually into tolerable servants and citizens. Besides the fall in wages, other circumstances led to what to some extent must be called reform, for station life not only put a stop to drunkenness and theft by the absence of grog and of anything worth stealing, but the constant absence of temptation had a tendency to throw the convict's mind into a better groove. It also struck me that

the intercourse of the convict with an occasional
free fellow-labourer, and also with his master, to
some extent educated him to better principles,
and to thoughts and ideas which were not of the
prison.   Probably, also, the possession of a reasonable freedom went towards creating a healthier
tone of mind.   After my men had realized that
they were free, and found that circumstances
had in a great measure cut them off from
drink, a desire for property sprung up amongst
them ; so that though the old convict custom of
going to town once a year " to have a spree,"
or spend in three or four days' drinking the
earnings of the twelve months, did not go out of
fashion altogether, it at least became modified, by
the men investing a portion of their wages in the
purchase of horses, guns, prime sheep, dogs, or
something of the sort.   As a rule the horse (or
more often the mare) once bought was kept, and
commonly before commencing the annual spree,
when, of course, his owner rode him to town,
some clothes were purchased and the stabling
paid in advance, so that when the debauch was
over his owner might return to his usual avocations without let or hindrance.   The more property a man acquired, the less he used to drink,
so that acquisitiveness, once set agoing, not
unfrequently beat inebriety.   At Tongala the
result of the change was, that most of my
servants had one, and several three or four brood

mares and their offspring on the station, and some more, the possession of which I found excellent guarantees for the good behaviour of their owners. Having a few head of horses, for the grazing of which no fee was charged, tended also to render men stationary ; and, indeed, several of my men remained with me for periods varying from five to ten years. As they improved in their conduct I naturally came to have a kindly feeling towards them, which soon became mutual ; and though I was a little stern with my rogues, and kept them at arms-length, I experienced several instances of goodwill on their parts which proved their disinterestedness. As our sheep increased fresh shepherds of course had to be hired, otherwise there was little change in my staff of men, and a good many of them used to talk very complacently of the little burial-place on the sand-hill as undoubtedly their last resting-place. However, that was not to be, for the discovery of gold changed everything; and, as I have often thought, how unfortunately for the majority of us.

Whether it arose from the lonely life the men led, or what, I cannot say, but we used to notice that a few of them became somewhat eccentric after several years' residence on the station, and that occasionally men passing by inquired for work who were evidently somewhat silly. Others escaped anything of the sort, and even improved their minds a good deal by reading. As an instance, I may mention lending a shepherd a trashy romance, which he kept for months, and read and re-read until, I fancy, he must have almost known it by heart. To this man of the prison, hulk and chain gang, who had probably known little of anything but misery and vice from infancy, the scenes depicted by the author, which day by day he pondered over under the shade of a gum-tree whilst shepherding, no doubt were glimpses of fairyland; and I used to fancy that a certain nobility of feeling, with which the writer had imbued some of his characters, had not been without effect on the heart of his convict-reader, as I found his sympathies were with the hero and not with the ruffian of the story. When he returned the book, it was with expressions of admiration so strong as to make me smile, and at the same time imprint the circumstance on my recollection. That he thought the tale a true one was evident, and for some time he seemed to dwell in imagination on the scenes without any wish to enter on new ones. One day, however, I sent him a second book, after which he took to supplying himself now and then with one of the Waverley novels, or some biographical work, which he purchased from a hawker who latterly used to visit the station from time to time with his waggon-load of wares. The result was that reading became a habit with the man, and, finding himself once without books, he asked me to lend him one. On inquiring what he would like to have, he said he had never read anything like the romance I first lent him, and that, as he had not seen it for three or four years, he would be glad to read it again. My reflection was that he must indeed be a low animal to prefer such maudlin stuff to Scott. However, I sent him the book. A week or two later I saw the man again, when he referred to the romance. " I used, sir," said he, " to think it the finest book that ever was written, and was never tired of thinking over it, but somehow, I don't know how it is, it seems all changed now ; a poor childish sort of book, and not a bit like ' Guy Mannering ' or ' Kenilworth,' so that I have hardly been able to read it through." So I saw the man's literary taste had grown, unknown to himself, and his endeavour to read the old book was like trying to put on the boots which had fitted him in boyhood. His case was by no means a solitary one.

Besides the eccentricity induced by station life, there seemed to me a tendency to insanity in some of the men when left without companionship. This we had frequent opportunities of noticing, as, when our flocks had become large and the Blacks got quieted down, we often left a trustworthy shepherd quite alone for weeks in some corner of the run. On such occasions one of us visited him every ten days or so with rations, had half-an-hour's chat, and left. After six or eight weeks, and in some cases in less time, we generally noticed an alteration in the conversation and demeanour of the recluse, and that he had become somewhat eccentric, excited, and childish. Strange to say, there was little or no complaint of loneliness or wish for the solitude to cease, the man seeming engrossed with his business and content with his surroundings. Those who were not injuriously affected in this way were usually rather impatient under their banishment. I used also to think that solitude was more prejudicial to the expiree convict than to the free man, but I could never satisfy myself why it should be so. Concerning mental culture, I think, as the result of prison discipline, that the convict had not unfrequently the advantage of the free labourer; on the other hand, the free labourer was seldom so thorough a drunkard as the convict, neither had he the same craving for tea, strong tobacco, and stimulants of every sort. As a rule, the convict was short-lived, and I am not aware that, of those who tended my father's flocks thirty years ago, there is one now alive. Truly, a heterogeneous lot they were—horse-stealers, machine-breakers, homicides, disorderly soldiers, drunken marines, housebreakers, petty thieves, and so on. Amongst them there always remained more or less of the freemasonry of their class, and one was apt to keep the other in countenance in any little misdeed. When several were together, and conversation flagged, it was not unusual for one of them to exclaim, "Well, So-and-so, why don't you say something? Tell us how you were lagged (convicted), man!" The history of that event was always thought to be a man's best story, and I should think the histories of my men would not have been a bad stock-in-trade with which to commence another "Gil Blas."

In my experience the new chums (as lately-arrived emigrants were called) were the least satisfactory servants, though often sober men; as, besides being poor hands in the bush, they were generally dissatisfied, and had a very faint idea of obeying orders. Old soldiers were better in this respect, but less intelligent than others, and generally drunkards. On questioning one of this sort, whom I was about to hire, concerning his antecedents, he said—

"I have only been in the country a year; before that I was in the army. About eighteen months ago we were playing long-bowls with the Afghans."

"How long were you in the army?"

"Eighteen years. I have seen a good deal of service on many stations."

"And which station did you like best?"

"Oh! the Mauritius, sir; rum there was only twopence a glass, and *illigant* rum one shilling a bottle."

Fortunately for us, rum was not to be had very easily at Tongala, *illigant* or *inilligant*. Several of my men had had varied experiences of life of a certain sort. Two of them, for instance, had served in the British legion in the first Carlist war, and their tales interested me somewhat, possibly because not so long before (whilst at college, and just in my teens—*Consule Planco*—) I had myself been possessed by a strong desire to take service on the other side, under Zumalacarregui, the great Carlist general. One of these men was an Irish Londoner, long in my service, a hot-tempered, good-natured little fellow who rejoiced in the name of Ben Hare. Except on the subject of some valuable plunder which he said he had buried in the Peninsula, Ben was decidedly averse to speaking of his campaigns, notwithstanding which I used to draw him out occasionally.

On one occasion, whilst busy pressing wool, I said to this hero—" Ben, I'm tired, and whilst we rest, and smoke our pipes, you shall tell me something about Spain and the legion." At first my little Irishman was unwilling to enter on the subject, and excused himself on the plea that he did not like to think of those times; but, once started, he got on well enough, and gave me some descriptions of rough campaigning scenes which have now pretty well passed from my memory. One, however, I recollect, which was as follows.

"The weather was hot and sultry one day, and as we were passing by a country place about a dozen of us straggled off from the line of march and began to grope about for something to drink, when one of the fellows happened on a wine-vat, which was a bricked place in the ground. They were all terrible sharp at finding drink of any sort—dead hands at scenting out anything in their line, from a demijohn of *hogadent* (*aguardiente*) to a plug of tobacco. So one called to another, and all came flocking round; and, as many hands make light work, we lifted the wooden top off the vat, and sat down round it to have a drink fair and aisy. Of course, we kept our knapsacks on, as we intended to follow the route after a spell. Most of us, too, had our firelocks handy, as it was quite likely the villagers might try and mob us, for Spain is a very unruly country, sir, entirely. So some of us lit our pipes, and all drank away at the wine with our canteens, and in a quarter of an hour or so, owing to the heat of the weather. got very merry, as soldiers will do. Whilst we were enjoying ourselves quite orderly and peaceably, however, a very drunken boy from London overbalanced himself as he was filling his can, and fell into the vat, knapsack and all. As he could swim, he came to the top at once and clutched the edge of the vat, and I thought the men near him would have pulled him out. But how it was I don't know : I think the devil must have got into the fellows' heads, for, instead of pulling him out, all hands began to laugh at the thing as a good joke, and set to work to trap his fingers with the butts of their muskets when he caught hold of the edge of the vat ; and the more the poor fellow begged to be pulled out, the more they laughed. So the end of it was he was drowned before we suspected anything was wrong, and went down just as our captain, who had missed us, rode up and ordered us to fall in and march, which we did, without a word about the boy in the vat."

This is a sample of Ben's yarns about the British legion in Spain. Three or four years later, it was my chance to pass some time in the Peninsula, where I knew several Christino officers, who had served in the Carlist war, and it seemed strange to me to find how much the stories they related in Seville resembled those I had heard from the British convict in Australia. One of them was as follows :—

" On one occasion several companies of our Peseteros had entered a village in the morning, the inhabitants of which had given up to the *facciosos* (Carlists) the mother of General Cabrera (if I remember right), who forthwith shot the old lady in reprisal for the numerous massacres of Carlists ordered by her son. This outrage we had been directed to avenge ; so we forced all the villagers, men, women, and children, into the *plaza*, at the point of the bayonet, formed across the street at each end, and set to work to shoot them down, whilst others bayoneted such as took refuge in the houses. It was a frightful business; unarmed men and women tried to force their way through our lines—of course in vain— and most of the crowd had fallen, when a boy of ten years of age or so, bespattered with the blood of his relatives, rushed up to a captain who stood at the head of his company, seized him round the legs, and entreated him to save his life. Our orders, however, were imperative that none should be spared, and I felt that the captain's case was a bad one, as he dared not disobey orders, and the boy, who refused to let him go, was a fine little fellow apparently, and his appeal for life touching in the extreme. However, there was nothing for it, so he said to the child, 'Go; you shall not be shot!' and, putting his hand into his pocket, he drew out an orange, and, rolling it along the ground, said, 'There, my little fellow, take that!' The child accordingly ran after the orange, and the captain ordered a soldier close at hand to shoot him, which he did at once."

I have already said that most of my old servants came to their ends shortly after I left the station, when the discovery of gold introduced high wages, and, of course, disorder and drunkenness; and I heard that poor Ben met his fate in his cups one night, by stepping out of a window in Bourke-street, which he fancied was on the ground floor.

CHAPTER XXXI.

CONCLUSION.

I HAVE brought the reader to a close of my recollections of bush life. Glancing over the pages, it may perhaps be noticed how little I have had to say of my real business as a squatter, the result, I think, of the circumstance that a squatter's life furnishes in the main but little to write about, at least that anyone could be expected to read ; a fact which I shall be happy if the reader does not, as it is, find exemplified in these pages. Let me add a few words about the results of my sheep-farming.

Bearing in mind that my father's sheep were of an inferior description from the first, that they never averaged quite two pounds and a half of wool, that I was not allowed to take the necessary steps to improve them, that the prices of wool and wethers were low ; and then remembering that the £1,500 so ill invested in Wolfscrag and the £500

30

worth of sheep received from Steele's Creek had been producing, for several years before I left, a net income ranging from £1,000 to £2,500 a year, I think it will be admitted that the undertaking was brought to a successful issue, especially when it is remembered that, in addition to the thirty thousand sheep which I left on the ground in 1851, the run secured was of first-class quality as squatting country, and capable, with the help of a few tanks, of depasturing a hundred thousand sheep. Indeed, I believe I was as successful as any sheep-farmer of those times.

Whilst describing the more prominent features of my life at Tongala, I did not think it necessary to mention that, in 1846, my father gave me a flock of sheep, with which I took up a small run near his, which, as the reader has seen, I still continued to manage. When I gave up the management of Tongala my sheep had increased considerably; and, being desirous of a change, I let them and my run for three years, and went to travel through some of the countries about which I had interested myself from boyhood.

I had, however, scarcely reached the shores of the Mediterranean when the discovery of gold was made in Australia. The results of this discovery changed everything, and swept away the old order of things, so that when I got back, three years after, I found the squatters—who, during

the first fifteen years of the colony, had established
a great trade in wool, and built a thriving city—
being denounced as monopolists of land and
enemies to the public weal.   The epoch was
quite a turning point in the history of Victoria,
and I remember, on landing, stopping to listen
to a tall, burly, good-tempered looking Scotch-
man, who was holding forth to a little audience
of new chums, or persons like myself, who
had just returned to the colony.   After inveigh-
ing for some time against the injustice of the
new comers, he said, turning towards me—
"Here's a man that doesn't know me, but I
know him.   Three years back there were not
three men in the colony who didn't know his
father—the father of separation, as we used to
call him—or who wouldn't have sworn to his pair
of roan horses anywhere.   Well now ! I'll give
this gentleman a week to find a man who ever
heard of his father, or of separation either.   Why,
these new chums, who have overrun the colony,
seem to think, by George ! that they are the first
comers here, and that this wharf, and the houses
and bridges we built, and the roads we made, and
the stock we brought from other colonies before
they ever heard of the place, grew of themselves
like the gum-trees."

   And so, since the brawny Scot stood venting
his displeasure on the wharf, time has not ceased
to bring its changes.   Of the little circle who

used to be merry at Tongala five-and-thirty years
ago—alas !

" Kaled, Lara, Ezzelin are gone,"

and the two who remain are old ; and the writer,
in lieu of the stirring pleasures of youth, has learnt
to content himself with a book and an easy-chair.

Walker, May, and Co., Printers, 9 Mackillop street, Melbourne

Lightning Source UK Ltd.
Milton Keynes UK
UKHW030620251122
412773UK00011B/761

9 781241 442064